In the Lap of Tigers

In the Lap of Tigers

The Communist Labor University of Jiangxi Province

John Cleverley

ROWMAN & LITTLEFIELD PUBLISHERS, INC.
Lanham • Boulder • New York • Oxford

ROWMAN & LITTLEFIELD PUBLISHERS, INC.

Published in the United States of America
by Rowman & Littlefield Publishers, Inc.
4720 Boston Way, Lanham, Maryland 20706
http://www.rowmanlittlefield.com

12 Hid's Copse Road
Cumnor Hill, Oxford OX2 9JJ, England

Copyright © 2000 by Rowman & Littlefield Publishers, Inc.

All rights reserved. No part of this publication may be reproduced,
stored in a retrieval system, or transmitted in any form or by any
means, electronic, mechanical, photocopying, recording, or otherwise,
without the prior permission of the publisher.

British Library Cataloguing in Publication Information Available

Library of Congress Cataloging-in-Publication Data

Cleverley, John F.
  In the lap of tigers : the Communist Labor University of Jiangxi Province / John Cleverley.
    p. cm.
  Includes bibliographical references and index.
    ISBN 978-0-8476-9937-7
    1. Chiang-hsi kung ch'an chu i lao tung ta hsüeh—History. I. Title: Communist Labor University of Jiangxi Province. II. Title.

S539.C6 C64 2000
630'.71'151222—dc21

99-056024

Printed in the United States of America

∞™ The paper used in this publication meets the minimum requirements of American National Standard for Information Sciences—Permanence of Paper for Printed Library Materials, ANSI Z39.48-1992.

"Ninety nine li at one leap,
Day and night in field and forest,
Asleep in the lap of tigers,
Naught shall stop us."

— Song of the Jinggangshan Branch

Contents

List of Photographs	ix
Abbreviations and Terms	xiii
Preface	xv
Map	xvii
Introduction: Setting the Scene	xix

Part I: **Establishment**

One
Great Expectations   3
Two
The Founding   15
Three
Branches of Gongda   25
Four
A Dark Side   41

Part II: **Educational Work**

Five
Classroom and Farm   51
Six
"Staffers, Laborers, and Researchers"   63

Part III: **On Politics**

Seven
Guidance from the Chairman   75
Eight
A Role for Ideology   87
Nine
On Political Movements   95

Part IV:	**Steps Back and Forward**	
	Ten	
	Famine and Fortitude	107
	Eleven	
	A Letter from Mao Zedong	117
	Twelve	
	Good Friends Rally	125
	Thirteen	
	"The Golden Years"	135
Part V:	**Cycle of Revolution**	
	Fourteen	
	Cultural Wars	145
	Fifteen	
	An Open Door	161
	Sixteen	
	Trial by Media	173
	Seventeen	
	Attacked by Left and Right	183
Part VI	**Life and Legend**	
	Eighteen	
	Decision Point	195
	Nineteen	
	Life after Death	203
	Afterword	213
	Notes	215
	Select Bibliography	233
	Index	237
	About the Author	249

Photographs

1. Main Campus, Communist Labor University.
2. Eighty-five percent of students claim worker or peasant origins; new enrollees, 1964.
3. First-year students in the classroom, Department of Agricultural Economics, c. 1965.
4. Early buildings, Damaoshan Branch.
5. Administration building, Taihe Branch.
6. Meeting hall, Taihe Branch.
7. Jiangxi brick kiln.
8. Wang Dongxing speaking at the opening of the Main Campus of the Communist Labor University, 1 August 1958.
9. Liu Junxiu teaching cotton planting at his experimental plot, Main Campus, 1965.
10. Shao Shiping lecturing at the university, 1959.
11. Party Secretary of the Communist Labor University, Zhang Yuqing, talks on teaching reform, 8 December 1964.
12. Zhou Enlai meets representatives of the Communist Labor University at the Nanchang Hotel, 18 September 1961. From front row, left: Luo Ruiqing (Secretary General of the Military Commission), Yang Shangkui (First Party Secretary, Jiangxi Provincial Committee), Zhou Ehlai, Liu Junxiu, Shao Shiping, Fang Zhichun (Party Secretary, Jiangxi Province), Peng Mengyu (Vice Governor, Jiangxi Province), Li Chao, and Wang Jin Xiang.
13. Zhou Enlai's inscription, Communist Labor University, August 1959.
14. Zhou Enlai chats with Xiao Gao, a student from Shaoxing, Zhou's hometown.
15. At Lushan Branch on 17 September 1961, Zhou Enlai talks with Yang Shangkuig, fourth from left, Yang's wife, Shui Jing, and Yang Cai (Party Secretary, Lushan Branch).

16. A student forestry class from Damaoshan Branch.
17. Silkworm factory students gathering cultivated mulberry leaves.
18. Carting logs, Damao mountains, c. 1972.
19. Animal husbandry students from Taihe Branch examine domestic animals for common diseases.
20. Worker-peasant-soldier students return from the countryside under the Zhou arch, c. 1973.
21. Yunshan Branch student musicians, c. 1965.
22. Zhu De sits alongside Dai Shuirong in a mathematics class at Yunshan Branch, 12 March 1962.
23. Zhu Min (center) visits and talks on her father's concern for the university following his death. From left: Zhu Jingshu, Zhu De's nephew and Gongda graduate; far right: Wang Jin Xiang.
24. Wang Jin Xiang orientates new students to university life in the Main Campus exhibition hall, 1960s.
25. Graduates of Nancheng Branch return to the commune.
26. Shao Shiping's inscription congratulates the Communist Labor University on its first anniversary: "Persist in carrying out the principle of combining education with productive labor and open up the road for all those seeking to enter university."
27. Zhu De's title for the magazine of the Communist Labor University: "Furnace of Jingganshan."
28. Mao Zedong's study, No. 1 Lu Lin, Lushan.
29. July 30 letter by Mao Zedong to comrades of the Communist Labor University, 1961.
30. "Knees as desks": Mao lecturing at the wartime institution, Lu Xun Academy of Arts, Yan'an, 1938.
31. Mao at the construction site of a Ming Tombs reservoir, 1958.
32. Slogan on the wall of the main teaching building, Main Campus: "Three key issues in university administration: i) Party leadership, ii) mass line, iii) the combination of education and productive labor."

PHOTOGRAPHS xi

33. Students from Taihe Branch listen to veteran Zhou Wenkai at Mao's stone seat outside his former residence at Ciping.
34. Students of Yunshan Branch listen to a peasant's story of his family's "bitter past."
35. Scene from *The Break*. Principal Long holds up the hand of the blacksmith Jiang Danian: "To enter our Communist Labor University, the first qualification is to be a laborer. The thick callus on the hand is the qualification!"
36. Cinema, Taihe Branch.
37. Living room: peasant home, mountain region, Southern Jiangxi.
38. Kitchen: peasant home, mountain region, Southern Jiangxi.
39. External: peasant home, mountain region, Southern Jiangxi.
40. Graduation certificate of twenty-one-year-old Wang Jin Xiang, who studied at the Communist Labor University from 1 August 1958 until 31 October 1962, majoring in political education in the Department of Social Sciences. Signed Liu Junxiu, president, 17 November 1962. Seal of the Communist Labor University.
41. Wang Dongxing with author (center) and, from left, Wang Xiaoyan, his third daughter; Wang Yanqun, second daughter; Du Li, Beijing Agricultural College, Liu Guimin, secretary; and Xu Xiangyang, third son-in-law; Beijing, October 1998.
42. Administration building, Jiangxi Agricultural University.

Abbreviations and Terms

CPC	Communist Party of China
Fen	One hundredth of a yuan
Jin	Half a kilogram
KMT	Kuomintang
Li	Half a kilometer
Liang	0.5 grams
Middle	High (School)
Mu	0.066 hectares
PLA	People's Liberation Army
PRC	People's Republic of China
RMB	Chinese currency
Yuan	Basic money unit

Preface

My personal involvement with the Communist Labor University arose from curiosity. Coming across its claims as a model Chinese agricultural institution in the early 1970s, I wrote to Jiangxi inquiring of progress twenty years on. A courteous reply invited me to visit the onetime Main Campus where I found an institution with a past deserving the telling. Here I am indebted to the authorities of what is now Jiangxi Agricultural University for their ready access to staff and students and an opportunity to inspect ex-branches of the Communist Labor University in the mountains. Visits were made to several locations, among them, Wenyuan, Tiahe, Ji'an, Donggushan, and Ciping, and to various associated museums that still display memorabilia.

Staff, student, and graduate interviews were undertaken at Jiangxi Agricultural University in June 1991 and September/October 1992; in all, over forty-five staff, individual students, and graduates were interviewed. During the next seven years, I talked and corresponded with other ex-staff and graduates, including Wang Dongxing in Beijing, one of the founders of the university. My writing particularly identifies Wang Jin Xiang, an ex-student, teacher, and administrator of the university, but I owe as much to others who have contributed important facts and opinion.

Recording the Communist Labor University has its challenges. Access to records remains limited, and published sources are frequently overlaid by the propaganda of the day. Of course the political genre of that period attempted to shut out contrary argument, which must be sought elsewhere. While discourse changes rapidly, I have aimed to recognize the language of the university and the fervor of it. The time was not so far back. Much content necessarily depends on word of mouth, yet individual memories are selective and fading and these and other accounts, and statistics as recorded, can fail to corroborate one another. I should add that *In the Lap of Tigers* represents my own reconstruction of the events of the day.

In the translation of material I am grateful to Zhang Changzhu, Zhang Lizhong, Liwanna Chan, Du Li, Nian En Wang, and He Guanghua, and, for secretarial help, Lorraine Wildman, Teresa Wise, and Meddie Lee, and, for support generally, Margaret Teo. I am appreciative of the assistance provided by Susan McEachern and Rowman & Littlefield, as publishers.

Photographic material has come from my own collection, ex-Communist Labour University staff, Xinhua Tongxunhe (Mao Zedong), and Chinese texts representative of the period. *The Communist Labour University* (1960), *Training New Type Personnel through Half Work and Half Study* (1965), *The Red Sun Shines over the Journey* (1978), *China Reconstructs* 21:9 (September 1972), *Remin Hua Bao Press,* no. 334 (April 1976), and two other titles, *Founding and Evolution of Jiangxi Communist University* (1996) and *The Road of China's Rural Education* (1997), published in Jiangxi, contain further illustrations.

Inside China there is evidence that the university's claims for recognition are being reassessed, with information released by Jiangxi Provincial Party Committee and by Jiangxi Agricultural University. Most alumni of the Communist Labor University I interviewed remain fiercely loyal to their institution and their life there: but a number would wish this early chapter of the beginnings of Jiangxi Agricultural University closed for good. It is true that the happenings of yesterday touch a living nerve, and that readers will make their own assessments. History is always of the present.

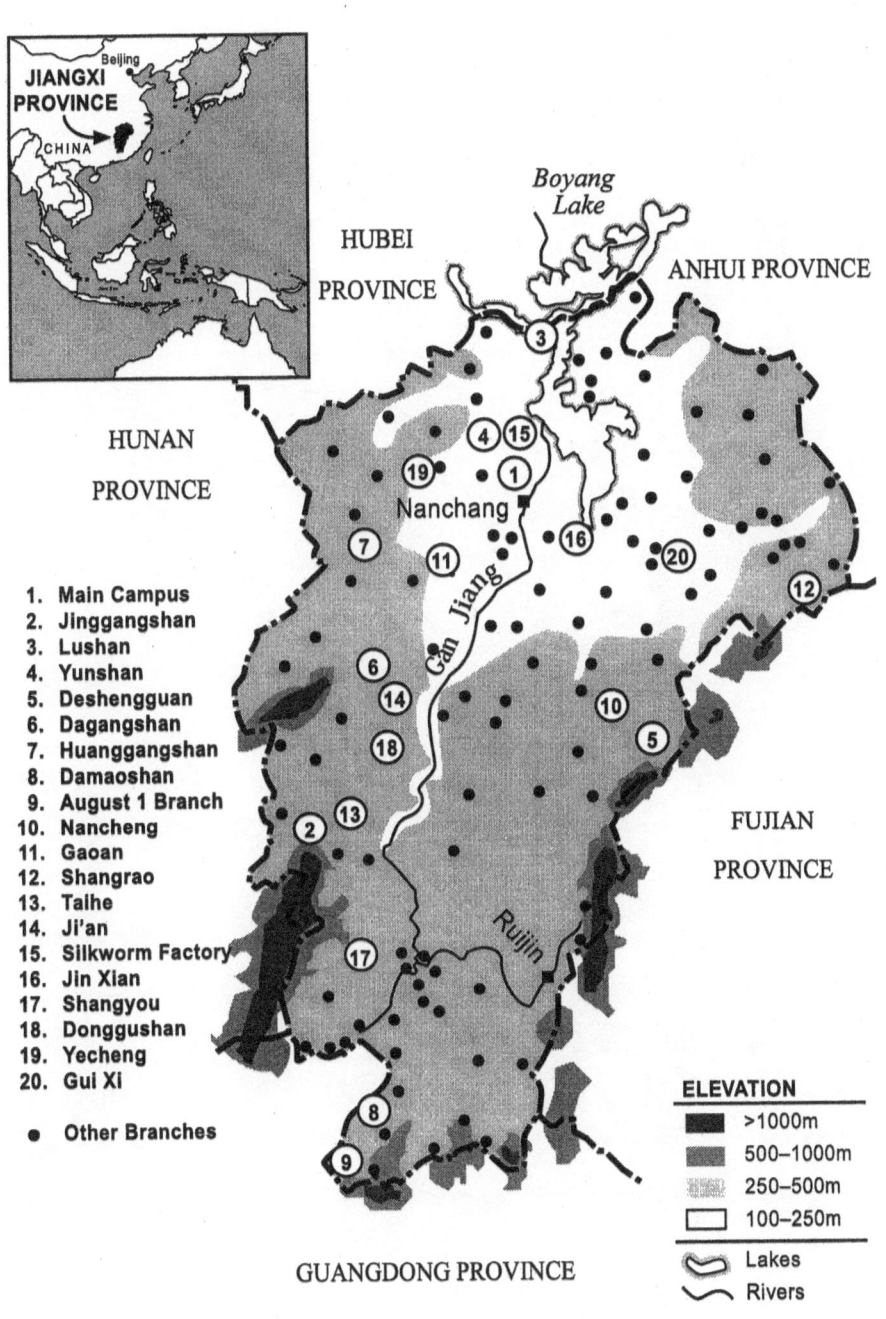

Introduction
Setting the Scene

"Realize the Great Leap Forward in education."

—Wang Dongxing, Party Secretary, Communist Labor University[1]

There is a saying about Lushan, the green and misty mountain resort in Jiangxi Province: "To see Lushan, you must see Lushan from afar." Likewise the story of the Communist Labor University should be viewed in scale and time. This unique social experiment set itself the task of educating generations of farmers and workers for their own immediate improvement and the anticipated coming of communism. Founded as a part-work and part-study enterprise in 1958, it became a model for China's higher education sector in the 1960s and 1970s.

The "university" in China was itself an importation from the West, the institution having emerged during the death throes of the Qing Dynasty when Western schools had followed in the wake of the foreign armies, traders, and Christian religious. Imperial China sought to utilize Western science and technologies and European languages for its own ends, arguing the dictum, Chinese learning for "essence," Western learning for "application."[2] However, the shock of the new destroyed the power of the neo-Confucian knowledge base of the Qing and, by 1905, the centuries-old civil service examination in the classics had been abandoned, opening the way for graduates trained in modern schools to enter public life.

Leading communist men and women attended the higher education institutions of their day. Among institutions open to them were the state-supported universities and colleges of the late Qing Dynasty such as Capital College (later Peking University); missionary-backed institutions such as the Episcopalian St. John's University in Shanghai; private universities like Fudan, also in Shanghai; and Kuomintang centers of learning such as Zhongshan University in Guangzhou. The nation's best, they drew students from across the country. Beneath them was a second layer of public, missionary, and private institutions offering professional subjects and teacher education, and various technical institutes attached to government ministries and large industries.

The first-generation communist leaders who involved themselves directly in the affairs of the Communist Labor University — Mao Zedong, chairman of the Communist Party of China (CPC); Zhou Enlai, premier of China; paramount chief Deng Xiaoping; and Marshal of the People's Liberation Army Zhu De — had imbued a Confucianism in elementary school that valued the admonitions of the sages above all. Exposed to modern education, principally in second-layer institutions, their Western learning and social purpose led them inexorably to the philosophy of communism. Theirs was a world of intellectual crossings: as agents of social change they must hate what they had been taught to love — the harmony of a time-sanctioned universe — and value what they had been taught to fear — chaos in the body politic. Mao himself recognized the importance of this re-education process in the business of revolution, telling his biographer, Edgar Snow, that of all titles he wished to be remembered as Teacher.[3]

Higher education in the Republic years (1912-49) was driven by contention and disagreements in which the communists played their full part. Underfunded by the state, government institutions were prey to the arbitrariness of local warlords and racked by expressions of student nationalism and political feuding, and the missionary universities, whatever their quality, had to defend their foreign origins, fight charges of proselytism, and counter attempts by authorities to regulate and control their extracurricular and religious activities. Many of the smaller private institutions, established in times when wealthy entrepreneurs sought "three treasures" — a newspaper, a bank, and a university — taught their clients a smattering of the cheapest subjects on offer.

Many universities were so small in size as to deny the claim of the title. Across China, thirty-four universities were open in 1931, accommodating some 17,000 students in all. A large one, Yenching University in Beijing, formed from an amalgamation of four missionary colleges, had 830 students enrolled, including 230 women; smaller places, such as West China Union and Fuhkien Christian universities, held 300 apiece or less.[4] The Japanese war brought the enforced evacuation of East Coast institutions to relative safety inland at great cost to academic life: staff and students were killed by the Japanese and university buildings razed. By 1947-48, there were fifty-five universities and colleges with an enrollment of around 148,000. Institutions had risen, fallen, and combined with a too-familiar regularity.[5] It could be said truly that higher education was more elitist than mass and more foreign than Chinese.

Yet the higher education sector, with its international associations, had a disproportionate influence on social life. The activities of intellectuals, whose ranks included men like Cai Yuanpei, the first minister of education of the Republic and chancellor of Beijing University, the left-wing intellectual Chen Duxiu, and the liberal scholar Hu Shi, were complemented by a politically active student movement which struggled against warlord and political repression and Japan's encroachment and invasion. Increasingly sophisticated, the men and women educators of the political left and right learned and networked: they emerged towards the end of World War II capable of guiding a national educational system, although at odds over its direction.

The Communists were no less blind than other intellectuals to the weaknesses and limited strengths of their own tertiary studies. Their opportunity to introduce a reformed school system came in the 1920s and 1930s, when they took control of large tracts of territory in the south and north of China. Among the harbingers of the Communist Labor University were the Red Army University, the Anti-Japanese Military and Political University, the Marxism-Leninism University, and the Chinese Women's University, which together met demands for Party organizers, propaganda workers, army personnel, and technicians. The Communists also sent promising youngsters abroad to study Marxism and Leninism at places like the Sun Yat-sen University of the Toilers of China in Moscow. As the civil war of the late 1940s swung in the Communists' favor, their troops entered and took responsibility for regular campuses in northeast China.

By the end of 1949 the CPC found itself master of a university sector not of its own making. It was uncertain about how best to engage, given that its own propaganda depicted orthodox higher education as representing many of the worst features of cultural imperialism. Careful to take over the university sector in running order, the Communists' accession to power was generally welcomed by staff and students. It was Mao who put forward the government's policy for the future: "The education of new China should use the new educational experiences of the old Liberated Areas as the basis, should absorb the useful experiences of the old education, and should make use of the experiences of the Soviet Union."[6] This would prove an impossible recipe.

Of the three options, the preamble of China's Constitution of 1954 came down decisively on the "indestructible" association of the Soviet Union and China. It does not surprise then that the Ministry of Education turned to "elder brother" for advice. It could be argued that this was no bad thing given the importance accorded higher education in Russia, and the opinion among some rank and file Chinese revolutionaries that university staff were class enemies. Altogether, China would employ over 10,000 Russian experts in the decade from 1950[7], and many senior cadres and academics, including better-educated staff at the Communist Labor University, came to speak Russian as their second language.

On Soviet advice, the comprehensive universities were reduced in number and consolidated, and priority was given to specialist institutes designed to fulfill the manpower targets of China's first Five Year Plan (1953-57). Longer term, this reorganization was regretted as it inhibited innovation by discouraging the fertilization of ideas across major disciplines. Russian experts' assessment of Chinese higher education did not flatter: they attacked the weight it put on humanist and basic studies, and the absence of a full range of professional and specialist studies. Astonishment was professed at the practice of lecturing in English, and experts pointed to a failure to link industry and research activities. Students were switched from learning English to Russian; course outlines were to follow Soviet teaching plans; Russian textbooks dominated the classroom; and hundreds of young staff and postgraduates were sent to the northern neighbor for training and upgrading.

The second half of the 1950s brought a severance in the filial relationship. Among the reasons for the dissolution was Khrushchev's attack on Stalin and the unwillingness of Russia to help China's atomic bomb project. Signs of division were apparent in the mid-1950s when collectivization in agriculture was stepped up against Soviet advice. Particular Chinese leaders became alarmed at the influence the Russians were gaining inside the country and in the army, with Mao himself fearing for the ideological purity of his revolution. The Chairman went so far as to quiz Liu Shaoqi, then responsible for the Ministry of Education, as to whether he was running "a Soviet Ministry of Education or a Chinese one."[8]

As the pendulum swung again, Chinese academics revealed that many had not thought particularly highly of Russian expertise. Teaching content, especially in agriculture, was not appropriate for local conditions; and syllabuses had become overloaded with Soviet extras. The teaching method commonly applied the "three copy" practice, whereby a teacher's lecture notes were copied from the Russian textbook, and copied again by the students. Mao himself noted, "Some comrades feel dismayed when they do not borrow."[9] For their part, the Russians complained that the Chinese wanted a magic wand approach to complex problems.

Indigenous solutions came to the fore once more in 1958, the year of the Great Leap Forward movement and a period of enormous enthusiasm for Chinese answers to Chinese problems. As the first Party secretary of the Communist Labor University, Wang Dongxing, put it: "The coming out of the university was not accidental."[10] Rather it was a manifestation of the enthusiasm of the "red and expert" high tide. In days of excitement and anticipation, Mao had challenged the country to catch up with Britain's steel production in fifteen years, before overtaking the Soviet Union and the United States. Attacking what he saw as the overcautious approach of his Soviet economic advisers and the complacency of leading officials content to live with past achievement, the Chairman launched his movement in May. Digging out a reservoir near the Ming tombs outside Beijing, the man set a personal example of the work ahead.

The Great Leap Forward was accompanied by large-scale collectivization through the movement to found giant communes. In 1958 the educational divisions of these communes founded hundreds of thousands of new schools based on work-study regimes, the Communist Labor University among them. The editorial of the *Jiangxi Daily* of 2 August boasted: "The Communist Labor University is born in the year of the Great Leap Forward in the construction of socialism, when one day's achievement is equal to twenty years." The new university was to tutor undereducated farmers and peasants in the advantages of scientific agriculture through planned work-study education. Unlike many of the ill-considered ventures of the day which quickly folded, the university would survive into the post-Mao era.

This story of Gongda, as the university was familiarly known, takes up its establishment at the high point of political and economic enthusiasm, a red star university praised and supported by China's veteran revolutionary leaders. Outlasting severe famine, the consolidation following the collapse of the Great Leap Forward, and the devastation of the Cultural Revolution, it ultimately confronted Deng's reforming zeal. The peaks and lows of its progress mirror the cycle of expansion and contraction of higher education down the years and also point to the tensions within the CPC as to the best kind of school system for China. In sum, they chart a watershed in educational policy from Mao to Deng.

Some in China still consider Gongda a product of "ultra left" political thinking, not a fit subject to delve into. Others dismiss it, along with the social extremes of that generation, as Utopian and doomed to failure, its idealism a shell, an outcome of manipulation and self-delusion. All such romantic schemes, they argue, lack a human face, with injustice and savagery justifying the end.

Yet the Communist Labor University experience has remained alive in the memory of teachers and graduates in Jiangxi Province. Original staff members have a strong attachment to their past, many regarding the early days as the height of a personal contribution in life, and men and women can be met in senior posts in the Jiangxi countryside who were taught there and weigh it from personal experience. Although written off by professional educators and others, the institution stood locally as a place where tens of thousands of Jiangxi youngsters learned basic skills in modern agriculture and forestry. Here the Communist Labor University addressed rural poverty through innovative work-study approaches. Although the university can be regarded as an indigenous model of higher education, one based on the pre-1949 experience, it did orient itself to the demands of New China, and its thinking and practices crossed the boundaries of orthodoxy. The creation of an educated labor force dedicated to work in the countryside remains an important and outstanding task for China's national and local policymakers.

Part I

Establishment

One

Great Expectations

"educating peasants was the starting point."

—Wang Dongxing[1]

On a mild June afternoon in Shanghai in 1958, a newly graduated senior high school student, Wang Jin Xiang, was working his way through the columns of the local *Xin Min* evening paper in his family's small flat. His eye switched to a notice inviting applications for a new university in Jiangxi Province, the Communist Labor University.[2] Wang knew his history of the Chinese revolution and was well aware that the province had harbored the Communists in the late 1920s, having been the base where their fighting force was created. What was so special about this institution was its aim to bring higher education within reach of Jiangxi's local peasants and laborers. Wang made a commitment to join then and there.

> I was fascinated by the idea of belonging. I longed to go to this university. In my mind's eye all was new, buildings and facilities. Imagination took charge of me. A member of the Communist Youth League, I'd been educated by the Party for many years and had embraced the saying, "Go wherever the conditions are hardest. Go wherever the country needs you most." Determined to follow whatever the Party said, and labor and learn alongside peasants and workers, I

talked things over with six of my closest friends: all of us decided to go to Jiangxi to attempt the entrance exam.

My parents, relatives, and friends just couldn't understand my way of thinking. Since I'd been born and raised in Shanghai, and had never been away from home before, they thought I'd be unable to withstand the certain hardship I'd encounter. Yes, there was nothing lacking at home and I could have attended a university there. But my mind was not open to them. On 26 July, I boarded the train for Nanchang city. Along with my six classmates, we headed for the middle reaches of the Yangtse River.

The seven young men in search of adventure and a chance to serve New China presented themselves at the stone gray Jiangxi Hotel in Nanchang where the university had an enrollment office. Their names were written down and they were shown a large room with beds and lockers where they spent an anxious night. Early the next morning the seven, along with other hopefuls, sat for a short examination. When the list of successful candidates was posted, Wang and four others had places.

After good-byes to the two who missed out, a truck arrived to take the five youngsters from the outskirts of Nanchang across the narrow Bayi River Bridge to the site of the Main Campus at Ba Mao Ling. As the truck moved into the foothills against the backdrop of the dark green Meiling Mountain, the youngsters glimpsed their chosen institution.

Curiosity was put at rest. The campus site of roughly cleared ground and tall yellow grass accommodated several long wooden and stone huts, once the property of Nanchang Forestry Technical College, whose 600 occupants had been summarily drafted as its first students and staff. The Nanchang College itself had been through an amalgamation only five months before, when it had absorbed the Ganzhou Forestry Technical College, following an inexplicable government decision that two provincial forestry training centers were not needed.

The arrival of the first batch of students for the Communist Labor University, familiarly known as Gongda, brought the foresters from their quarters to stare at the newcomers. Conflicting thoughts rushed through Wang's head:

> This place was completely different from the universities I knew in Shanghai — Fudan and Jiaotong. Where were the professors, experts, big buildings and advanced equipment? The university had nothing. It awaited building.

On the first day, 920 students of different ages and backgrounds overflowed the rooms and corridors, most being young men and women from the Jiangxi countryside.[3] Students were put in classes according to their school attainments and Wang found himself in Class 109, a group of forty senior middle school graduates which included seven women. The majority of students had completed only five years or less of primary school, and the remainder had either junior or senior high school qualifications. Wang himself was assigned to the Department of Industry in Mountainous Areas before moving to Social Sciences.

On the second day, Class 109 received its first lesson. Students were issued hoes, baskets, axes, and shoulder poles and shown how to surface a road. New road works were essential if building and other supplies were to be brought up to the university site. This hard initiation did not suit three of the Shanghai recruits, who slipped away in the first few days. Dropouts among urban students were frequent: these were attributed to the unaccustomed physical labor, health problems in a parasitic and mosquito-ridden region, the unfamiliar spicy food of the locality, and tears for loved ones left behind. Those who survived had a saying:

> Head touching the blue sky
> face turned to the wilderness
> feet planted in grass
> no room to live in
> no bed to sleep in
> classes and meals in the open
> a university in the hands of teachers and students.[4]

Accommodation made ready for the new recruits and staff comprised crude, wooden-framed shelters with woven sides, matting floors, and grass thatched roofs. These makeshift structures lasted until the thaw of spring when they were replaced by a second version, higher off the ground, with mud walls and a wooden roof. In putting up their shelters, the newcomers drew on the traditional building skills of the locality. Those on the Main Campus would occupy temporary quarters for over a year before learning to fashion gray and red clay bricks, dig out and fire kilns of their own, and mix mortar. While staff and students were erecting these shelters, other youngsters were given temporary lodging in local villages, temples, clan halls, and farmers' homes. Some of these men and women were hired by nearby farms and communes, earning the university extra funds which it spent on iron and other essential building materials.

How was it that such an institution came to open in Jiangxi in 1958? Although sparsely populated, its 30 million and more people among the poorest in China, the province had a wealth of primary products, minerals, and water. Rural life seemed idyllic. Still, the lot of the peasants was unremittingly hard, not least the reason why many disgraced Chinese leaders were sent to exile there. Jiangxi suffered burning and looting in the civil war of the 1930s, and the unchecked felling of timber saw the tributaries of the Gan River course red with soil from denuded hillsides.

Certainly the need for educational services was apparent to all. A survey undertaken by the nationalist government in the late 1930s recorded a male illiteracy rate of 78 percent, and a female rate of 97.[5] Rural Jiangxi had been slow to recover from the fighting of the 1930s and 40s, the place crying out for improvement. While demand for educational services has never guaranteed supply in China, new organizational opportunities opened up in the mid-1950s with large state reclamation farms bringing virgin land into production. Two provinces, Jiangxi and Xinjiang, were the recognized national leaders. One hundred and fourteen farms, based on conglomerates of agricultural cooperatives, provided the first agricultural centers in many parts of the countryside.[6]

The staff of the new centers drew on the 50,000 educated and skilled personnel sent down from Jiangxi's cities on Mao Zedong's orders in the winter of 1957.[7] Uprooted along with their families, these urban conscripts were assigned to rural work units, their current salaries guaranteed for three years. The "sent down" educated men and women proved a key rural resource: without their talents and belief in the importance of education, the Communist Labor University could not have moved past the drawing board.

The genesis of the Communist Labor University was a discussion between Mao, chairman of the CPC, and his onetime bodyguard, Wang Dongxing, then vice governor of Jiangxi Province. In 1958 Mao held unchallenged power in China, a living colossus equally feared and revered, and, of all Chinese, Wang was the individual closest to him, his vice governor rank belying the influence. "Between Mao and me it was not a superior inferior relationship. We talked of all kinds of things. We were friends and comrades."[8] The bonding between the two was founded on action in the field:

> Yes, I saved Mao three times. In 1947 we were in North Shanxi having retreated from Yan'an. Mao was conducting the war across China. Against us were two Kuomintang army groups —some 90,000 men were mobilized. Mao himself was about fifteen kilometers from the front and refusing to move until he saw the enemy with his own two eyes. I said I'd go to look for him as I knew the lay of the land. We had some small earthworks. The enemy commander had boasted he'd take our positions by 9:00 a.m. Taking a small force, we counterattacked at 8:30 a.m. and drove the enemy back twice. Zhou Enlai took the opportunity to get Mao to move back as soon as the shooting began. It was very dangerous.
>
> The second time was in 1948 in Hebei after we had been betrayed by one of our own. Mao had worked into the night and was in deep sleep when we had news of a plane coming. Mao wouldn't leave his bed so we began to carry bed and all into the shelter. We were covered in sweat. He finally entered a trench just before bombs destroyed the house.
>
> The last time was in 1971 when I discovered plotters so we advanced Mao's train timetable by ten days to avert an attack by Lin Biao's Warship 571 party.

Born in Yiyang County in 1916, Wang attended a local school for three years learning Confucius's sayings and the abacus. He joined the CPC in 1932, the same year he entered the ranks of the 10th Worker and Peasant Red Army. The soldier went on to study at the No. 1 Army School in Jiangxi staying on as an instructor, and he and his 180 students and staff joined the Long March. At this period the school took the role of protection unit.

> I had always wanted to learn and apply. We were taught tactics and applied them in fighting. To me the army and society at large were a school. Later on I learned something of agriculture. Mao Zedong said of me, "People like Mr. Wang got their education in the practice of the revolution." That was true.

From an instructor in the 1st Battalion, Central Guards Regiment, in 1937, Wang rose to head the Central Bureau of Guards, his responsibility the security of the senior leaders in the Zhongnanhai complex in Beijing. Mao had given him time out to study in a nine-month stay at the Central Party School in Yan'an before 1949, and he entered the Central Cadre School in Beijing in 1957 for a similar period, reading the Marxist classics.

"Mao told me that all cadres should be able to read and write — and not just listen and act. All should learn some literature, and engage in research and study." Wang remembers that one of his teachers was the Chinese translator of *On Capital*.

Instead of returning to Zhongnanhai, Wang was sent to Jiangxi Province, it was said because he and Mao had argued over security and other arrangements.

> How did I come to be in Jiangxi? That I was sent down is untrue. In fact I had just graduated from the Party school. Mao asked me how I enjoyed my studies there. I told him I'd like some time to practice what I'd learned. However I wasn't very good at science or industry. Mao said to me: "Let's make an agreement between two gentlemen. Let's make it for three years in three different places? Where would you like to begin?" I said "Jiangxi." Mao said "Hunan is OK." I said I'd prefer Jiangxi. "Why?," he said. "Because I know Jiangxi better and am more familiar with the accent." "But you know how they talk in Hunan?" "All right I'll go wherever the Party wants me to go."
>
> Mao asked me what job I wanted. I suggested Party secretary of a county. Mao said it was too limited. I suggested Party secretary of a district. Mao said no: "What about vice secretary of the Provincial Party Committee of Jiangxi and Director of the Land and Reclamation Farms?" I was called back to serve Mao in Zhongnanhai after two years.

Wang's social ideas had been strongly influenced by his mentor. He first met Mao in 1933 and was in the audience a year later when the Chairman had spoken on the importance of combining labor and study at the Second Session of the National Soviet Conference in the Jiangxi enclave. Wang followed his leader in supporting the various practically oriented wartime training institutions of Jiangxi and Yan'an, believing their graduates better equipped for life and struggle than those from conventional places. The security chief also helped Mao establish two training schools in Zhongnanhai for his soldiers and staff after 1949, taking lessons in one of them himself. Not surprisingly, Wang valued the efforts made by some of the new Jiangxi reclamation farms which had begun to open technical training classes to meet their own immediate manpower needs.

Wang, who had arrived in Jiangxi on 10 March 1958, was called to Beijing two months later for a national meeting on state farms and reclamation work, where he received an unexpected call to wait on his old boss. "Mao was happy to see me, standing up and shaking my hands. 'How've things been going over the last few months?'" Wang, in charge of reclamation efforts in the province, had visited most of its state farms, observing the poor living conditions, low production, and deficient services. "My heart was heavy during these months of investigations. Where should we start to make a change?" The vice governor told Mao how he'd been out surveying conditions. Things are "not too bad in Jiangxi," he reported, telling him, among other things, about the reclamation farms running technical classes for adult peasants. Mao's ears pricked up: "That's a good idea. Thirty years ago, when I investigated the peasant movement in Jiangxi, Hunan, and Fujian, many peasants were illiterate and couldn't express their feelings and write what they wanted to say. In this situation, isn't it impossible to develop agriculture? When you go back talk about it with Governor Shao Shiping and try to educate these peasants. How does this sound?"

Wang had heard what he wanted: "I had become acutely aware that educating peasants was the starting point." The suggestion that more effort be put into educating Jiangxi farmers was taken up in early June with the provincial governor, who responded: "Beginning from education, agricultural production will be strengthened and expanded. Our school should be self-supported and self sufficient."

A new institution would prepare farmers and workers for degree and lower qualifications in agriculture, rural accounting, forestry, animal husbandry, fisheries, horticulture, social sciences, and industrial production in the mountain areas, and its influence would be spread and enhanced by a network of branches undertaking their own specialties such as herb cultivation, bamboo and timber processing, "walking-tractor" maintenance, and sericulture.[10] Short courses like driving and bookkeeping would help meet local needs, and larger branches could open attached technical schools offering vocational training. Course lengths would be a standard four years for the university qualification, two years for the short course, and one year in an attached technical schools. All students would have to work and study. The average man or woman, it was calculated, would labor 200 days a year, which should return 240 yuan in cash or kind for living and medical expenses. About 120 days were set aside for study.[11]

Wang Dongxing served as Party secretary and deputy principal at the Communist Labor University from its establishment until February 1961, when he was recalled to Mao's court. He took his administrative functions seriously, lecturing at the university and occasionally joining staff and students in the mountains. As importantly, he would later intervene on the university's behalf both during the famine period and in the Cultural Revolution. During these years in Beijing he would direct the General Office of the CPC, eventually becoming vice minister of public security, vice president of the Party School under the CPC Central Committee, and Politburo member. A younger man than his superior, he was nicknamed, "the Little Red Devil." In Wang's eyes, the university was an evolving institution in the inevitable transition from socialism to communism. If senior university staff visited Beijing and failed to report, he was aggrieved and said so. Wang used these reports and his connections in the capital to help resolve their particular problems. His would prove a pivotal role in the innovation and its maintenance and, it would transpire, in its denouement. The man's creative achievement, granted the many hands involved, was a truly remarkable one.

Governor Shao Shiping was the driving force behind the university's on-ground establishment and, like Wang Dongxing, he was born in Yiyang County. Son of a hired laborer, and one of a family of seventeen children, he had been lucky to enter regular schooling in his teens. Caught up in the May 4th Anti-Japan demonstrations, the youth had gone on to win a scholarship to Peiping Normal College, training as a teacher. After a study period in Russia, Shao operated as a fighter and Party cadre in the Jiangxi enclave and in 1934 joined the Long March to Yan'an, where he gained a reputation for exceptional bravery. In the north he became deputy principal at the Second Branch School of the famed Kangda, the Anti-Japanese Political and Military University. The man proved a ready ally for Wang.

> The university is a good suggestion which we should consider. When learning at the Labor University of the Soviet Union we students worked while studying, supported our school and earned our own living expenses. I think Jiangxi could run a similar institution of benefit to the economy.

Calling in at Gongda on an almost weekly basis, Shao gave regular lectures. It was said of Shao, "He worked six days of seven from his office and, on the seventh, he was found at the Communist Labor University."[12] He was known for his advice: "Seek learning from practice, and practice what you've learned."

Shao's commitment to the university went beyond mere personal or political advantage. In the hospital in November 1962, he found the time to call in the newly appointed dean of studies at the Main Campus, Chen Ping, for a briefing. The dean remembered:

> After breakfast Li Chao and I went to his ward. Comrade Shao pulled himself up in the bed and asked me to sit beside him. Holding my hand he said, "Chen Ping, do you know that it was I who sent you to the Communist Labor University to direct its teaching? With more than ten years experience in the countryside and in the Propaganda Department and the Party School of our Province, you're the man for the job." I answered frankly, "Comrade Shao, I've never worked in higher education and don't know much about it. But I'll do my best." [13]

In 1965, this time on his deathbed, Shao brought the leaders of his university together for final words of encouragement.

A third man, Liu Junxiu, secretary of the Provincial Party Committee in charge of agriculture, completed the triumvirate. From Jiangxi's Yongxin County, Liu's first experience of school had been forty-five days in a winter class at age twelve. Despite having the good memory essential for an education at that time and relatives who had rent from fields belonging to an ancestral temple, there was insufficient cash to send him to a boarding school in a country town. He had to continue as best he could herding cattle, cooking for laborers, and carrying coal as a hired hand: "By day and night, I struggled just to survive in the most abject poverty."[14]

Liu was twenty-three when accepted into the Communist Party, taking the oath to be faithful, brave, and death-defying. He would work hard, obey the organization, observe discipline, keep secrets, and never betray the Party. The good of the whole, he promised, would always be above personal benefit. In 1927, Liu was directed to a secret training school in his home county where he studied Marxism-Leninism and how to launch land reform and fight local tyrants.

More lessons were learned in 1933 at the Marxism-Leninism University in Jiangxi's "red capital" of Ruijin. Conditions in the town were hard, with killings and pillaging daily events. The revolutionaries were allocated a ration of twenty liang of rice a day, later reduced to twelve, and there was little cooking oil and no salt. The people's government was penniless and could barely supply vegetables. For all the hardships, Liu maintained enthusiasm, reading his roughly printed Marxist texts conscientiously before graduating in 1934. Joining the 6th Army Group, Liu took part in the Long March. In all, the communists covered 9,600 kilometers, through eleven provinces, only one in ten of the original force arriving at the northern base camp. While Liu's own unit was defeated by the Qinghai warlord, he fought on as a guerrilla for three months traversing over 3,000 kilometers in the northwest.

In February 1942, Liu was sent to the First Branch of the Central Party School where Mao lectured him on the art of politics and war. "I had the great honor of being Chairman Mao's student." When Shao invited Liu to take up the post of president of the university in the making, he queried his own suitability. Could he be president without ever entering a university? Shao retorted that he had studied at the Central Party School, hadn't he? "Comrade Mao Zedong held the post of president. You're a university graduate then. The place where Chairman Mao was president is the real university."[15]

With President Liu it was always "his staff," "his students," "his university."[16] Practically minded, he was well liked on campus, where he is remembered for his energy and chain smoking. Nicknamed "the Cotton President" because of an obsession with experimental cotton plots, the leader had the habit of inspecting his beloved plots before dealing with university matters, academic or administrative. Despite his communist credentials Liu, as university leader, would find himself a live target for the Red Guards of 1966-67.

While the three men, Wang, Shao, and Liu, were immensely powerful, they still had to gain approval for the project from the Provincial Party meeting, where opposition to the new institution surfaced. One faction openly opposed setting it up, insisting it would distract from the main work of the newly established reclamation farms. There was not enough money, either. Nor were peasants keen to study and, if enrollments were down, how could a university start? Others agreed with the university idea in principle but wanted its program tied to the work of the reclamation farms. Farms should determine enrollments, courses, fees, and management, according to local conditions. Students would labor and study under the farms, this way the financial question would be manageable.

More information was requested before a final decision, so Wang and Liu volunteered to visit particular reclamation farms and counties over several weeks to gauge local sentiment. Wang inspected eleven and Liu nine. Their advice favored a main campus and branch network, and the findings were put up to Shao Shiping, powerful First Party Secretary of Jiangxi Provincial Party Committee Yang Shangkui, Fang Zhichun, Bai Dongcai, and other Party leaders. Although a decision to move forward was taken, several at the Party meeting remained unconvinced. "There were always two opinions about us." Opponents, though, would need to bide their time.

Official approval for the university came on 9 June from the Party Committee of Jiangxi Province and the Provincial People's Congress. Within six days, the governor had called a meeting at the Meiling Mountain site of the Nanchang Forestry Technical College, attended by provincial Party and administrative leaders and their counterparts from twenty-four state reclamation farms. The new venture, they agreed, would open on 1 August 1958. So confident were they that they were following Mao's express direction, no further attempt was made to seek higher approval.

A final decision, on the name of the institution was taken in mid-June. In the Confucian tradition of the significance of naming, authorities sought the best of titles for their prototype, coming to a decision only after much discussion.[17] The first name considered was Communist Labor Team, which was rejected as it was thought to underestimate the scale of the project, while Jiangxi Labor University, which took its cue from Moscow Labor University, was turned down because it seemed to minimalize political "redness." However, it was agreed that Communist should be in the title, signifying the spiritual, and Labor, standing for the material.

The institution would also carry the title *Daxue*, or "big school," the description accorded a university in China. *Daxue* was thought justified on account of the size, scale, and communist objective of the project, and because the communists' wartime institutions had carried the title. The name Communist Labor University (*Gongchanzhuyi Laodong Daxue*) finally satisfied all criteria. Its familiar title, Gongda, came from the shortening of *Gongchanzhuyi* and *Daxue*.

The very idea of a self-sustaining university for peasants appeared an attainable vision in these days of great hope. In this case, the institution had moved from conception to realization in a brave three months. By September 1958, the Main Campus had recruited a core of staff and administered an entrance examination to some 2,500 applicants, most of them having come from Jiangxi, although nineteen provinces, municipalities and autonomous regions were represented in all. Jiangxi itself was comparatively homogeneous in population, speakers of Gan dialect predominating, but provincial authorities were proud nevertheless to have attracted students from across China.

The Party secretary, Wang Dongxing, spoke movingly when he promoted his university as the country's largest in size and enrollment, and least costly per student. It was another step toward the communist objective of making higher education universal, toward a time when every commune would have its own university.

> Society changes and our people make progress continuously. What our forefathers did, we can do now. What our forefathers could not do, we can do now. We won China through hard fighting. Problems were there to be overcome. The Communist Labor University is the youngest of universities: it is the product of struggle and toil. As long as we keep going, and trying, there is nothing we cannot achieve. Our university has great expectations.[18]

Two

The Founding

"Getting on the horse before the saddle is ready."

—Donggushan Branch[1]

The ceremonial opening of the Communist Labor University on Friday, 1 August 1958, started at 8:00 a.m. in the hall of the onetime Nanchang Forestry Technical College. After the sounds of gong, drum, and firecracker had died out, Wang Dongxing, the master of ceremonies, moved to introduce President Liu to guests, staff and students, and family members. Casually dressed in a white, short-sleeved shirt and wearing cloth shoes with straw soles, Liu spoke from the rostrum microphone on what he called "Double Happiness Day," the birthday of the People's Liberation Army and the day of the founding of the Communist Labor University.

Liu explained why "Communist" was put first in the university's name: "because it is the guide of our actions, the goal of our struggle, and our ultimate aim."[2] Although the nation was now in the historical period of transition from socialism to communism, he said, the period of waiting would be short: "Our lofty ideal is realizable within the foreseeable future." "Labor" in the title signified the key to the creation of New China. "Marx and Lenin tell us labor creates wealth; labor transforms the world; labor will remake the future." Had not Karl Marx asserted that in a reasonable social order, every young person would become a productive worker? A similar prophecy, Liu divined, was true for China. Like the early communist theoreticians, he regarded a working childhood as a fact of life.

His students were warned against the classical assumption that brain always triumphed over brawn, a pointedness directed at the doctrines of Confucius and his disciple, Mencius. The Master had put the contribution of the "superior man" above that of farmer, while Mencius preached the supremacy of mind over body. Such traditionalists, said Liu, had no understanding of the virtue and rewards of human labor. The conventional university had taught such a bourgeois lifestyle, whereas his university would write a new page. Liu looked ahead to a time when they would have "fine classrooms and excellent facilities," and when "miracles" would flow from their graduates. However, attitudes and habits several thousand years old would need to be shed.

There was much to be proud of already. The university owned a powerful name and had demonstrated an immediate attractiveness, shaming its critics by enrolling 20,000 students across thirty campuses in less than two months. Already 11,000 had arrived.[3] Entrusted with 6,000 mu of waste land by the state, ambitious plans anticipated the graduation of 480,000 skilled personnel by 1972.

The president's speech on 1 August emphasized the liberating role of communism. The challenge it threw down, the creation of a just education system owing nothing to Russia or the West, was well received. Like most present, the man had embraced the Party's objectives with zeal, accepting that the Party's victory on the battlefield had brought stability to China and that the future was rosy. A beneficiary of the times, he revealed no reservations, though later he would admit to having had fears about how his untaught peasants would perform. Liu warmly commended all present who had laid down the hoe to commit themselves to this socialist-inspired community. Applause followed the President to his seat, as Wang stood to read a congratulatory letter from Governor Shao Shiping, himself in the Jinggangshan Ranges officiating at a local branch. The speeches and ceremony ended at 11:00 a.m., prior to lunch.

Initially the province had allocated 300,000 yuan for the establishment of the university and for the salaries of staff transferred there and had allowed 30 yuan per student for recruitment costs, 70 yuan for construction money, and 40 yuan as a monthly subsidy for up to five months. Students were given 30 yuan in hand on joining, which they mostly spent on tools.[4] After food, medical benefits, and other charges were paid, students retained three yuan monthly for pocket money. Specific disbursements from provincial funds, or internal transfers across branches, were permitted in an emergency.

The Main Campus staff and students received a monthly grain ration of 28 jin, two jin below the ration granted regular institutions like Jiangxi Agricultural College and four below that allowed Nanchang secondary school students.[5] This was despite the heavy physical work required of them. The university submitted several reports to the governor's office making the case for more grain. Shao, however, was silent. Unless the Main Campus could contribute substantially to its own funds, the leadership was acutely aware it would not survive long. Hence it must apply its student work force to return an immediate income, labor gaining precedence over study.

In early September 1958, the university's president, Party secretary, staff, and students assembled for an immediate push into the countryside. Three labor teams were formed. A small party stayed on campus to plant green vegetables, build shelters, and undertake road works. Of the rest, about a quarter was sent north to the shores of Boyang Lake to build dikes for land reclamation where they established the Nanhu farm primarily for rice production; and the third and largest group, some 1,000 staff and students, was dispatched to Dagangshan in Fengxin County in an expedition to fell bamboo. Among this party, led initially by Wang Dongxing, was Class 109 and Wang Jin Xiang who recalled:

> We started off in September and came back the following May. I had never done bamboo cutting before. I had never seen a mountain in Shanghai. So we had to receive a course, "How to cut bamboo." Later we put its details into a textbook, and we offered villagers bamboo-cutting classes. Another subject for study was bamboo transportation. One way we managed it was by water. We lashed the bamboo into rafts to float down the river. This meant opening up the river: rocks in the way were dynamited.
>
> We had to cart the bamboo by land as well. A U-shaped sluice was designed with five bamboo poles lashed together for each of the three surfaces. It ran for more than 10 li. A catapult was devised to send single poles of bamboo on their way down the sluice. We even built a bridge to cross a valley using strong rope. You could say our transport was by air, land, and water! Many generations had lived in Dagangshan but no one had ever seen such a sight.

It was dangerous work, especially when we used our slide at night. We would blow whistles when we sent the bamboo flying. The force was great, and we had to keep the bamboo walls along the base and sides of the slide in good repair. Once our slide needed attention. The student Zeng Shengxuan volunteered for repairs and he stood straddling both sides. A piece of curved bamboo flew down and cut into his calf muscle. It would have been okay if he had fallen off the slide. But he fell into it. The top of the slide was 5 li away. Nobody could see him and the bamboo kept coming. This classmate was killed. Although he died more than thirty years ago, we all remember him, and his tomb can be found on the campus. When we came back to the Main Campus we had money, houses, pigs, and vegetables. We were ready to sit down to study.[6]

Harvesting bamboo returned 380,000 yuan and another 110,000 yuan was earned mainly from road building in the first year.[7] However, this kind of labor had its disadvantages. Academic study was not readily linked with the physical side, and too much time was wasted traveling to and from projects. It did provide a significant cash return, though, and was a stimulus for the second stage of the Communist Labor University, the creation of permanent production bases.

Where the university would be best sited in the higher education structure was an issue of moment. The Communist Labor University was not one of the centrally supported institutions under the Ministry of Higher Education, and it could not have been sponsored by it without obeying Ministry rules and regulations. Nor was it attached to a government authority such as Light Industry or Finance, which ran their own colleges. In the event, it was decided to place it directly under the Provincial Party Committee and its Provincial Propaganda Department, and its branch campuses under the Party committees of the host farms.

Putting the university directly in the political domain was unusual — although there had been Party universities before 1949, and the Chinese People's University in Beijing had such a connection afterwards. While the act gave it special status, enabling it to side-step the demands of the regular education sector and much regulation and red tape, it also removed it from a common source of university income, the higher education budget. Nevertheless it could still draw on academic advice from the Ministries of Higher Education or Agriculture in disciplinary areas. Within its resources, the provincial political division proved active making decisions and issuing much official documentation on its behalf.

Shao, Liu, and Wang, the three leaders, held senior government positions concurrently, which associated the university with the center of political gravity in Jiangxi, though this was not invariably to the university's advantage. President Liu once told the staff that he must be careful making government decisions benefiting the university, fearing charges of favoritism across the table. Professional education advisers were not happy either about what they saw as too close an association between matters academic and political. In 1958, though, the university's political credentials were considered its great strength.

The first set of teaching plans would put the communist ideals unabashedly up front, insisting that "in every department and unit, unified studies of Marxism, Leninism, and Comrade Mao Zedong's writings will be enforced."[8] In the auditorium of the Main Campus two slogans were inscribed on the side walls: "Education must be combined with productive labor" and "Education must serve the interests of the proletariat." Political exhortations were painted on the external walls of teaching buildings too, imprinting the communist message on pliant minds. About a quarter of the original intake joined the Party or took Youth League membership, and thousands were singled out as "activists in socialist construction."

Governing regulations were drawn up quickly, publicized and applied. The first set stipulated the university open its doors to men and women aged seventeen to thirty from the ranks of adult peasants, workers, shop assistants, and army veterans, and from school leavers with the minimum standard of junior middle graduation. All students must present their identity cards, records of employment, residence permits, oil and grain ration entitlements, and three half-body photographs. They should have a clean political slate, pass a physical examination, and disclose their medical histories. On graduation they were promised a job, either assigned by the state or found by themselves.[9]

An Enrollment Committee decreed that every entrant be examined academically. Students destined for the four-year degree courses were to be tested in Chinese, mathematics, physics, biology, and political knowledge and given an oral, while those seeking two-year placements should pass an oral and produce evidence of practical experience. The same committee was empowered to admit excellent men and women recommended by the reclamation farms. This practice went against tradition and orthodox practice, which preferred the examination mode of entry as favoring quality and being meritocratic in operation. Main Campus administrators and large branch heads wanted examinations applied, arguing that nomination was open to nepotism and corruption, with those in power promoting their family members and friends, or accepting inducements. Recommendation, they said, worked to shut out the most able and best qualified.

Against this opinion, supporters of recommendation put the philosophy of political "redness" and equity, saying it aided the entry of students from poor districts with only minimal educational services. It also favored minority nationality entry. Certainly the university made some provision for minorities, e.g., for individuals who did not eat pork, but the staff did not seek out minority entrants, arguing that entry was open to all. Gongda having been founded in the Great Leap Forward, a period of the Anti-Local-Nationalism movement that underweighted differences between the Han and ethnic groups. These were the years of assimilation and the "language fusion" policy which proclaimed the importance of all Chinese learning *putonghua*, the common speech. Recommendation generally helped minority nationalities gain entry to tertiary education as they were among those least able to complete under the conditions of the regular Han examination system.

Reclamation farms and the smaller branch campuses were also strong supporters of recommendation, promising to maintain the supply of youngsters if this happened. Field workers openly disparaged examinations, arguing that students recruited on their marks took longer to adjust to physical labor, were less interested in politics, and were more likely to drop out. It would be difficult, said branch leaders, to recruit a high proportion of worker and peasant students were examinations to be applied.

Gaoan County's Hualin campus demonstrated the model recommendation arrangement. Intending to train four technicians for each of its 297 production brigades, it circularized neighboring communes and organized teachers to visit production teams, reassuring the leaders as to the return of their young people. Individuals seeking places had to complete a questionnaire as to their personal commitment, physical strength, and parents' expectations and were tested in the basics for grading purposes.[10] One enthusiastic assessor claimed that the recruits of Hualin held their school, "dearer than their families."[11]

Recommendation versus examination remained a tension point throughout the university's history. Eventually the university came to the compromise that entry to the higher-level courses would be by examination, whereas lower-level programs would take recommended students. Likewise the best qualified graduates could expect a government appointment, and the least qualified would return home. Here the university assumed that all graduates would be readily employable across Jiangxi's 3,000 communes, 25,000 production teams, and 460 state farms.[12]

Despite offers of a quota of students, not all reclamation farm leaders supported the Jiangxi experiment. Several large units refused to provide letters of introduction or withheld residence permits from prospective students. Fearful of losing their best young laborers, they threatened them with dismissal from the production brigade or loss of Party or Youth League membership. A number were accused of the political sin of "individualism" and threatened with reform through labor. Others released for study had their oil and grain rations held back and passed to others. While the university attempted to negotiate students' rights in such cases, they were seldom successful, for the units asserted near-absolute control.

The quality of the in-house leadership and management of the university was an early feature. From a farming family, the highly capable Li Chao, vice president and vice secretary of the university's Party Committee (formed in November 1958), proved an outstanding manager.[13] Li had become deputy head of the provincial Financial Department and head of the Taxation Bureau before being sent down to the countryside in December 1957, where he was appointed director of the Comprehensive Reclamation and Cultivation Farm at Yunshan.

One day in October 1958, after a branch campus had opened at the Yunshan farm, Li hosted an overnight visit by Shao, Liu, and Wang. The three recognized an outstanding talent, despite his lack of middle school qualifications. The Yunshan director was invited to return to the Main Campus as Liu's deputy in December. There he would work continuously for the university (with the exception of two years during the Cultural Revolution) until he moved to vice director of the provincial Education Commission in 1980. His administrative skills and good sense were a byword.

The second vice president, Lin Zhong, in charge of formulating university teaching and study plans, had been sent down from the China

Science Academy, Beijing. A graduate of Zhongshan University in 1924, Lin was considered the best-educated man on campus. He was also a close friend of Governor Shao and the brother-in-law of Lu Dingyi, the national propaganda chief. Its third vice president, Qu Shaojian, had been recruited from the reclamation farm and branch campus of Deshengguan.

Two other prominent campus figures were Zhang Yuqing, who would replace Wang Dongxing as Party secretary in March 1961, and the long-serving Tao Mao, later to become a vice president of Jiangxi Agricultural University. Tao had been sent down to Jiangxi from the Central Propaganda Department, becoming deputy head of the university's Propaganda Section and head of its President's Office.

Records of the first 18 months count over 46, 650 students enrolled, of whom some 18,000 were second-year admissions, attending the Main Campus and its seventy-seven branches and thirty-eight attached technical schools.[14] Eight out of ten of them were listed as being from worker and peasant families, and the same proportion had between two and five years employment experience. Only 4 percent of students had a senior middle school certificate, the usual qualification for university entry. Allowing for some exaggerated reporting, it was evident that the target population was being tapped.

The Main Campus and branches managed sixty-six farms, with over 16,000 pigs, and there were 243 small-sized factories for bamboo and timber products, soap manufacture, insecticide production, and printing and paper making from local grasses. There were tool-making plants and shops for mechanical repairs. Explosives for quarrying were manufactured, and cement mixed and bagged. Branches had sericulture farms with mulberry plantations, spinning wheels, and weaving frames, and there were bees, rabbits, and fish ponds. Effort was also put into processing pickled vegetables, peanuts, and bean curd and the firing of pottery containers. Several campuses soon had their own vineyards and distilleries. Altogether 42, 750 mu of farmland and 142, 050 mu of forest were worked. Nearly seven out of ten branches claimed early self-sufficiency, although this figure cannot be taken at face value given the onset of the 1959-61 famine.

Production aggregates and material advances are seldom the things individuals best remember. Asked what he recalled of the early years of the university, a county agricultural head and graduate replied: "It was the Gongda spirit."[15] Wang Jin Xiang expanded on the same theme when he spoke of his own growing attachment to the place. After less than a year of the hard life, the young man developed stomach ulcers and was sent to Nanchang hospital for treatment.

> The vice president of the Communist Labor University, Li Chao, asked whether the student who had stomach ulcers had returned to Shanghai. "No," he was told. "He's back in the dorm." Li sought me out. Did I miss home? Did I want to go to Shanghai? I said I'd like to think about that. He told the head of the cookhouse, Zhao Daoqiu, not to give me rice, but noodles like we have in Shanghai. After lunch I went to look for Li Chao and told him I would not go home. I would go back to the mountain to cut bamboo. He said, "No, not yet." So I went secretly. My leaders and classmates were good people. I stayed with Gongda.

Among the first cohort of students was Mao Bingjie from Sichuan Province, a woman whose enthusiasm matched Wang Jin Xiang's own. "Whatever men can do, I can do," she protested, as she joined in the Dagangshan expedition, cutting bamboo and hauling it to water. One morning she slipped into the boiling race of bamboo trunks. Thanks to a teacher, Dong Peilin, who risked his own life jumping in to haul her out, she was rescued alive. In July 1962, after graduation, she and Wang Jin Xiang married.

The two refused an opportunity to return to Shanghai in 1962; Wang's elder brother had joined the army and been posted to Harbin, so under the rules, Wang was entitled to return to care for his parents, both of whom were over seventy. Later, in the Deng era of the early 1980s, educated youth sent down to rural labor were allowed to return to the cities, and Wang's Shanghai family found him a job in a local work unit. Again, the couple determined to remain in Jiangxi.

The public face of the university was revealed as early as 3 October 1958, when it supplied material and photographs for an exhibition on education and productive labor in Nanchang, and it exhibited in Beijing at the Jiangxi Hall the following month where the display was "much praised."[16] In early August 1959, during the Eighth Plenary Session of the Eighth Party Congress, Premier Zhou Enlai received a report from Governor Shao on the university's first anniversary. In an act of grace, he inscribed the name, Communist Labor University. By omitting Jiangxi from the title, Zhou affirmed that the experiment was a truly national one.[17] Shao returned with the prized calligraphy, which was reproduced in letterhead and teachers' and students' badges. Zhou's act was especially valued because Gongda was a "red brick" university, with no history. Now its utilitarian landscape had a fountainhead, a gateway of pillar and arch, which proudly proclaimed the Zhou calligraphy and his faith in them and the school's future.

Three
Branches of Gongda

"Like a willow tree taking root and budding wherever it is planted.
Like a pine tree withstanding the trials of wind and frost."

— Gao Xiaoren, Yunshan Branch Graduate[1]

Wielding ax, shovel, and hand-saw, students and staff began the task of clearing a site of timber and undergrowth, bamboo, thistle, and bramble for the Wuyishan Branch in the mountains. New arrivals stopped over in the huts of farmers or slept out in makeshift tents: "Sleep in the dew, eat in the wind."[2] When their roughly hewn dormitories of bamboo and thatch were up, these doubled as classrooms, stones hauled to the site by rope as became seats, and knees desks. At last the time arrived to put up the branch's name board. Improvisation ruled. With no baskets available, pairs of trousers, their ends sewn together, provided storage and carry bags for rice. Young men and women cut and hauled timber, tapped resin from pines, and collected chestnuts and wild herbs for the table.

On the flat, students harnessed themselves to the plow, turning the muddy soil in paddy fields for the first crop. They worked in planting and harvesting and rotating the water wheels, keeping the sun off with straw conical hats, palm bark or woven leaf capes, pants rolled up high, feet bare. As the months moved into winter, firewood and coal were collected for cooking and heating, and students and peasants shared a warm rice brew after a stint in forest and field.

Branches worked one to four mu of farmland per student, and about twenty mu of forest and orchard.[3] Some of the fields allocated grew only one crop of rice instead of the usual two a year: the lakeside plots were much more fertile but subject to flooding, accepting that the university normally took up unwanted tracts. With the land secured for cultivation, roads, bridges, and ropeways were constructed, consolidating ownership and cutting time and expense in traveling.

While a few large branches had access to reasonable resources from the start, most had to fend for themselves. Those campuses backed by reclamation farms had land readily available; others expanded meager holdings by managing state forests or came to agreements with communes and cooperatives to lease plots. Title of unfenced waste land worked by a branch was usually transferred to it when the expanse was salvaged. The going was hard. Even if the Main Campus wished to help its outstations, many branches had no access roads suitable for wagons or trucks, supplies having to be hauled up by pack and hand carts under conditions of ice and snow in winter.

Physical effort and ideological motivation were yoked. The Huanggangshan Branch, Yifeng County, had as its base a small mountain hamlet which overflowed with 1,200 students occupying ancestral halls, temples, and storehouses. The streets of Huagguangshan had seen bitter hand-to-hand fighting between Red Army and KMT soldiers in the early 1930's, and signs of the revolutionary past survived for the reading. As the youngsters filed down the lanes and into their temporary quarters, they could still make out the worn outline of characters scrawled on the walls in black ash and red soil: "Long Live Soviet Power!" and "Long Live the Communist Party of China!"[4]

Kept busy at labor from dawn to dusk, Class 202 was bedding itself down on red cogongrass mattresses in a dilapidated Confucian hall when an argument erupted:

> Suddenly there was an altercation in the dark place. We guessed it was about the old question: "A university should look like a university." "How can our branch be called a university!" "What's your opinion of a university anyway?" "A university should have. . . ." We were so tired after clearing wasteland all day, we couldn't bother with their squabbling.

Early on the Tuesday morning of 2 September 1958, students were told to assemble for a special lecture, an unusual happening and a break from classroom and field. Gathered for an early breakfast in the "dining hall," a space of leveled land under a large camphor tree, they were less happy to hear that one of the Huanggangshan community had left for home without saying good-bye or even eating. A fractious and tense atmosphere across the trestle tables forced the duty teacher to blow his whistle defensively: "Will you stop all this questioning! We are a university! Our own teaching buildings, libraries, and laboratories will be available soon. Hurry up with your breakfast. And listen for the bell!" Students were not reassured. If their university awaited building, what was their situation?

The surprise guest was Shao Shiping, governor of Jiangxi Province. Here he was, he told his greeters, ready to give a free speech, communist style! All activities stopped as teachers, students, and workers hurried to the main clearing, maneuvering for a sight of him. The leaders of the Huanggangshan reclamation farm were favored with places staked out on the grassy slopes; others stood on rising ground among the tall tallow trees. The community watched expectantly as a square table, borrowed from a nearby peasant hut and decorated with a vase of mountain flowers, was carried to the center of the clearing and admonitions of Mao Zedong, black characters on red paper, were hurriedly pasted on the trunks of two trees for the backdrop: "Education must serve proletarian politics and be combined with productive labor," and, "Our education policy must enable everyone who receives an education to develop morally, intellectually, and physically and become a worker with both socialist consciousness and culture."

The scene set, Shao entered his open-air hall to deafening applause, settling himself comfortably in a large cane chair. After welcoming staff, students, and friends, he made two points clear: that the Communist Labor University had its own characteristics; and that these features redefined the concept of "university" in China. The audience was engaged immediately: "How many of you were farmers, or workers, or in the People's Liberation Army? How many elementary school graduates, middle school and college graduates are there?"

Peasant students were quick to acknowledge some elementary schooling. "Ah, so many — most of you," Shao said with a smile. No student could claim college experience. "Well," he shot back at them, "You have all entered university. The topic of my lecture is the Communist Labor University. What is a university? Is our university a regular one?" The rhetorical questions went to the heart of anxieties. Shao continued:

> All schools embody the characteristics of their times. Different times have different schools. Feudal society had its feudal schools — the Confucian scholar taught twenty or thirty students using Confucius's writing for their text and his students had to kow-tow to a Confucian tablet everyday.
>
> Capitalist society provided its schools — universities had many teachers and classrooms with their platforms and desks, and various

modern subjects. These so-called Western schools were much more progressive than feudal schools, yet the ruling class of the feudal society accused them of irregularity when they first appeared. When Kang Youwei carried out his political reforms and attempted to run Western schools, the empress dowager, Cixi, declared him a rebel. Orders were given for his arrest and beheading. Western schools were not able to replace feudal schools until the bourgeois revolution led by Sun Yat-sen overthrew the Qing Dynasty.

If the bourgeois could abolish the feudal schools and establish their own, why can't and shouldn't we abolish their schools now that workers and peasants have become the masters of our country and are striding towards communism?

"Yes, of course," students chimed in. Shao went on:

We must abolish the bourgeois system. It is the inexorable law of historical law that capitalism will be replaced by socialism. How? By establishing the Communist Labor University, we are abolishing their schools. People who criticize us are full of filthy bourgeois ideas. They judge our proletarian schools by their own social class criteria. This is ridiculous!

As he built his case, the governor revealed his own school experiences, which had seen him expelled from class and listed among the KMT's wanted.

You could not be admitted to the university in my day unless you paid a large sum of money, and a tuition fee annually. Children of workers and peasants like me were so poor we hadn't enough food to eat or clothes to wear, let alone the money to go to school. Almost all students were the children of landlords and the exploiting classes. They studied for ten years — no wonder they served their own class. Now a fundamental change has taken place. We are in the transition period from socialism to communism. Anyone who has studied for a few years in school and worked in the factory or on a farm for a few years can be admitted to our university.

"Where does knowledge come from?" Shao stirred up the audience. "From a dream? No. It comes from excavation!" They laughed in anticipation. "How can we undertake industrial production without digging a mine!" He continued:

True, mental labor is important, but manual labor is more important. We cannot live without food. Food, as you all know, comes from the grain produced by peasants. If everybody had a university education, and knew how to read but didn't know how to farm and grow food, we'd starve to death among our piles of texts.

By now it was 11:30 a.m., scorching hot, and Shao's white shirt was drenched with sweat. When the bell rang out for the dismissal of classes, he rose from his chair and stood confronting the audience: "Therefore I say to you the Communist Labor University will create its own small world of communism!" Shouts of approval and clapping echoed around him as he walked down from the clearing to the car.

Records from Huanggangshan suggest that the governor's speech had an impact on morale. At dinner on the day of the visit, the duty teacher changed his tack, rewording his advice of the morning:

> What I said at breakfast was too one-sided. While it's true that we should have teaching buildings, libraries, and laboratories, we cannot regard these as the essential characteristics of a university. This university is of our own making.

The class's only graduate from senior middle school, who had handed in an application to leave the university two days earlier, asked for it back, joining his classmates carrying bed roll and ax into the high country. When bad weather prevented the cutting and hauling of bamboo, the youngsters attended classes held in a thatched hut.

Although it was known that Yunshan Branch worked the hilly fields of its reclamation farm, demand for places was high. The first intake exceeded 500 young people.[5] One young woman, a Hunan peasant, walked for seven days to find the campus, carrying her own charcoal for cooking; her rice exhausted, she endured on a diet of pumpkin and water. Yunshan's twelve senior staff, released by the host farm to move things along, led the students in clearing 70 mu of land for a central site in the opening week, including 30 mu for a vegetable garden. Among them was the soon-to-be appointed vice president of the university, Li Chao. His first classes at Yunshan were taught outdoors. Office staff, teachers, and students worked and ate alongside each other by day and, at night, rifles were issued to protect the encampment against intruders — wild animals, feral pigs, and stray cattle.

A large wooden dormitory was erected where staff and students slept beside each other on the boards, accommodation later augmented by small sheds each accommodating ten men or women. During a night of wild wind and heavy rain, the roofs of several of these small dormitories were blown off, and the students were left huddling in rain capes on the flooded floors, covering their bed rolls and grass mattresses with coats and oil cloth. Several cried aloud, the soaked bedding and belongings spread out around them.

Over time the Yunshan community constructed three kilns, which would bake the 750,000 bricks for the living quarters, classroom, and storage sheds. The major branch edifice, a three-story teaching block, was built with help from a few skilled carpenters and plasterers: the leader of the carpenters was a member of the social science class, and an engineering student headed the bricklaying teams. As labor costs were generally half the total cost of a project, branches sought to utilize student labor to the maximum.

Yunshan soil was poor and yields low, one mu of field at the foot of Yunshan mountain reaping just one basket of rice. This was about one-eighth the average yield set for the province by the state planners. The branch moved quickly to improve its agricultural base, opening 300 mu inside two years and reclaiming another 3,000 mu of hillside land for timber, oil-yielding palms, and tea plantations. Compost was a valued resource: leaves, grasses, palm fronds, everything degradable was collected.

For all the hard work, Yunshan nearly closed when the creek it relied on for drinking water suddenly dried up. After much searching, a large spring was located in a cave, and water for the branch's vegetable plot was carted by human chain passing along buckets and basins. It eventually mobilized its labor to build several small reservoirs, staff and students surveying the sites themselves, measuring the storage capacity and catchment flow, and planning the construction. In 1962, Yunshan Branch joined the main and other campuses in digging out and constructing a major dike project; students joined their colleagues in the communal activities of rock breaking and carting. Moved by their great efforts, Governor Shao wrote a poem in celebration:

> Vitality and high spirits
> Remove mountains and drain seas
> Enrich the red soil
> Build paradise with our own hands
> Open up our vision to the world.[6]

The day a campus became self-sufficient, defined as covering the food and cash expenses of its students, was a milestone in its history. Some achieved it in a year, most took three to five years, others never did and their name boards were moved to other places or abandoned. Newly irrigated land, which typically doubled rice yields, helped Yunshan move from 85,000 jin reaped in 1961 to 635,000 jin and self-sufficiency in 1964. The final accolade was public announcement of a branch's capacity to pay taxes and sell surplus grain and meat to the state.

Earning a cash income was essential for many branch purchases. Yunshan's cash-in-hand came from a small winery of three sheds and seven vats which started its pressings in 1959. Red berries picked on the mountain slopes for the main product, Yunshan High Grade Red Berry Wine, were fermented and bottled, drawing on outside technical advice and machinery borrowed from a Nanchang vineyard. An early vintage won a first prize at the local Rural Industry Conference. In its first six years, the winery earned a net profit of 350,000 yuan, part of the income paying for a township building purchased as an investment property.

Branches had to be careful to obtain a balance between cash income and subsistence; however, in difficult times in China, money could not always buy grain, a government-rationed commodity. Yunshan combined yield in kind with cash return in gardening and horticulture by growing fruit for sale in the north. An orchard and vineyard, planted in 1960, were watered from two homemade wells 30 meters deep. Technical help to run the farm came from Beijing's Evergreen Commune, which had six Yunshan students assigned as apprentices. After several years of experimenting with grapes and grape hybrids, the branch had an annual output of 50,000 jin, an achievement applauded in a celebratory letter from the Fruit Tree Research Institute of the China Academy of Agriculture: "Led by the radiance of Mao Zedong Thought, you persisted in scientific research and succeeded in growing grapes. Your efforts have great significance for production and scientific farming in the broad lands south of the Yangtse River."

Academically Yunshan offered its students an ambitious program of five courses at three-year senior technical level, despite pressure from nearby communes for shorter courses which would free students to return to their units. Later, the branch's offerings would be cut back to three subjects — forestry, agriculture, and gardening.

Yunshan's best-known student was the peasant recruit Hu Rigao. Hu had read the enrollment notice for Yunshan branch campus on an office wall in the Zhu Hu Brigade, Boyang County, an advanced agricultural cooperative. Though he could barely stumble through the text, the peasant understood this Communist Labor University offered free tuition and board and that those with work experience were encouraged to apply. An application was put in immediately: "Such schools cannot be found even with a lantern!"[8]

Under questioning at the university office Hu's story came out. His father and brother had been killed, and his mother had died from tuberculosis despite begging forays by the young son to pay for her medicine. Afterwards the boy kept himself alive by shepherding sheep and pigs. Hu's first lessons were learned when his village opened a night school during an anti-illiteracy campaign.

The day his red stamp of admission arrived, word was already around his village, which hummed with the excitement of a wedding day: the youngster admitted to lying awake until after midnight worried about how he would acquit himself. Wearing a straw hat he had woven himself, a cloth bag slung around his neck holding his old begging bowl, Hu set out for Yunshan. At this time the branch was just a couple of sheds, one having an inscription painted on the side: "Study while laboring now: Fight while laboring in the future. This is the style of Kangda. Defeat all enemies." Hu found the small encampment busy with tree felling, the sawing of boards, and splitting bamboo for weaving. He felt quite at home, unpacking his belongings and joining the labor without a word spoken.

The young man quickly moved through the preparatory classes to mastery of the junior middle curriculum. By the time he left in late summer 1962, among the first cohort of graduates, the young peasant was something of a local hero, having badly burning himself raking out a flaming charcoal kiln. Speaking on behalf of the students at graduation, Hu held his red certificate aloft in triumph.

Yunshan took a special place in the history of the university when Marshal Zhu De visited the branch in 1962. Chairman of the National People's Congress, Zhu was of a poor tenant family himself, born in 1886 and one of thirteen children, five of whom were drowned at birth.[9] His relatives banded together to pay for his attendance at local schools, including one taught by a scholar who welcomed modern thinking despite knowing little of it himself. Entering Chengdu Higher Normal School, Zhu graduated as an instructor in physical training. Then he moved on to Yunnan Military Academy and was in Europe after World War I where he met Zhou Enlai in Paris. In April 1928, Zhu allied himself with Mao in Jinggangshan, and formed the Fourth Red Army, of which he was commander and Mao political commissar.

The marshal's interest in schooling for army men was well known. In the earliest days in Jiangxi, he had headed a special Officer Instruction Regiment which provided a core of skilled persons for his military units and, in the Yan'an years, he taught at Kangda. Learning of the Communist Labor University inside its first year, Zhu wrote an inscription for its journal, selecting the name "The Furnace of Jinggangshan."[10] On the 6 March 1962, he and his wife, Kang Keqing, took an opportunity to inspect the Main Campus and, six days later, the Damaoshan Branch. Accompanied by provincial leaders, Zhu walked around the campus, approaching a classroom where a lecture was in progress. Moving inside he sat next to a student, Dai Shuirong. Telling her that he was here to learn, Zhu stayed until the end of the lecture, which went on for another 30 minutes.[11] After his math lesson alongside the young woman, the marshal toured the branch's forestry and bamboo processing centers.

On the 18th, the husband and wife inspected Yunshan where 1,400 teachers and students gathered to greet him: he responded with vigor, waving, clapping, and grasping hands. Zhu was especially impressed by Yunshan's small winery and distillery, which utilized wild fruit and berries, saving public grain. "It's good to make do with what's available. We should make full use of wild fruits, increase production, and lessen the university's burden on the state." As Zhu left, he reiterated advice that staff and students should "keep the glorious tradition of Kangda and run the school well."

Back in Nanchang and excited by the tasks the university had set itself, Zhu called his younger brother's son long distance, suggesting he leave Beijing to study at Gongda. The plan was approved after two more telephone calls and a family conference. When the relative eventually arrived in Lushan, the uncle was delighted and presented him with a set of *Selected Works of Mao Zedong*. The young man enrolled himself in agricultural accounting in 1963, going on to complete the three-year qualification.[12]

Marshal Zhu and Kang Keqing inspected the Communist Labor University for the last time on 7 February 1966. Their backing remained unequivocal:

> Chairman Mao said in Yan'an that intellectuals should serve the proletariat. Did they? No. Only in the last two years have intellectuals turned around, and doctors have started to go down to the countryside. Emperors, kings, generals, ministers, gifted scholars, and beautiful women are no longer seen on our theater stages: only by such a turn-around will the dictatorship of the proletariat be ensured.
>
> The combination of education with labor was proposed by Marx and Engels a long time ago but was not put into practice. It was only practiced after Chairman Mao backed it. It has never been practiced in the Soviet Union; that's why revisionism has arisen in that country. [13]

The old marshal was in feisty mood, reminding the staff that the problem with the teachers was their unwillingness to engage in production alongside workers and peasants. He went on:

> Your merit does not lie in the tens of thousands of students you have trained only, or in the wealth you have created. These are of course very significant. But, what is more important, you have introduced new ways of doing things, and broken a new path for socialist education.

An inscription was left behind:

> The Communist Labor University is a new kind of school integrating theory with practice, mental with manual labor, and production with education. In the last eight years you have made great strides and led the way in creating a socialist education system. [14]

Zhu, like Mao, saw the Communist Labor University as a realization of his hopes for universal higher education under communism. "For eight years," he told them, "you have taken the lead." On his return to Zhongnanhai, the marshal sought out Wang Dongxing, recounting his visit and telling him how it had broadened his thinking. He invited Wang to see what he had written: "Have a look." The security chief approved. "More schools," Wang agreed, "should be run like this."[15]

In the early days, Governor Shao, President Liu, and Vice Governor Wang took a direct role in managing the largest branches. Shao took care of the Main Campus and Yunshan Branch; Liu, Jinggangshan and Huanggangshan; and Wang the August 1 Branch, most of whose teachers and workers were PLA men and women. They also initiated an annual meeting of branch presidents where progress was reviewed and three-year plans discussed.

Usually new branches either petitioned the network for admission or were directed to join it. The campus of the Silkworm Factory was an exception. Wang Dongxing, always on the lookout to extend his beloved institution, seized an opportunity in the mid-sixties to capture a Shanghai silk factory after its directors had been ordered to move inland in the context of Mao's prediction of the inevitability of atomic war. Wang obtained a valuable consignment of timber from the university's mills and entered a barter arrangement which paid for the factory's relocation in Jiangxi and membership in the university network.[16]

Rural extension activities complemented formal education. Hualin Branch gained a reputation for its mix of long- and short-term teaching and distance education: "The whole county was our classroom."[17] When local farms received their first allocation of small, bright red tractors, the teachers ran a three-month course for the drivers, the fifty men and women steering the machines back to their farms in a public celebration. Hualin also offered correspondence classes for the hundreds of young people sent down to the countryside, staff undertaking regular tutorial circuits of the holding centers across Jiangxi. At one camp, the youngsters asked teachers Li and Jiang from its Agriculture Department how to prevent tortoises damaging their crops. Never having heard of the problem, the two men talked it over with the locals and at brigade level, before taking it back to the university. The solution was a ditch around the seedlings filled with chemicals: as the tortoises left the plots at night, they were poisoned in the trenches.

A branch campus was typically small in size, usually 400 to 500 students, with the camaraderie of youth mostly high: "We live in our own houses, walk our own roads, and eat our own food."[18] While there was a considerable number of dropouts, especially in the famine years and in poorly managed branches, individual students were known to remain on course despite being offered good jobs outside. Many took cuts in personal income to join classes, payment of 14 yuan monthly being accepted in place of the 50-60 yuan previously earned. Of this 14 yuan, nine was set aside for food, three for pocket money, one for medical expenses, and one for study costs. Very poor students were fitted out with padded clothes, quilts, and mosquito nets. Almost all could earn cash for extra work, up to 20 yuan a month, the thrifty sending RMB home, as much as 70 yuan a year. But there was always the risk of a student going back penniless if a branch failed.

Students were worked hard as one Huanggangshan man recounted:

> In our branch there were around 800 mu of paddy fields as well as a group of employed farmers whose job it was to grow vegetables and take care of the fields. We worked in rice-seedling transplanting, tilling, and harvesting and helped farmers with plowing. There was a "walking tractor" in the school but mostly we used buffaloes. There were dozens of buffaloes in the care of specially appointed workers. We were soon producing more grain than we consumed.
>
> The district had rich resources in bamboo but was short of laborers. Local people had no way of transporting bamboo out of the mountains so the resource was not exploited. We students went into the ranges once a year — twice for the students of forestry — and, after paying local production brigades a small fee, we'd stay for a month cutting down bamboo trees and carting them down the mountains to highways or riverside where they were bound into rafts and let drift down the creeks. The money we earned helped with school costs and our food allowance.
>
> Not long after I was enrolled in late autumn, my class was sent into the mountains just for this. We walked and climbed 25 kilometers to get there by midnight. We rested the next day, then began work. Some entrants were little children from the cities, sixteen- and seventeen-year-olds who'd had never done physical labor before. They could only pull one bamboo shaft a few meters — then the tears rolled down. After practice they learned to pull two and finally four. We knew it was good for us.[19]

Women comprised seven to ten of each forty-student group.[20] Communist Labor University planning was conscious of the importance of recruiting and training women, and the numbers increased when short-term courses directed at local demand became available. If women married while in the program, or became pregnant, they were usually asked to leave, although individual married women were admitted at various times. While they had to join in labor equally with the males, women were allocated tasks thought less physically demanding, such as trimming timber rather than sawing trees; others were placed in horticulture and accounting courses. Periodically they were released from the paddy fields as a guard against infection, washing clothes or carrying food for other student laborers.

At the Nancheng Branch, located among red earth mounds and low hills, women had their own agricultural projects, which included a large four-row piggery — they cut timber, baked bricks, and mixed and laid mortar themselves.[21] Nancheng itself was regarded as one of the best of the branches — strong in growing top-grade rice seed and in supplying meat for local markets. Wang Jin Xiang spoke up for the qualities of the female contingent:

> It was traditional in Jiangxi Province to look down on women. Their labor was seen as of less value and we had only a minority of women on campus. Of course there were many excellent female students. One good friend of mine from Zhejiang, Lou Jinglin, who was eight or nine years older than me, had only a primary school education. She had entered an arranged marriage when very young and had children. At university she helped me in the fields and I helped her at school work. Now she holds down a responsible job at a hydroelectric station in Xinanjiang.[22]

When the university was established, Wang Dongxing had cited the achievements of the Chinese Women's University in Yan'an as one of its models;[23] however, few women ever reached senior positions. An exception was Ma Chaomang, who was deputy principal of the Revolutionary Committee from 1972 to 1980. Women held positions on the Students' Union executive and chaired subcommittees which dealt with activities considered relevant; Shao Yilan, a female student from Damaoshan Branch, was chosen to represent the university in Beijing on 1 November 1959, celebrating the tenth anniversary of the founding of the PRC. Even so, the negative attitudes toward women typically found in Chinese agricultural colleges, and the poor conditions, were not appreciated by female teachers who frequently sought transfers after arrival.

One activity in which university men and women were equal participants was games. All students engaged in a program of physical education and sports as part of the curriculum, volleyball, table tennis, and basketball being the most popular. Three hundred of them attended the Jiangxi Provincial Games in February 1959,[24] and four years later the university won nineteen first places from twenty-three opportunities and first place overall. The Main Campus and branches were especially strong in team games and field sports such as shot put and javelin. Bronzed by sun and the elements, the university contingent stood out in student gatherings: they were proud of their physiques and their labor and sports skill. On the expressive arts side, their troops of song and dance performers were considered the equal of professionals.

University spirit was evident in the friendly rivalry in class, the noisy congregation of friends and coworkers in the fields, and the recreation of sports, singing, and games after hours. Visitors to the branches were caught up in the bustle of their daily activities. Building, road construction, gardening, and landscaping were vigorously pursued outside classrooms, which themselves were filled with youngsters and adults learning the day's lessons. At night, comrades caught up on their studies by the light of oil and reed lamps and cooking fires. Staff and students appeared thoroughly engaged and recognized their own achievements.

In the small isolated communities of Jiangxi, which had few schools between them and only primary schools at that, a *daxue* had appeared. Substantial buildings, some designed to last generations, were constructed at remote sites, and the services they offered augmented the trained people available in local communities. The branch factories — rice and flour mills, oil presses, cotton gins, wood processing and machinery repair shops — contributed to the whole.

Once the land was reclaimed and roads opened, plots were turned into farmland, orchards, and tree plantations. Winding paths became roads and improved transportation enabled local products to find new markets. Electricity brought light to remote villages, introducing radio, film, and the ubiquitous loudspeaker. Better management techniques in irrigation, forestry, and storage arrangements increased crop yields and the quantity and variety of timber products.

In the mid-1970s three Gongda staff members visited Huanggangshan Branch some twenty years after Governor Shao Shiping made his opening address. They reported remarkable progress:

> Standing on the site and looking far into the distance, you can see terraced fields between valleys. Factory machinery can be heard and rows of poles from hydroelectricity stations crisscross the landscape. Former barren hills sleeping for more than 1,000 years are the bases for our teaching, research, and production. [25]

It is easier to grant educational institutions their achievements than account their costs. Lessons had been learned. The university as a whole could recognize that its labor demands had been excessive, a point forcibly brought home by a large number of dropouts from the student body early in 1959, which led Party Secretary Wang Dongxing to mount a vigorous rectification campaign.[26]

Gains can be attributed to the effective linking of labor and knowledge and the introduction of appropriate skills and technology. Others came through the social organization that accompanied the branches, the newly founded schools, theaters, meeting halls, first aid stations, and libraries serving many isolated communities for the first time. When the dean of studies, Chen Ping, visited more than sixty branches in 1962, he reported back: "They have changed their mountain valleys beyond recognition."[27]

Four
A Dark Side

"Big feats had individual deaths."

—Wang Jin Xiang [1]

For all the early effort, the Communist Labor University had a dark side. Being a student there was a dangerous occupation. Two young people were killed during the construction of an earthen and rock dike on the Boyang Lake reclamation site, and three forestry students were trapped in a fire, burned and suffocated to death in 1965. Others died in accidents chopping bamboo, mishandling explosives, and cutting roads, or were maimed for life. No less serious were the effects of various diseases such as schistosomiasis, typhoid, malaria, and hookworm. Of these it was *Schistosoma japonicum*, also known as Bilharzia after its discoverer and as "big belly," which extracted the greatest human toll.[2]

Schistosomiasis is a chronic disease of poverty in rural areas in Africa, South America, and Asia . Not officially recorded in China until 1905, little effort was made to chart its extent until 1951, when surveys revealed it endemic in eleven provinces, including Jiangxi Province and the Yangtse basin.[3] Over 10 million had the disease itself and another 100 million were constantly exposed to infection. In Jiangxi's Yushan County, schistosomiasis had been rampant for over 100 years and peasants were stunted and emaciated and died early, entire families vanishing from the lists. Shangyanpun hamlet, which contained 500 inhabitants in 1920, had only 144 in 1949, of whom 115 were infected.[4] The place was known as "the village of widows."

The deadly parasite is waterborne, its prime host an amphibious snail which releases large numbers of minute, free-swimming cercaria capable of boring into human skin immersed in water. The parasite matures in the veins of the liver, gut, or bladder, releasing its eggs in about 30-40 days through urine and feces.[5] These eggs hatch into miracidia, also free-swimming, which complete the cycle by entering the snail. Several domesticated animals, including cattle, pigs and dogs, can act as reservoir hosts.

Signs of infection are tiredness and general lethargy, which some university staff and students attributed initially to fatigue from hard work. Later the telltale signs of blood in the urine, diarrhea, and cramps testified to its progress. Untreated, it leads to a distended stomach due to excess fluid, gross enlargement of the spleen, cirrhosis of the liver, and cerebral breakdown if the eggs aggregate in the brain. The severity of the reaction varies from manageable symptoms to eventual death, dependent on the number of worms carried.

The waste land the Communist Labor University worked — swamp, marshland, and backwater — was the classic breeding ground for the snail carrier. Much of the university's holdings had been left untilled by locals precisely because the land was infected. Snail density was also high in the paddy fields, especially those which were single-cropped in hilly regions. Cutting reed, clearing weeds, fishing, planting rice, bathing, and washing clothes were all sources of contact; the disease was even spread through dewdrops and water film infected by crawling snails. While specialist staff were fully aware of the dangers of schistosomiasis and urged caution in clearing land, the pressure for grain was irresistible. At first, some individuals refused to work in contaminated water. However, a vice Party secretary criticized them for lacking a self-sacrificing spirit and plunged in himself; staff and students had to follow. In this instance, the young and vigorous were the most vulnerable and inevitably a price was extracted. Across the lifespan of the Communist Labor University, an estimated 10,000 staff and students contracted schistosomiasis.[6]

Treatment of the disease at that time was principally by antimony tartrate through an oral dose or an intravenous drip. In mild cases, treatment lasted three to four days in more moderate cases, 25 to 30 days. In advanced cases, the spleen was removed by surgery. Treatment frequently had serious side effects, including weakening of the heart and occasionally death. Chinese medicine, for example, powdered pumpkin seed, root extracts, and various shell, animal, and plant products, were available and used independently or in association with antimony treatment.[7] Those infected went on a regime of nonstrenuous convalescence.

The hospital at the Main Campus had 150 beds and a staff of 60-70 doctors who treated staff, students, and locals. Larger branches had their own hospitals and smaller branches had clinics. If treatment failed, or symptoms were thought too advanced or facilities considered inadequate by staff or parents, patients were sent to county or township hospitals. Some university staff were sent to Nanjing for attention. When urban parents heard that their children had been infected, they were worried and angry, and staff visited homes to explain matters and provide comfort. The task was the more difficult to handle as the university prided itself on the care shown its young people. Further, it was possible to catch the disease several times over; Wang Jin Xiang himself survived two attacks.

In 1950, the First National Health Conference laid down policy which paid attention to the health needs of workers, peasants, and soldiers, emphasizing preventative medicine and combining Western and traditional Chinese medicine.[8] A Nine-Man Subcommittee under political leadership was established in November 1955 specifically to target schistosomiasis, and plans were announced to eradicate the disease inside seven years.[9] One task of the committee was to publicize the case for prevention through newspapers, popular readers, and films such as "Spring Comes to the Withered Tree."

During the Great Leap Forward movement in 1958, after thousands of specialized workers and hundreds of prevention and treatment units applied shortened treatments and claimed high cure rates in rural areas, the timetable for elimination was reduced to one year. Undoubtedly these initiatives produced results, although claims by Committee Member Wei Wenbo in 1960 that schistosomiasis was under complete control cannot be credited.[10] Two and a half million sufferers were still counted in 1977,[11] and, for all the new drugs, the World Health Organization's Division of Control of Tropical Disease currently lists schistosomiasis as endemic in Indonesia, the Philippines, Thailand, and China.

Mao Zedong took a personal interest in rural health, being a forceful advocate of galvanizing the rural community: the introduction of the commune system was to provide the organizational structure. A physical cultist himself, Mao made frequent statements on health issues and the well-being of students, perhaps the best known being his charge, "Health first and study second," passed to Ma Xulun, his minister of education in 1950.[12] The Chairman would tackle schistosomiasis in his own way. He raised the importance he put on eradicating the disease at a Party meeting in Hangzhou in 1955, the Nine-Man Subcommittee being one outcome.[13] Then he took direct action himself.

Reading in the *People's Daily* of June 30th, 1958, about the stamping out of the blood-fluke in Yukiang, my mind became so turbulent. I couldn't sleep. A soft breeze blew warmly and the rising sun sparkled on the window. Looking far into the southern sky, I began to write.

> Farewell to the God of Plague
> So many green streams and blue hills, but to what avail?
> This tiny creature left Hua To powerless!
> Hundreds of villages choked with weeds, men wasted away;
> Thousands of homes deserted, ghosts chant mournfully.
> Motionless, by earth I travel eighty thousand li a day,
> Surveying the sky I see a myriad milky ways from afar.
> Should the Cowherd ask tidings of the God of Plague,
> Say the same griefs flow down the stream of time.
>
> The spring wind blows amid profuse willow wands,
> Six hundred million in this land all equal Yao and Shun,
> Crimson rain swirls in waves under our will,
> Green mountains turn to bridges at our wish,
> Gleaming mattocks fall on the Five Ridges heaven-high;
> Mighty arms move to rock the earth around the Triple River.
> We ask the God of Plague: "Where are you bound?"
> Paper barges aflame and candlelight illuminate the sky.[14]

Clearly the poem contrasts China's historical past with modern achievements. Hua To was the famed physician from the Three Kingdoms (200-204 A.D.), and the mythical "Cowherd" lived on a star in the Milky Way. "Six hundred million" Chinese now stood together with Yao and Shun, ancient emperors of great virtue. Five Ridges and the Triple River represent the whole of China.[15]

A decade later, an English surgeon in China, Joshua Horn, reported that no snails were found in Yujiang County and that stool tests revealed no infection.[16] Snails were destroyed when swamps were drained and earth turned to bury them. The clearing of vegetation along the ditches, burning of infected grasses, and submerging the snails for long periods were also effective.

The Communist Labor University made its contribution through land reclamation and dike construction. Staff were well aware of the fatal practice of storing night soil in pits or jars along rivers, which were prone to overflow thereby spreading infected feces and urine. They encouraged their work groups to use communal containers, which were sealed, enabling the generation of heat and ammonia to kill eggs. Student teams also collected the host snails from along waterways.

Cattle and draft oxen were other sources of serious infection on university land, particularly in grassy marshlands where they were the most significant vector. Indeed, parasites were found to survive longer in cattle manure than human feces under the same environmental conditions. According to a 1957 estimate, about 1.5 million cattle carried schistosomiasis.[17] Schemes were put in hand to remove large animals from the rundown shelters of individual dwellings and place them in collective shelters that provided manure containers for heat fermentation. The university undertook a research project, part of the State Plan advocated by Mao in the 1970s to eliminate the disease in cattle. Fresh land was opened up in 1973 for grazing a small experimental herd, and students undertook surveys of infection in nearby counties. Applying a newly devised mouth injection treatment, cattle were inoculated and anatomized.[18] Four years later, the findings and recommended treatments were reported nationally.

Parasitology was taught as a subject by the Department of Animal Husbandry and Veterinary Medicine in 1959. Apart from a few branches which offered specialization in Health Hygiene, knowledge of the dangers of schistosomiasis was spread mostly by word of mouth and incidental reference. In 1960, the large Damaoshan Branch engaged directly in rural health when it provided a qualification for rural doctors and, by 1965, it was providing four-year training — one year of basic medical study, one and a half years of clinical medicine, and the same period of supervised practice. The course offered parisitology, pathology, microbiology, pharmacy, gynecology, acupuncture, and so forth, putting an emphasis "on the prevention and cure of commonly occurring diseases in the country and mountainous areas."[19] Graduates, who reached the standard for practitioners serving mountainous regions laid down by the Department of Public Health, were said to both treat patients and engage in physical labor.

The anti-schistosomiasis campaigns of the mid-1950s, backed by vigorous educational programs that utilized radio, exhibitions, slide shows, and broadsheets, were designed to change attitudes. Many peasants believed the disease the outcome of unfavorable *feng shui* around family teams, or the machinations of evil spirits in the nearby lakes, or bad deeds of ancestors. However, the years of famine of 1959-61 worked against "human sea" campaigns, as rapidly falling incomes and a severe shortage of grain were disincentives for the mobilization of public labor. Similarly the added responsibilities given production teams discouraged what seemed unproductive labor. A greater tolerance of living with schistosomiasis became apparent. Mao himself avoided mention of mass campaigns in health until the economy began to pickup in 1964, and then they proved more difficult to promote the second time around.

Under instruction from Zhou Enlai, the Main Campus opened a Department for Rural Medicine in 1965, which offered a three-year diploma course for students, who were to return to their commune on graduation. This direction from Zhou was consistent with his known attempts to protect the regular hospital system, medical training, and medical research from serious dilution under short-term political policies. Approved in February 1966, the university program would teach Western and Chinese medicine to 300 students, initially on a trial basis.[20] As well, the Main Campus three months later prepared a set of Temporary Regulations that stressed the importance of the physical well-being of students, including adequate rest periods. Mao's affirmation at the Third National Congress of the Communist Youth League, "Good health, good study, and good work,"[21] was cited in support.

Neither Zhou's proposal nor the Temporary Regulations survived the onset of the Cultural Revolution. Major rural health initiatives of these years came from sending hospital teams down to the countryside and the "barefoot doctor" schemes. Young people, some of whom came from families of traditional medicine practitioners, received a three- to six-month course in a commune hospital or clinic before moving into rural areas to undertake basic medical work. The innovation was hailed as another anti-schistosomiasis measure. Overall though, enthusiasm for public health was subordinate to political activity. The Nine-Man Subcommittee was dissolved, and new leaders told farmers, "Forget about the little worm, grasp the big problems of class struggle."[22] The disease raged again in some localities where it had been previously controlled. A further initiative from the time was the opening of a pharmaceutical factory at the Main Campus, part of a national trend to cheaper medicines and a means of earning extra income for institutions.

The considerable number of infected staff and students reduced the effectiveness of the university's total workforce, despite treatment being timed to coincide with periods before and after the busy season. One estimate put the average loss at 40 percent of an individual's capacity to labor.[23] Infected men and women were treated under insurance at the university; however, no compensation was paid immediately. Staff who suffered were regarded as injured on duty at retirement and were entitled to 5 percent additional pension. If a breadwinner died, an additional 50 yuan a year was paid for 20 years. Those seriously incapacitated were prescribed light duties or returned to their original units or sent home.[24]

On foundation, the university had promised to give great attention to health and safety, echoing Mao's charge to end overwork and overstudy.[25] More than 20,000 mu of swamp and marshland was salvaged by 1964,[26] and leaders from the early days set their losses against the achievement. Wang Jin Xiang put it with vigor: "The university must have land. Without it we could not survive. It was a price we paid willingly, a necessary sacrifice. We would give our lives for Gongda."[27] Yet the cost in individual suffering was undeniable.

Part II

Educational Work

Five
Classroom and Farm

"By struggling against nature we are struggling for the revolution."

—Wang Jiming, Director of Education[1]

The busiest period for the university was the late summer, which brought the harvesting of the April rice crop and the plowing, irrigating, and planting of the crop to follow. Seed rice was germinated in water before transplanting to a nursery, where fires were lit to bring on the plants or the nursery was cooled to delay growth. From germination to planting took about a month. Soil was prepared, turned, and manured with natural compost, and planting began under water. Mature plants were irrigated at night, the water let out by day to give them access to sunlight. If plants were kept too long in water, they would rot. A second crop was gathered in October, when red flower grass was usually sown and later dug into the soil as fertilizer. On fertile land, 800 jin per mu was grown, but on the poorest, only one crop enough to fill a basket of rice could be harvested. Rice was grown for subsistence; as a cash crop it brought only 10 to 20 fen per jin: "It is said no one can grow rich from agriculture — it is better to try industry."[2]

Students had to learn to move backwards in line and push rice plants deep in the soil, not just throw them in. Weeding the plots was harder work still: the students had to kneel down, "back to the sky, face to the land," as they moved slowly through the rows. Cuts to legs and arms easily became infected and leeches attached to ankles and bare feet. The rice was harvested by hand using a sickle, the most skilled students harvesting one mu a day. Rice straw was then stacked. Winnowing also required much physical labor, as students beat the plants on a stone floor or rolled a stone over them by hand or bullock, shovelling the gathered grain into bags of 50-100 jin made from local fiber. The students soon sported the wear and tear of toil and sunburn: "In July and August we worked so hard our skin became red, then brown. A layer of skin was shed and we lost weight."

Women were thought especially adept at planting and harvesting: "My wife was more careful and quicker than I, and she moved backwards more surely." For city girls, the required work hours were built up gradually: "At first we women carried a 'flower basket,' then loads of 30-60 jin, and even up to 100 or more. When I came I couldn't manage my luggage." Female students were introduced to the fields from beginning; it might take almost a year for the city-bred to reach full capacity. Physical demands were considerable as boys learned to carry 140-150 jin, girls up to 120.[3] In places where the labor force was adequate, men normally took over the heavier duties.

Hard though it was, the labor expected from rice growers was of a lower order than that of forestry students. Foresters were required to climb mountains to collect seed, germinate it in a seed bed, plant the saplings, soften the soil and add fertilizer, cull their plots, and eventually cut down the product.

> First of all we selected our tree. Next we cut it down by hand ax (which we learned to make ourselves) or by saw. We tried to cut it as low down as possible. The fall was controlled by ropes, not always successfully as the tree could shift and some of us would be hurt. Branches were cut off next and the trunk rolled down to the water. We had no sawmills at first; everything was cut by hand and stacked to dry. When we did get power saws we pushed the wood forward for cutting. This was quite dangerous — students lost limbs.[4]

Timber was selected for building purposes and university furniture, with some earmarked for sale: "Among the trees, we found sweet-smelling wood which repelled insects." Students also collected fruit from the tung oil tree, which looks similar to an apple; when peeled and crushed, its oil could be used as varnish.

> The new students from the cities would take a fruit and sneak into the lavatory to have a bite. They could lose a tooth! There was an oil tree in Jiangxi which was planted in the mountains. It made the mountains green and us a profit. Its oil was said to have medicinal benefits and reduce cholesterol — one reason why the locals had longevity.

All students at the Communist Labor University worked for periods in field and forest without exception. One city mother from a well-to-do Shanghai family offered to buy her son out of field work. "Wasn't Labor the name of our university — that was impossible!" Usually the Main Campus and its branches adopted block time for labor. Forestry course students would camp out, so their teaching and production comprised three- to four-week blocks; other courses generally alternated a one-or two-week cycle of study and work. In July 1961, the maximum hours for labor were fixed at eight a day, or, where study and labor were combined, not more than nine.[5] Most students took a one-month vacation in winter.

The advantages of a keen young workforce had not been lost on many farm hosts, whose leaders needed reminding that they were managing a university campus not a labor camp. Some farms appeared immune to a high dropout rate among students, quickly filling the vacancies with new youngsters. Control over excessive demands put on students soon became a major issue. After a good deal of contention and over a year's negotiations with the farm branches, it was agreed that all centers would strictly adhere to fixed labor periods: six months in the first year, five in the second, and four in the remaining two years from 1960 on.

Of course, there were deaf ears, some branches continuing with a 50-50 split throughout. Others increased the physical labor component on demand, or "volunteered" their labor to outside agencies for private benefit. A few branches adopted an incentive scheme, allowing students more study time when labor targets were met. At the commencement, students had been organized in two teams — one for study under a teacher, the other for labor under a farm leader; it was now determined that the teams would be amalgamated and led by a university lecturer. Branches that had surplus laborers would release students for periods to work their home plots, where the experienced youngsters toiled effectively in the production teams.

Hard work was evident in the classroom, too. Most of those enrolled in branch campuses had low entry qualifications, understandable given the opportunities in the countryside where four to five years of primary schooling was an achievement in its own right. Campuses had considerable autonomy in the methods they applied to raise standards among their students. Several could draw on the background of staff with experience in the postwar accelerated schools opened for Party organizers who had missed out on schooling during the fighting. These older men and women had been taught the basics in shortened courses before taking up higher-level posts or entering university. Similar learning strategies were applied at the university, where branch staff demonstrated the same confidence as the early communist educators, accepting that men and women could attain academic prerequisites in a remarkably brief period given a will to learn. As Wang Dongxing explained at a meeting of farm leaders in 1959, "It is not necessary to go to middle school to learn natural science if students come equipped with enthusiasm and indomitable spirit."[6]

Preparatory students joined undergraduate ranks in half the time normally set aside in the regular school system. Students with five or six years of elementary school who entered courses which required junior middle entrance (equivalent to three years of high school) were given additional hours and intensive study in the core subjects of Chinese, mathematics, physics, biology, and chemistry. One or two years' study was considered sufficient time to attain accelerated entry.

The least-educated entrants with incomplete elementary schooling attended remedial classes where they were coached by "little teachers," their fellow students. At the very least they aimed to graduate with a knowledge of 5,000 to 6,000 characters and the ability to write simple reports on such topics as best practice in cotton and rice cultivation, or prevalent pests and plant diseases.[7]

Many stories record the remarkable progress of individual "catch-up" students. One head of an agricultural cooperative, with only four years' primary schooling, reached the second-year level of junior middle school at Damaoshan branch after less than a year's study. A young woman caught up after learning her lessons by candlelight, taking short walks in the night air to keep alert. Other students maintained the pace by reading their books under burning pine branches. The stories are reminiscent of the exemplary tales in the reader *The Three Character Classic*, compiled in the Song Dynasty and reprinted down the ages, which tells how the ancient sages read by the light of glowworms or tied their hair to beams to prevent themselves nodding off during their assiduous study of the classics.

When Party Secretary Wang Dongxing told people that the results of his experimental university would reach and doubtless surpass those of China's other institutions, however, it was largely passion which backed his claim.[8] Little accessible material was available for guidance in work-study beyond experience from the communists' wartime political and technical schools. The works of the country's best-known adult educator, Liang Shuming, had been proscribed following his fracas with Mao over the origins of social class: the Chairman had denigrated Liang as the assassin with a pen. And the famed Yan Yangchu, who managed the model Ding County project in rural reconstruction in Hebei Province, had left China for Taiwan on the communists' victory.

The writings of another significant adult educator, Tao Xingzhi, a graduate of Teachers College, Columbia University, and manager of a rural teacher training center outside Nanjing, were similarly out of favor despite Tao turning to Chinese peasant life for inspiration. "I went through a moment of awakening, like the Yellow River breaking its dikes, and rushed back to the way of the common people."[9] While his philosophy of education was attacked by the communist cultural powers in the early 1950s, his writing was reassessed and he returned to popularity after 1980.

Closer to home, Jiangxi Province itself had experienced rural reconstruction programs supported by missionaries under the Nationalist government in the 1920s and 1930s. Among the Methodists was George Sheperd, who cooperated with the Nationalists in his Lichuan County project.[10] Also Chiang Kaishek, the KMT leader, made Nanchang the headquarters of the New Life Movement, through which he aimed to restore the allegiance of the local population in the one-time Soviet enclave. The Nationalists planned to enlist intellectuals not committed to city life for rural reconstruction. Their most sustained effort was the backing of ten welfare centers providing education, agricultural extension, cooperatives, and health services in the Jiangxi countryside in the 1930s and 1940s. Some centers were located in the same villages and counties as the university branches of 1958, including Nancheng, Ji'an, Gaoan, Shangrao, and Taihe. While the various projects promoted social service and application in learning, they were very much a transplant from the cities and prey of their social context. The salaries of their staff, for instance, were frequently delayed or not paid at all. Neither missionary partner nor KMT officialdom achieved long-lasting benefits and all had closed by 1945.

Another contender for educational influence was the system of cooperatives and vocational projects of New Zealander Rewi Alley, who had set up his Gung Ho (Work Together) movement in 1938 in Jiangxi, where he made use of lathes and machinery from other centers in the north buried to avoid looting by the Japanese and dug up and freighted downstream later to his headquarters at Ganzhou. Youngsters were prepared for cooperative activities in Bailie Schools, named after the American Joseph Bailie, who supported reforestation and technical training in China, sending students to the United States in the 1900s. Alley had been appointed to lead the Sandan Bailie School, a vocational center in faraway Xinjiang.

> Rewi brought in an advance truck load of students, huddled in their sheepskin coats against the cold of the desert, and began lessons in an unheated building on Christmas Day, 1944. Half work, half theory, was the school's idea from the start, and the advance students were quickly at work within the buildings Rewi had rented — helping to build the *kangs*, (clay stoves used also as beds in Northern China), and clearing out the main temple.[11]

Sandan was eventually moved to Lanzhou in 1952, where it became a technical school for training workers for the oil industry. China's leaders approved of Alley's cooperatives and educational activities. He was on terms with the KMT heads, knew Mao from 1949, and was friendly with both Zhou Enlai and Zhu De. However, Alley's ideas were not widely disseminated inside the country given the chaotic circumstances. Wang Dongxing thinks he remembers meeting him a couple of times, but said his educational ideas were unknown to him and they played no part in the conception of the university. When the New Zealander visited the Communist Labor University in December 1961, touring Daomaoshan Branch, it was more as publicist than educational expert. His role was similar when he inspected the university at the beginning of the Cultural Revolution. Certainly there were points in common between their two sets of opinions. Alley regarded the potential of "the illiterate children of illiterate peasants as 'second to none.'"[12] When work-study was applied, these youngsters would "learn even more of ordinary educational subjects than they will in the full-time classroom schools."

The writings of other individual international educators held little sway. American John Dewey's seminal studies on work and education had been condemned both by the Chinese Nationalists for their child-centeredness and by the Communists for their capitalist message. At the same time, the writing of Russian Anton S. Makarenko, famed for his Gorki Colony for orphans, was out of favor, with China busy weaning itself from Soviet influence.

In the Soviet Union itself, the innovative work-study experiments during the 1920s had been abandoned by Stalin, and it was the more conventional policies which were passed down by "elder brother" during the early 1950s, the time of borrowings. Taking Soviet advice, China cut back its comprehensive universities and increased its special-purpose institutes, especially engineering, in a move to expand the output of skilled personnel quickly. For all that, the Russians backed solid academic ways, calling for good buildings and facilities, qualified staff, and full-time students, preferably with senior middle qualifications. By 1958, however, educational ties with the Soviet Union had loosened, itself a reason why the Communist Labor University experiment, so different from standard practice, could be attempted at all.

Wang Dongxing believed that the Communist Labor University would surely find its own way: in Marxist terminology, it would make itself. All that was needed was homegrown confidence: "Why are our own ways inferior to foreign ways of doing things? Are not goods made in China labeled 'imported goods' in foreign countries? We must rid ourselves of any notion of inferiority and trust ourselves."[13] The words of Wang's earlier promise to outperform conventional universities would come back to haunt him. What he had really meant, he declared later, was that Gongda's enrollments would be greater, courses more practical, and research wholly applied. He also admitted: "We'd never run a university of part work, part study like Gongda — we weren't sure how to run it well."[14] To answer the situation, the university needed to attempt considerable trial-and-error learning over several years.

The Main Campus staff put much time and effort into ensuring the academic program as a whole appeared respectable. They insisted that core subjects be taught and basic levels of abstraction mastered first of all. The theory strand covered the essentials of Chinese, mathematics, physics, chemistry, biology, physical education, and political study, which included CPC policy, the history of China, and Marxist economics, philosophy, and ethics. Comparisons of basic study times were published, the university claiming that there was little difference between its hours of classroom teaching and those of conventional universities. Indeed, in some basic subjects the hours surpassed the national average. Over the five-year course, 29 months were set aside for teaching, 26 for labor, and 5 for vacation periods. The ratio for the four-year course was 25:19:4, and for the three year course, 18:15:3.[15] Approximately half the teaching time was face to face and the balance self-study.

Disciplinary knowledge was associated as much as possible with a student's designated qualification.[16] Chemistry for agricultural majors, for example, was taught as it related to soil science and plant physiology. After the classroom stage, a period was allowed for observation on site, and this was followed by farming activity, the particular learning cycle concluding with group discussion of theory and outcomes. Sequence in learning was demanded, classroom teaching being based on experience in the field and vice versa.

The production cycle determined the appropriate time for related teaching: rice and cotton cultivation, for example, was taught in spring and late summer, and wheat, rape, and manure crops such as red clover and legumes, in autumn. Forestry students were taught the plantation management of pine and spruce early in the new year, care of seedlings and young trees in summer, and seed selection and the opening of new forest areas for camphor and tung oil trees in early winter.

The activity of basic teaching, associated with the careful timing of studies, observation on site, production activity, and academic summary, was titled "on-the-spot teaching." This was an invention of the Communist Labor University and its prime educational principle. At first there was debate as to whether on-the-spot teaching sufficiently emphasized theoretical knowledge. Should knowledge and skills be taught mostly in the classroom, or mostly in the field? A public test was called for, with investigators briefed and sent to production brigades to get local views. When the results were collated, most of the staff were convinced, or agreed, that the second proposition was the better, that on-the-spot teaching enabled students to undertake operational skills with speed and accuracy and to better understand the total process and work independently. Students were deemed equally enthusiastic: "They say that one hour of on-the-spot teaching is more useful than 100 pages of learning from textbooks."

Class and farm work were coordinated to allow experimental small plot exercises, followed by involvement in field-scale projects. Some branches established special demonstration centers where model practices were on display, for instance, the Main Campus maintained President Liu's famed cotton center. If a branch was not farm- or forest-based, adaptive arrangements applied: the Nanchang campus, where the Silkworm Factory had relocated from Shanghai, offered its 375 students work experience in the cultivation of mulberry trees and cocoon rearing, as well as spinning and weaving.[17]

Innovative solutions were developed for assessing the classroom–field nexus. "Most examinations were open. Teachers posed questions — and local farmers, workers, and teachers joined together in rating individuals according to their abilities, skills, and results."[18] The university declared itself not bound by scholarly convention, having rejected the conventional wisdom that "the greater the quantity and depth of knowledge the better."[19] It would accept a narrow range of teaching options from small campuses where course content would be restricted and subordinate to production. However, courses could be too narrow: agricultural students at Nancheng Branch, redirected into horticulture in midstream to meet the manpower demands of local communes in 1965, had found themselves back at the early stage of the horticulture learning circle.

In 1958, only 500 characters appeared in national texts on the red earth of Jiangxi. As early as the first year, the staff started to modify these textbooks by introducing local content:

> The old teaching material dealt in detail with black earth, saline-alkali soil, and podsol, which Jiangxi does not have, but little about red loam which makes up over 60 percent of the soil in Jiangxi. The new teaching material focuses on red loam.[20]

Bamboo, a crop widespread in the province and an important commercial item, was another subject excluded from the national texts. Nor was silkworm raising on a small scale mentioned. Much in the official texts was thought redundant: staff halved multivolume works in size, reducing their characters from 600,000 to 200,000, thereby making them more pertinent and readable. Extra space was found for content on water and soil conservation.

> The national texts and references carried too much detail. And they were not written according to our production cycle. When we were planting, they were fertilizing. We couldn't stay in the classroom too long — we must catch the season.[21]

As early as August 1959, the university reported fourteen new textbooks, and a teachers' working group was assembled at Lushan under Governor Shao's supervision in September 1960 to transform class books into "living texts."[22] Course content was reorganized, overlap excised, and material like hunting considered obsolete dropped. Twenty courses were collapsed into twelve, with teaching hours reduced by 25 percent. Staff went into nearby communes to try out the new books: "We discarded the usual way of writing texts. We joined a production brigade in forestry laboring alongside the workers for several months. Many things were learned that were not taught in our textbooks, and things that were in our books couldn't be used in production."

Commissioned texts were published, among them books on how to better utilize Jiangxi soils, manage field work, and evaluate field experiments. The provincial bureaus of education, agriculture, reclamation, and forestry assisted in the compilation of texts and approved the final versions.

Effective teaching and production required careful planning. Wherever possible, labor was associated with teaching in specialist fields, allowing for value-added return. Monthly records and estimates of revenue and disbursements were kept by branches and balance sheets posted for public display. The university's senior students were closely involved in estimating these costs as part of their training. The open operation of much of the university's accounting represented its application of the "mass line" philosophy. The concept, developed in the Jiangxi enclave in the early 1930s, called for Party organizers to explain government policy to farmers who in turn would provide their own assessments before any final decision was taken. Also known as the "democratic management" style,[23] the Communist Labor University regarded itself as its institutional manisfestation given its reliance on local knowledge and advice. Supporting the idea, the university held annual meetings of its branch and farm heads to share experiences and swap ideas and to report and modify the three-year plans.

Branches were directed to aim for self-sufficiency for students before directing funds into building improvement. Broadly speaking, the class unit worked as the production team in the field, the department kept the accounts, and the university regulated the whole. Labor tasks were ordered according to priority, with the necessary workforce and projected output calculated in advance. Some reserves were kept in hand for unfortunate or improvident branches, but campuses were expected to store up in fat years for the certain lean ones to come.

The link of school, farm, factory, and research center and the blend of theory and application were the university's major contribution to the theory of part-work, part-study education. The leadership regarded the program as a socialist breakthrough. No longer could students pass their courses on paper by regurgitating the thoughts of others: instead they would utilize actual production activities in support of learning, a form of study leading to "true scientific knowledge."[24] The new way contrasted with that of conventional teaching, which "overemphasized scientific method, logic, and completeness." The university, though, needed to be careful to strike a balance. Farm leaders were not above quoting its own philosophy against it when they defended overworking students, insisting that "application is more important than study."

In all, it was the attention given learning procedures and practice which set the Communist Labor University apart from the many short-lived, politically serving ventures of the day. For all the inevitable waste of experimentation, the teaching and production linkage of the Main Campus was innovative and recorded for others to assess and attempt.

Six
"Staffers, Laborers, and Researchers"

"Jiangxi Communist Labor University has good experiences. It's said that its graduates can write and fight, and work as staffers, laborers, and researchers. They are the new generation."

—Liu Shaoqi, President of China, 1964[1]

The university boasted no professors in the usual sense of the word. Its main teaching force had been recruited from the urban personnel sent down to the countryside in 1957 and, for new recruits, authorities drew on demobilized army officers, college graduates, technicians, and exceptional students, "pulling up young crops."[2] Wang Jin Xiang was among those released before graduation in 1961 for various teaching duties. Among the best of the makeshift staff were the former local government cadres and technical workers who knew Jiangxi. Thought honest and reliable, if pedagogically inexperienced, they were to the fore in practical teaching and leading the "revolutionary teaching groups,"[3] whose members worked alongside students and farmers in the production teams. Much was made of the philosophy "Let those who know, teach," irrespective of whether the lecturer had any formal qualifications.

The skills expected from staff were diverse. The agriculture department wanted lecturers experienced in grain production, the cultivation of cotton and fruit trees, pig and cattle raising, and the extraction of oil from plants. Forestry section staff had to manage afforestation, commercial tree cultivation, tea plantations, and wood processing. Animal husbandry and veterinary science teachers concentrated on livestock farming, assisting with grain and forestry production as extras, and agricultural machinery personnel built and repaired machinery for the university's factories and local farmers. In the mountains, branches sought experts in handicrafts, bee-keeping, and road construction.

Eventually staff members were recruited directly from other universities; however, they were not thought especially effective. These men and women noticed a coolness toward the ethos they brought with them, if not towards themselves personally. Certainly a Jiangxi posting was not popular among conventional scholars; the hopes for a proper academic career of those assigned appeared dashed. A teacher's standing at his or her new home was made clear by the welcome from the Party secretary in the language of the day:

> Though we have adopted the mass line at our university, this does not mean that we ignore the contribution of the expert. On the contrary, in teaching production and research, we trust our experts and give full play to them. They are our great treasure. We will unite with those who want to serve the construction of socialism, help them remold their ideologies, raise their class consciousness, and integrate them with the people.
>
> Without the masses, experts are leaders without followers. If these same people consider themselves masters of the masses, superiors above inferiors, no matter how intelligent they are, they are not wanted here and there is no future for them. [4]

Ideology aside, Wang Dongxing took a softer tone: "Our teachers and students should trust one another; and help and respect each other; that is the main thing in our running the university well."[5]

His first caution to new academics required no reinforcement. Salutary lessons had been meted out to hundreds of thousands of non-conformist teachers in the Anti-Rightist movement only a year previously. In a campaign which swept the country, intellectuals and teachers remembered as having spoken out against government policy, or who were thought too Western in opinion, were imprisoned, hundreds of thousands being sent to labor camps, many being worked to death. Regarded as class enemies, these unfortunates and their families were legitimate prey. A student of the time reports:

> I was a bright boy at a country high school and my teacher backed me in my efforts to get to university. Because university places were cut back in 1957, my teacher joined a demonstration against higher education policy. He was named a "rightist." I tore up his picture and destroyed the notes I had from him. He was arrested and I dared not ask about him. Later I heard he had died in the fields. Today I am ashamed, and when I think of him it brings tears to my eyes.[6]

The Communist Labor University had a few proclaimed rightists which it inherited from its various cooperating institutions. However the group was small, for most had already been sent to labor in the countryside, only a handful remaining on campus by the end of 1958. An administrator explains:

> Yes, we had several rightists. We criticized them, of course. The branches had more of them than the Main Campus as some places used them as teachers. This was Wang Dongxing's idea. "I don't use them politically," he said. "I want them for their academic skills." Most were university graduates. Some leaders were against this opinion of Wang. He was quite brave in the matter. Eventually some rightists reached the rank of head of a department, a middle level position. We also took responsibility for the children of our rightists by finding them jobs.

One woman who had committed the sin of owning land was set to hard cleaning around the campus, where she was under constant supervision because the university was required report on her regularly. The sympathetic called her "Grandma." Down the years, most rightists returned to the Main Campus from the countryside after their "caps" were taken off, and the mid-sixties saw more of them rehabilitated. By 1980, seventy-one rightists had been formally pardoned, among them staff going back to the days of the Nanchang and Ganzhou Forestry Technical Colleges, as well as others from Jiangxi Agricultural College.[7] A few too old to move stayed in exile, not wishing or able to return. Of those that died, it would be admitted posthumously that they had been unjustly persecuted.

Unlike other educational institutions, the university lost little momentum from the purge. Implicit in the Anti-Rightist movement was an assessment that many academics from regular universities were contaminated by Western ideas. By contrast, Communist Labor University teachers were "new born."[8]

Within a month of arrival on campus, new staff members were dispatched to the fields to build up laboring skills. Assigned to individual farmers to speed their learning, they toiled with their students for three to four months a year. Apart from meeting the philosophical demands of the university, teacher labor was justified on the grounds that staff would otherwise be underemployed when their students were out of class.

Time in the paddy fields was not popular with those who genuinely doubted its educational value. Men and women with limited work skills feared the physical labor and the loss of face when their inadequacies were exposed. Some were given a hard time by a few farm managers who took advantage of their lack of experience and physical strength to repay some real or imagined slight. They suffered too when directed to supervise teaching at the production bases, where living conditions were primitive and dirty — complainants were told to "throw their bourgeois conventions to the winds."[9]

Quite young teachers recruited from regular institutions, with only a few weeks practical experience in their training, could find themselves leading more-experienced students and workers in major tasks such as building reservoirs. Not all were equal to it, many being transferred or retired to light duties. Teaching loads were heavy. Original projections had estimated one teacher to twenty or twenty-five students, but in some under-resourced places there was only one teacher for ninety students.[10] While large classes have seldom been considered a handicap in China's rote-learning schoolrooms, on-the-spot teaching required smaller groups, so additional field workers were hired for the practical training, which ensured staff-student ratios of around 1:7, dependent upon students' work experience. The educational attainments of most did not go beyond an incomplete primary schooling, though their skill levels were thought sufficient.

Demand for teachers was consistently high, and teacher training became increasingly important: it was mostly organized in-house, with the Main Campus and selected branches operating as demonstration centers. In 1961, 2,280 were counted as trained in courses helping academics understand basic production techniques and trade teachers reach senior standards.[11] Inexperienced lecturers were released for basic training in winter or after work and mobile teams of trainers operated in isolated parts of Jiangxi. Promising young staff were returned for periods to the Main Campus. The daily demands put on teachers left them with little time to consider higher studies and there were no senior academics to supervise them in the first decade.

Administrators visited and encouraged teachers — an intimidating policy although one designed to break down the administrative-academic divide. After a senior cadre attended a Gui Xi Branch man, a teacher considered ineffectual in his subject of meteorology, boring and hard to understand, the individual was motivated to make his lessons more interesting and relevant.[12] Opportunities were there for general staff members to join regular university classes, in turn they would pass on their clerical and management skills. Technicians, motor mechanics, bakers, and brewers all passed down trade secrets to younger staff and students.

Students' progress was limited by their teachers' capacities and the primitive equipment available to them. The first anatomy class in veterinary science had selected a dying horse for dissection, using a kitchen table for the operation.[13] The teachers, themselves less than expert, worked from a textbook as they cut specimens for students to view. The carving and slicing, and the identification of the parts, took all night, staff and students mastering their anatomy and dissection lessons together around the blood-soaked table.

An essentially rural intake was maintained until late 1961, when the composition of the student body changed significantly under an influx of nearly 10,000 young Shanghainese. Nine hundred and seventy-nine senior middle school graduates were sent to the Main Campus, and 8,497 junior middle graduates to the branches.[14] The catalyst for the new enrolment had been a suggestion in August from Shanghai's Party head, Ke Qingshi, to Premier Zhou Enlai that the university take on a share of unemployed urban youth whose idleness was a source of trouble and disaffection, and mouths an extra burden on the state's granaries. Further, Mao had a national plan to reduce the urban population by shifting numbers inland. A large party of these Shanghainese had been sent to Xinjiang Province earlier, but most returned inside three months. Ke and Zhou hoped that the training component of the university would keep the young people in the countryside.

On 23 October 1961, the university sent Lin Zhong and a small team to Shanghai on a recruiting mission. Before he left, Lin was briefed to select only youngsters from the outskirts who already had work experience. Wang Jin Xiang joined the team, addressing over 70,000 young people. The first batches of volunteers arrived back in Jiangxi late the same year.

Alas, it seems Lin did not act according to instructions. His students had not come with field experience from the city limits; rather, they had been recruited directly from the city's high schools with junior or senior middle school qualifications. Shao and Liu were infuriated and had a row with Lin that all staff heard about. To help ease things, the province paid the university a head fee per student, gave them a small settling-in sum, and allowed a grain and oil ration up to the end of July 1963.[15] After that the students should fend for themselves.

As the senior leaders had feared, the newcomers were ill-equipped for work-study learning. Inexperienced and immature boys and girls in their late teens were put in branches already struggling with food shortages under managers who took no interest on them or their plight beyond sending them to labor. Not able to build up their work skills, they became exhausted and sick: with little to eat, some were too ill even to swallow food. Parents and friends had to send money to keep them alive, then pay the branch to send them back. About 2,000 youngsters packed up their scanty belongings, many of the original items having been sold for food, and collected their bus and train tickets home.

Though the university accepted the debacle as a poor reflection on itself, it did not despair. With the approval of the Provincial Party Committee, the names and addresses of absconders were collected and a letter sent inviting him or her to return. The missive from the Main Campus was followed up by a personal visit from a staff member. Wang Jin Xiang reports:

> Our point was that it was not the students' fault — the problem had been created by the managers in some branches who had abused the students. Our personal contact was valued and accepted by many families, and about 1,000 of them returned to Gongda. Over half of the original 10,000 would remain for good in Jiangxi.[16]

An analysis of about half the total graduate numbers between 1962 and 1964 counted 5,500 graduates with junior technical qualifications, 7,100 at senior technical, and 790 at college levels.[17] By remaining in the countryside, graduates spread the word about their education, which helped keep up enrollments: the more the graduates, the more the influence. Nancheng branch, for example, supplied at least 100 graduates to several local communes, building its reputation in the process.[18]

While graduates found a variety of placements, most returned to their farms and communes with knowledge of new ways of doing things. They built rural schools, making the classroom furniture and finding the teachers, formed teams to survey and map extensive forest resources, and constructed access roads. Those from Shanggao Branch had returned to a place "where even mice died of hunger, and frogs of thirst, and young plants turned yellow if no rain fell for three days."[19] Said to have targeted water conservation and new crops, they boasted observable results. The young men and women were praised for their talent and trustworthiness, they were living images of Bao Gong, the honest and upright dynastic official.

Not all graduates returned to work worthy of their talents. There can be sympathy for the family of Wu Zhengcai, Class of 1959, who went back to his home village in 1961. "'Who ever heard of a No. 1 scholar becoming a peasant?' said his relatives. 'Others study to lift their heads,' his father added, 'but you return to work our fields with the hoe.'"[20] Some went to lowly jobs such as porter or cook, or labored for work points, based on a production team's output in the field, until better opportunities arose.

Given the need for skilled manpower in Jiangxi's production brigades, the graduate output was theoretically covered. However, many brigades found themselves too poverty-stricken to take on additional labor, especially in the early 1960s, and a number of the first cohort of graduates left agriculture. Over time, individual graduates used their university qualification and experience to rise to senior county and prefecture posts in and outside agriculture.

A university is known for its research, and the leadership called on branch staff, as well as that of the Main Campus, to establish research teams. A how-to publication was issued in March 1960, requiring all members of the community — teachers, staffers, and students — to initiate projects, the exception being a few campuses with very limited resources. Those in large branches had an advantage, being able to make use of existing experimental units belonging to their host reclamation farms, while those in smaller ones had to manage with a shed or two and a small piece of land for a hothouse or experimental plot.

The university's research effort was strengthened when the Provincial Forestry Research Unit was relocated to the Main Campus in April 1961. Eight years later, its capacity was substantially enhanced overall following the merger with Jiangxi Agricultural College. Among the experts who joined was Professor Zhang Shimei, renowned in pest prevention and control, who would become a vice principal. Between 1971 and 1977, eight research projects were undertaken for the central government and twenty-one for the province, in addition to projects completed for work units and the university's own campuses.[21] Full use could not be made of Jiangxi Agricultural College staff, however, because of the anti-intellectualism of the time.

Researchers applied basic scientific agriculture to Jiangxi conditions, questioning long-standing habits. Projects given priority were those thought likely to increase output in the major specialties, hence experimentation with rice hybrids was widespread. By utilizing improved strains, the Xin Gan Branch claimed to have tripled its average yield from 200 jin in 1959 to 655 jin in 1964.[22] Nancheng Branch claimed to have lifted output in some of its fields from 100 jin per mu on foundation to 1,400 in 1976.[23] Hybrids were said to carry more ears of grain and were declared sturdier and resistant to disease and insects. Less spectacular increases of around 20-50 percent were commonplace. The best rice varieties were tested locally and sold across Jiangxi's counties, and the university began exchanging hybrid seed with Guangdong Province and Hainan Island. The exaggeration of research rice yields and timber output has been admitted, although the university generally had a good name for its recording and its products. Later, seed rice would be fraudulently marketed under the university label, but not in the early days: "We were more honest at that time."[24]

Much of the university research was essentially small-scale and directed at local problems, and it was essentially self-funded utilizing low-cost techniques and equipment. Accounts of research in forestry and insect control, give a sense of the work in hand. The Jin Xian Branch experimented with growing China fir, one of earth's most ancient trees, which has more species in China than elsewhere. "Since ancient times, fir in Jin Xian county was scarce. Even small branches were stored for later use. In the words of locals, 'China fir is as precious as gold.'"[25] When the Jin Xian County Party Committee discussed planting more firs in 1962, the forestry authorities claimed that Jiangxi's red soil did not suit: even should they survive, they would not grow into valuable timber. "The vice secretary of the Party Committee, Comrade Yi, who was also president of the Jin Xian Branch, thought otherwise. 'Why did they grow very well around houses?'" Visiting villages with stands of fir and talking with experienced farmers, teachers and students learned that the trees grew where red soil was well manured. Chemical analysis revealed that the untreated soil had insufficient phosphorus and nitrogen. In the winter of 1964, staff planted fir saplings near the branch gate, digging deeply and applying fertilizer. A year later, 90 percent had survived and, with continued attention, the stand grew into usable wood inside four years. By 1976, Jin Xian Branch had 600 mu of China fir of its own, and the county, 180,000 mu.

Another project began one day when, as Teacher Liu was eating his lunch, a worker broke in with news that the red lady beetle was infesting the rice crop.[26] The man found little help from textbooks, which had nothing to say on the plague, but which did note that beetles could be a serious problem, eating pollen and turning rice into husks. A conservative estimate put the loss at 20 percent. Liu aroused class members from their midday nap, taking them into the fields to observe. Branch teachers sent around the county reported stories of swarms of beetles in other brigades. Despite the infestation, though, a bumper rice harvest was brought in. Instead of losing 20-30 percent, output actually jumped 30 percent. How could this be? After the next crop was planted, students and teachers observed the beetles over twelve-hour cycles. Following months of work, the research group reported that the red lady beetles ate destructive insects such as the yellow rice boll. The reason that there were so many of them was because of the other large insect populations.

Laboratories built by students mainly relied on secondhand equipment, an improvisation regarded as meritorious. During the Cultural Revolution there were instances of expenditure on quality equipment being canceled simply to make the point that it was not material conditions that determined research effectiveness. High-grade laboratories within closed walls were said to limit research, shutting out real-life conditions and effectively preventing contributions from farmers.

Among incremental improvements attributable to research were the extension of sunflower cultivation, increased fish egg production, antidotes for snake bite, the application of loose tilling and organic fertilizer in oil-bearing plants, and the sowing and cropping of herbs on hillsides. Ginseng was used to treat eczema in pigs, and other natural remedies helped combat pig diarrhea and sheep dropsy. Forestry projects experimented with the germination of seeds, and sapling growth and grafting. The Department of Agricultural Machinery had inventions to its credit, too, including the design of an electric stirrer, the recycling of chemicals in papermaking, and a rotary cultivator attachment for the No. 27 harvest tractor.[27] In the early 1960s, several metal manufacturing factories moved to the university, advancing its industrial capacities; and a new fertilizer, produced by the Main Campus chemical factory, was promoted at an national conference in 1971.

The close association between research and product development was evident at the August 1 Branch, whose research team discovered wild herbs thought to lead to longevity. Hearing of the success of the team's cultivation, Wang Dongxing invited them to the Main Campus to enter a manufacturing process. The task was given to the July 30 Medical Factory which produced "Lingzhi grass" in wine and tablet form; after being taken by State leaders, demand for the tonic exceeded supply, the medicine becoming a profitable earner for its business partners.[28]

Not all university research was successful. Under the political agriculture of the day, campuses introduced deep plowing and attempted close planting. Deep plowing was unsuitable for many areas, where it raised salt levels leading to land degradation; and close planting prevented the healthy growth of many crops. In some cases, new agricultural products were promoted in places where they required too much labor or fertilizer to be established commercially. In 1965 staff involved themselves in an exchange of personnel between a rice region and a cotton-growing district, a move represented as diversifying agriculture in both places. Unfortunately, the cotton grew very poorly in rice paddies, with an accompanying loss in production; without the right climate, soil, and knowledge, the production of rice in cotton areas was not good either. In some rice-growing regions, wheat was introduced as an experimental crop, but the local peasants, not knowing how to grind it, cooked it like rice and made themselves ill.

Nonetheless, President Liu Junxiu was immensely proud of his university's research record, which demonstrated "the incomparable superiority of the part work, part study way."[29] The teaching and research of the university community were publicized in 1960 in the book *The Communist Labor University*. In 1962 a journal detailing research activities was published, and a film on Damaoshan Branch and laudatory articles and propaganda pictures extolled their efforts.

> We haven't done a perfect and systematic job in associating scientific theory with agricultural production. Nor have we raised the integration of teaching and production to a theoretical plane. But we have demonstrated that students can learn natural science and gain research expertise by means of part work and part study — a good beginning. [30]

Part III

On Politics

Seven
Guidance from the Chairman

"Our university followed the example of the schools Chairman Mao founded in the revolutionary wars."

—Liu Junxiu, President, Communist Labor University[1]

Wang Dongxing left for Beijing in July 1959 to help organize the Eighth Plenary Session of the Eighth Party Congress. Mao Zedong's opening words on sighting his one-time chief of guards did not take the Jiangxi man unawares: "How's the university going, Dongxing?"[2] Impressive numbers of buildings, factories, and mu under cultivation were produced, and the students, Wang told Mao, were much liked by Jiangxi's *lao xiang* — respected country folk. "But due to such a short period of effort, the heavy tasks demanded, and the poor conditions, much still needs to be done. Teaching programs and suitable regulations are underway." Wang observed his ex-boss intently as he talked: "He never interrupted. I thought I'd talked too much and wanted Mao's comments. So I stopped and looked at him. Mao suddenly realized. Putting his cigarette in the ashtray, he took another. 'Keep going. Can you summarize the university's philosophy?'"[3] Confident again, Wang talked more of its principles and work-study methods. At the finish, Mao summed up: "It seems you are running things well. You must keep at it: the place has great potential." The Chairman's approbation was transmitted back.

In backing the Communist Labor University, Mao drew on a well-developed educational position. Son of a well-to-do farmer, his early days had been filled with the drone of the classics learned by heart in a village classroom. Knowledge so arduously gained remained for life. This dominance of traditional studies in the Chinese curriculum provided a common language for initiates and the Chairman was quick to call on classical allusion to add force to his argument. Closer to home, he named his two daughters Li Na and Li Min after a passage in *The Analects of Confucius*, "The superior man is slow in speech *na*, but quick in action *min*."

For all that, Mao was strong in rejecting the classics, these "stinking corpselike dead writings full of classical allusions,"[3] as a recipe for the times. "They [our teachers] are not aware that this is already the twentieth century; they still compel us to observe 'old rites' and follow 'old regulations.'" Professors, he insisted, treated their young students like criminals, locking up their lives in study. As well, their institutions petrified their teachers: primary school masters had hungry bellies and were made to eat chalk dust all day. Women in the ranks were treated shamefully.

Young Mao was quick to look for enlightenment to Western education, enrolling himself in several so-called modern establishments, though with disappointing results. After turning to self-study at the Hunan Provincial Library, he was attracted by an advertisement for a government teachers college in Changsha that offered free tuition, cheap board and lodging, and a qualification which guaranteed the security of a job on graduation. Applying his well-honed skills in traditional essay writing, Mao gained entry in 1913.

First Provincial Normal was one of several modern colleges founded in the last decade of the Qing Dynasty, and it was here Mao met the intellectual challenge of Western philosophical thought reading German idealists such as Paulsen and Kant. Although in two minds over the usefulness of German metaphysics, he felt no equivocation so far as Western learning theory went, coming down firmly on the side of environmental factors, rejecting claims of innate or hereditarian advantage in intelligence. The belief encouraged him to value the process of education and place it high in the pantheon of agents of social change. At first he sought to reconcile Chinese traditional thought and modern education; later he would oppose the concept of the Western school transplanted in China. It was not that Mao denied the salient principles of much of

European or American schooling, rather it was its irrelevance for China's countryside and the arrogance of its local propagators.

> When I was a student and was visiting my home in the countryside, I saw how peasants opposed "foreign-style schools," and I acted exactly like the average "students of foreign-style schools" and "teachers in foreign-style schools" — I thought that the peasants were wrong. In 1925, the fourteenth year of the Republic of China, I spent half a year in the countryside. I was then already a member of the Communist Party and I already had a Marxist outlook, and I began to realize that I had made a mistake. The peasants were right, after all! All the teaching materials used in the village primary school dealt with things about the city, which failed to satisfy the needs of the rural area. Moreover, the manner in which primary school teachers treated the peasants was so disgusting that they were not only not helpful to the peasants, but they became very undesirable.[4]

The time Mao spent learning the classics and modern subjects in formal institutions brought forth the uncompromising remark on graduation: "I will hate school for the rest of my life."[5]

In 1919 Mao opened the Culture Bookshop in Changsha, making use of three rooms rented by Yale-in-China, from where he disseminated Marxist and progressive literature, including socialist-oriented mass education textbooks. Yale-in-China was a project of the Yale Foreign Missionary Society which supported a nondenominational medical school in Hunan Province. Though the hospital had survived the antiforeigner riots of 1910 and had been handed to a Chinese Board of Managers in 1925, the extreme antagonism in Hunan against Westerners left the Americans no option but to evacuate two years later. Communist opinion portrayed overseas mission-controlled education as a form of imperialism and, in the streets of Changsha, local students walking with missionary teachers were reviled as slaves of foreigners.[6]

By the early 1920s, Mao had shed his liberal reformism and was applying the spectacles of Marxism to social problems and their solutions. Marxism was a truth capable of scientific proof, and it stood on the side of the oppressed and those treated unjustly. As a communist he believed he held the secret of discerning heresy and a capacity to foretell the future. Although the first communist theorists had said little about education, regarding it as a secondary force of change, Mao gave education and individual human will a much higher rating in the process of social evolution.

Marx had supported the concept of productive labor as a means of helping universalize schooling, and Mao agreed, advocating productive labor as an essential part of schoolwork. In truth he had come to his belief well before he converted to communism. Taking a special interest in the Shu Yuan Academy of old China, where staff and students labored together for their own support, he had set up his own version on Mount Yuelu in 1918. A year later, details of its educational program were released: four hours for lectures, four for self-study, and four for physical labor. As in Jiangxi, the labor component comprised common agricultural pursuits: gardening, farming, forestry, animal husbandry, and mulberry tree cultivation.

Physical labor, Mao believed, renewed the human spirit and led to a reformed lifestyle. Tramping the Hunan ranges, he swam rivers, bathed in ice-cold water, and shouted poetry to the winds to strengthen his lungs. He approved of George Washington chopping wood, and Tolstoy's claim that "to earn your living through labor is true happiness!"' In 1920, Mao wrote to a friend, "I think I would really like to devote a period of time just to doing manual work."

Quick to seize on modern views of the importance of teaching youth and adults, Mao recognized that a vast pool of untapped talent existed in the community, not least because China's population was more likely to have been brought up outside school than in it. Intensely supportive of adult classes, whether of a "catch-up" kind or for training purposes, he helped revive an alumni-supported night school while at teachers college. Recruiting young people for the Changsha school, Mao's announcement aimed at the illiterate:

> Do you know what is the greatest disadvantage with which you are all faced? It is precisely that, to use a common expression, "You can't write down what is spoken; you can't read what is written; and you can't do figures." Under these circumstances, isn't a man just like stick or stone?[8]

Literacy was essential given the human need to read the Marxist theorists, a prerequisite for intelligent life. This commitment remained. In July 1961, listening to a further progress report on the Communist Labor University from Wang Dongxing, Mao broke into the conversation: "While you are working to raise the standards of youngsters, don't forget that middle-aged and older people need literacy classes too. Can the university and the branches run evening literacy classes?"[9] Wang answered, "We'll discuss this with the Jiangxi Communist Labor people and solve the problem." Mao nodded.

In 1918, the young revolutionary investigated the possibilities of linking political doctrine and adult education in the cause of spreading socialism. Inspecting classes for workers' children and their parents at the Changxindian Railway Works, he observed how its instructors took an openly socialist stance. "Does everyone understand why we are poor?" he asked.[10] The usual answer, "Bad fortune," was dismissed as incorrect, and classes were told their misery came from exploitation by the wealthy, a state of affairs best rectified through worker unity and political organization.

Mao was at his most innovative when set the task of training socialist youth leaders and organizers. Students at his Self-Study University, an adult training center set up in Changsha in the autumn of 1921, introduced significant social problems for investigation. The instructors raised social issues and organized group study, circulating their students' papers for class comment. The Self-Study University compared its own liveliness with the atmosphere in regular training centers, which dulled minds and initiative. At Changsha there were no examinations, no diplomas, and no tuition fees. The institution became a forerunner of the Party cadre schools noted for their effective practical training. In spite of its attractiveness to Hunan's young people, or because of this, the university was closed down by the authorities in 1923, a threat to good order and public security.

Mao moved on to become director of the Peasant Movement Training Institute in Guangzhou. The institute had been established by the Communists and Nationalists jointly for training rural cadres who were to open the way in the countryside for the coalition's forces as they moved north against the warlord armies. In 1926 Mao led his students into the countryside investigating rent and interest charges, the state of local schools, unemployment, and women's issues. This Peasant Movement Training Institute was cited as one of the places on which the Communist Labor University was modeled.

The untrusting coalition of Communists and Nationalists ended in 1927 when the latter turned its army and camp followers on their allies, killing many Communist supporters and driving them from the cities. The decimation of its urban backers forced remnant groups underground and dispersed others in the countryside. Mao led a group in Hunan which engaged in an abortive attempt to capture Changsha before retreating with some 400 men to the peaks of Jinggangshan. The revolutionary's knowledge of the Hunan-Jiangxi border region had come from his days at First Normal when he and his friends had walked the countryside, an exercise that led him to recognize its suitability as a redoubt. Jinggangshan was a natural fortress in Southwest Jiangxi accessible only through narrow pathways cut through forests of spruce, fir, and flowering bamboo along precipitous slopes. Its heart, the village of Ciping, was located in a small basin where food could be grown to support the defenders.

Other groups of dispossessed soldiers led by Zhu De and Peng Dehuai joined with Mao's soldiers in Jinggangshan to create the Jiangxi Worker and Peasant Red Army in 1928. The new force expanded its territory as Communists driven from the eastern coastal cities regrouped, and new enclaves were established.

Disease and attitudes of human poverty were endemic in the region when this Central Revolutionary Base Area was declared in the years 1929-34. It was in this least hospitable of places in southern China that the Communists took sanctuary. Mao found himself challenged to establish schooling in the Base Area where he looked to communist principles, including free, state-controlled education and the combination of education and production as cited in the *Communist Manifesto* of 1848, probably the first socialist text translated into Chinese. Thus encouraged, the Communist educators set about creating a school system under central control, secular in thrust, and comprehensive in coverage which demanded only minimal school fees and allowed labor as a subject.

What eventuated in Jiangxi in the early 1930s was a loose structure of public and private elementary schools, a middle school in the larger townships, and the Lenin Normal School for teacher training in Ruijin. Youth movements were initiated, the Children's Corps taking in younger children, and the Youth Vanguard, adolescents. Primary-aged children learned a basic curriculum and political knowledge in the Lenin elementary schools.

At this time, Communist educators were influenced by progressive Western writers, especially those associated with Europe's New Education Movement. Their early teaching manuals adopted a child-centered educational philosophy which assumed that children were innocent and pure, shaped by their environment, and brought to understanding by curiosity and creativity. For best results, children must want to learn, boys and girls should be taught together, and class teaching had to take account of the everyday world.[11]

Where the Communist educators had been singularly inventive was in the theory and practice of productive labor. Their theorist was Yang Xianjiang, whose book *The ABC of Educational History* (1929) was a sustained Marxist analysis of schooling. As early as 1920, Yang had called for the introduction of labor in schools across the country: conventional education in China, he argued, was too closely tied to the literary tradition. School lessons in morals should include practical learning, social science demonstrate the achievements of working people, and mathematics have relevance for real life. Trainees would be taught "labor is sacred."[12]

In truth the early Jiangxi schools under the Communists were not especially effective. Attendance of pupils was irregular, and the best school buildings were soon commandeered by the military, their tables and fittings frequently confiscated and used in shoring trenches and air raid shelters. Directors of education were ill-trained and changed frequently. Many local officials had little heart for the work, preferring to be sent to the front line. Educational headquarters, given its reputation for leisurely tea drinking, was nicknamed "the red restaurant."[13] Once teachers were trained, they were frequently directed to other work, and many Party men, illiterate themselves, treated them like class enemies.

Mao's work with adults continued in Jiangxi and he frequently engaged himself in devising literacy and training programs. He backed the decision that the army provide classes for troops, helping draw up the simplified textbooks for teaching the ranks to read, write, and count. The same soldiers, he insisted, must join political classes to counterbalance any exclusively military outlook. The public duty side of the Red Army's work required that they build roads, dig drains, construct schools, and reclaim land. In 1929, Mao drew up ten points to guide teaching in the Fourth Army:

1. A stimulating style (abolish the "pouring-in style").
2. From the near to the distant.
3. From the shallow to the deep.
4. Speak in a colloquial style (new terms should be explained simply).
5. Speech should be understandable.
6. Speaking should be interesting.

7. Use gestures to aid speaking.
8. Later sessions should repeat concepts from earlier sessions.
9. Prepare outlines.
10. The cadre classes should use the discussion method.[14]

The ten commandments were applied at the Red Army University, known as Hongda, established at Wayaobao in North Shanxi in 1936 for training army officers. Cadets learned politics along with war and labored outside class hours cutting grass, collecting firewood, joining the harvest, and tending livestock and gardens. Many Hongda buildings were constructed by the young soldiers themselves. Again, the influence of Hongda on the Communist Labor University is noted in the Jiangxi archives.[15]

Encircled by Nationalist troops, the Red Army broke out of its Jiangxi enclave late in 1934 and retreated north to the Shanxi-Gansu-Ningxia Border Region, a march for survival which lasted over a year. The Communists eventually settled in the ancient town of Yan'an, located in a river valley overlooked by a fine Song Dynasty pagoda, where they dug out caves in the soft yellow loess of its cliffs. These cave dwellings were bricked inside and plastered, and their wooden fretwork entrances covered with rice paper to let in light. For all this, the cave quarters and cave meeting rooms were damp and gloomy. Fear of arthritis added a spur to outdoor physical activities. Soldiers, students, and office workers were seen at dawn, exercising in the traditional Chinese martial arts and running between the vegetable gardens and up and down the river cliffs. Basketball was the popular pastime at midday; there was physical labor in the gardens after work and dancing in the evenings. Exercise materials were homemade: stones on poles for weight lifting, iron nailed on wooden bases for skates, and stuffed animal skins for balls.

Student City, as Yan'an was known, was filled with youngsters attracted by the Communists' willingness to fight the Japanese invaders. Japan had began its brutal expropriation of Chinese territory in 1931, its forces attacking and occupying China's large cities in the north and east six years later. From the Communists' view, it was important that their young be trained quickly in the science of war and social reconstruction and in loyalty to the CPC. Among the institutions they set up were the Chinese Women's University, the North Shanxi Public School, a political training center where Governor Shao Shiping served for a period as a registrar, and the Central Party School, all of which were named as influences on Gongda.

However, it was the Anti-Japanese Military and Political University (a reorganization of the Red Army University), known as Kangda, with which the university most closely identified. Kangda students dug out their own classrooms and grew much of their own food. Their instructors worked alongside them in fields and classroom and they slept in the same dormitories. Its lecturers stressed the combination of theory and practice in class, with key points summarized; examination questions were released in advance; relevant reading was listed; and students' answers were discussed in class afterwards.

Kangda's student body was organized into military formations — battalion, company and team — and a friendly rivalry was encouraged in the spirit of socialist competition. Students' backgrounds were discussed at self-examination meetings, and recruits were attached to homerooms where their companies met regularly to exchange information and join in games, singing, and plays. The motto of the university was "United, alert, earnest, and lively," and its school song proclaimed Kangda graduates "the finest offspring of the Chinese people," in the vanguard of saving the nation and liberating humankind.[16]

Kangda graduated around 200,000 political and military personnel from its various campuses between 1937 and 1946, most of whom specialized in political work and military strategy in courses of six months' duration. Mao Zedong headed Kangda's Education Department for a period, and his lectures there produced some of his best-known tracts on social policy and strategy in the revolutionary war.

The institution's fame spread across China into Nationalist-controlled territory. Yan Xishan, commander of the Second War Zone in Shanxi, established the National Resistance University where he taught army recruits political organization and guerrilla tactics, although his followers were said to lack "the fiery idealism of the long-haired, grass-shoed students of Yan'an."[17] After 1949, Yan'an-type activities were to the fore in periods of revolutionary fervor. A major exhibition of Kangda memorabilia opened in Beijing early in the Cultural Revolution where the university was promoted as "a college of the newest type," "most revolutionary and progressive," and "entirely in accordance with Chairman Mao's thinking on education."[18] Educators attending the exhibition were urged to "run all schools and colleges in the country on really Kangda lines."

Governor Shao Shiping adopted Kangda as his model when the Communist Labor University was established. He had firsthand knowledge of the school, having been promoted to vice principal of its Second Branch in 1937. Under his influence, the Jiangxi university considered itself a national leader in reviving and recreating the spirit of Kangda for the times. Whereas Kangda had been the spearhead in war, Gongda would lead the battle for agricultural production in peace. In one of his first lectures at the Communist Labor University, Shao made special mention of this Kangda mettle:

> Kangda had ample land, sunshine, and fresh air! It used Mao's works as teaching materials and welcomed everybody. If we were short of food, we grew it; if we had no spare accommodation, we built cave dwellings ourselves; if we had no teachers, we asked each cadre to give three lectures in turn. The students we trained built a new China. [19]

Kangda, Shao said, warranted imitation. "Why isn't it good now? Some people are against part-work, part-study. But many of our leaders graduated from this kind of school. Don't you think it good?"

The Kangda experience confirmed Mao in his thinking about the best direction for communist education. He had already begun to question the effectiveness of the regular Yan'an school system seen as failing in much the same way as had the Jiangxi arrangements, and times had become increasingly hard in the northern enclave as Japanese units penetrated its perimeter and the tax base shrunk. The central government needed to reshape priorities. Making a virtue from necessity, Mao supported a major reorganization of education in May 1944, with local schooling becoming essentially utilitarian in aim and increasingly self-reliant. By the end of the year, the education system had been restructured, the central government limiting itself to a general oversight and help for some township schools, with county schools coming under the villages or lower-level units. Elementary and middle schools aimed for self-sufficiency. Teachers labored as part of their duties, and pupils collected herbs and firewood and made charcoal. Peasants released land for school gardens and pig raising, accommodated the schools' teachers, and set their spinning teams to weaving teachers' clothing. School textbooks were revised to emphasize productive activity and political input was introduced. Party leaders themselves set the example in practical self-help: Zhu De collected manure for the gardens, Zhou Enlai took to spinning, and Mao Zedong grew vegetables and helped dig drainage lines.

Before the Communist Labor University was founded, the revolutionaries could claim thirty years, experience in educational work. The practices they promoted before 1949, especially in Yan'an, excited the revolutionary imagination. Not only did they match the Marxist principle that learning and labor were indivisible, but they proved a valuable vehicle for carrying the political messages of the Party. Furthermore they were economical and people-run: "We showed in Yan'an that the belief that only the state could run an education system was untrue."[20] The leaders of the Communist Labor University were products of the Yan'an years, and they proved educational disciples of Mao, following his example in founding classes.

Of course, within the CPC there were those who rejected the Yan'an enthusiasm, seeing a quite different future for China's education. Such men and women favored a core of traditional Chinese teaching for its moral and cultural qualities or else wanted a form of Western or Soviet school practice. Despite outward signs of consensus, rival theories of education struggled for ascendancy behind Party doors. Given the nature of the debate, particular educational practices became labeled, their advantages and disadvantages obscured and overshadowed by their attachment to some "left" or "right" political line.

Eight
A Role for Ideology

> Zhou Enlai: "Which study comes first at your university, politics or science?"
> Shao Shiping: "Politics takes the lead."
>
> —Discussion at Nanchang, 1961[1]

Believing that politics should be "caught" as much as "taught," the Jinggangshan Branch marched new students to the front yard of Mao's one-time residence at Da Jing ("Big Well"), a small yellow-plastered hut fronting a narrow cobbled track which served as the main street. The site of the building had been the Chairman's headquarters during the KMT's first campaign against the Red Army. Burned down by the Nationalists and subsequently rebuilt, a stone seat remained from the early days, around which students clustered to learn their CPC history and how Mao had organized his schools in Jiangxi under much poorer conditions than they themselves faced.

The first project of the Jinggangshan Branch led by the fifteen ex-army men and cadres assigned to it by the Jinggangshan Forest Pioneer Farm was cutting a road to the outside world. Large classrooms and dormitories were built, and stone and wood pens for chickens and pigs, the backbreaking effort relying on ax, shoulder pole, and handcart.[2] Life was especially hard for the those from the cities, who soon had cut and bloodied hands and raw, red shoulders. Days at Jinggangshan began with morning exercises and finished after dark with study revision, hobby groups, and the school song:

> Ninety nine li at one leap,
> Day and night in field and forest,
> Asleep in the lap of tigers,
> Naught shall stop us.[3]

An energetic outdoor life did not make studying ideology indoors a popular pastime. Taking a practical approach, Jinggangshan teachers exploited their access to the battlefields of the 1920s and 1930s, new staff and students joining 20- to 30-li marches in the mountains, camping at night in clearings or inside abandoned sentry posts. Among the historic places on the circuit was Xiao Jing, a one-time Red Army hospital, where the newcomers were shown the gully in which more than 100 sick and wounded soldiers, taken from their mattresses, had been gunned down. Another was the deserted mountain village of Yan Zhu Hu, at the junction of three roads where 100 people once lived and a small restaurant served travelers. Nationalist soldiers overran its defenses in 1929, slaughtering the population in a bloodbath of gun, bayonet, and fire. Only ruins were there to see.

Along the way, students learned that heroes roamed. Halfway down a foot track rising from the floor of the main valley, and cut into the heart of the mountains, stands a Mongolian oak. Under this tree Mao Zedong and Zhu De had unloaded heavy packs of rice and supplies, resting before the final haul to a higher fortified camp. University classes visited the site regularly for outdoor readings of the leader's works. Once the Topographical Survey Class of 1960 was caught out in a heavy downpour midway through pegging the high points; ready to give up and retreat to camp, students caught a glimpse of the big oak through the mist and weather and a shape of Mao humping his 200 jin load. They renewed their task with fresh purpose.[4]

Jinggangshan staff also brought men and women onto campus from a nearby "home for the aged" to narrate personal stories — how they had survived blockade and the Long March by eating grass roots, tree bark, shredded sweet potato, and wild vegetables, and by chewing the leather from belts and cart harnesses. Old army men offered good advice on guerrilla tactics:

> Take the small path and not the big road
> Take the mountain track and not the small path."[5]

Students were further exposed to local revolutionary history during fieldwork. At the Shang Jing Forestry Brigade, the Party secretary of the local production brigade, Luo Shangde, told her tale. Having joined the revolution at fourteen, she fought with the Fourth Army before transferring to propaganda work at headquarters. "Little Lark," as she was known, frequently visited the Red Army Hospital at Ciping where she sang for patients and staff and helped in the chores of nursing.[6] After the Communist troops were forced to retreat, Luo stayed behind to care for the wounded. With no food for the men, she left her party to search for grain. After three days, during which she herself ate only herbs, 10 jin had been collected, but when she returned the twenty-eight men under her care had been discovered and killed.

Many individuals and groups from the Main Campus and other branches visited Ciping, touring the township's lanes and its forest hideouts and walking along the Communists' supply lines in their personal recreations of history. Already, students perceived themselves as fighting for survival, reclaiming land and growing crops in harsh terrain: they related readily to the scenes around them and the stories of sacrifice from this "vivid and inexhaustible textbook of the Chinese revolution."

The "big men" of the Communist Labor University were dedicated Communists; young people at the start of the revolution, they were still pursuing their objectives in middle age. Communist business dominated their public and private lives. Through the provincial Party structure, and the network of Party Committees (larger campuses) and Party Branches (smaller campuses), they controlled decisionmaking in the university. Down the line, heads of the branches were normally Party secretaries of the host farms, who reported back to county and district CPC branches. From the top down, political orientation was a priority. During the first two weeks of student enrollment, which included a brief introduction and a visit to the Main Campus exhibition room, discussion sessions were called. The gatherings, "applying the method of speaking out freely, airing views fully, holding great debates, and writing big character posters,"[7] began with carefully crafted questions: "Should a Communist Labor University have been established? Can work-study promote effective learning? Is our university a real one? What of the future?" Students' answers were noted and corrected where necessary. When a bold individual raised personal worries, the answers given were constrained by the prevailing belief system. They heard that their university was an essential state institution for the education of peasants, that the work-study method enhanced learning, and that labor enabled the state to meet its education costs. Sacrifice and hard work would assure the morrow. Any continued querying of the university's status was regarded as a reflection on the questioner's class bias.

The first taste of politics in the classroom came when instructors explained the rationale for the university as set out in its establishment documents. Students learned they were the beneficiaries of a great social experiment, itself part of the general line for socialist construction. And their political instructors reminded them that their subject was not one of those which could be studied once and for all — its lessons were there throughout life. Students would graduate to more substantial writing by Mao and others later.

Government policy on international events, including the program for the recovery of Taiwan, was also presented. Here a "friends and enemies" approach was taken: they should support the "anti-imperialism united line"[8] which recognized the virtues of nonaligned nations in Asia and Africa, and pro-China Eastern Bloc countries like Albania. Enemies were pointed out by the recitation of Mao's prophesies that "the East wind prevails over the West wind" and that "imperialists and reactionaries are paper tigers." However, those visiting the university from abroad were welcomed and treated courteously as representatives of friendly nations or progressive individuals.

The time set aside for formal lessons in politics depended on whether students were in classroom or field. At larger branches, lessons were held twice a week followed by discussion sessions and self-study periods at night. Across the university, political studies were set at a minimum of 10 percent of the available teaching hours.[9] Benchmarking was applied, the university claiming the 410 hours it allocated to politics compared favorably with the 355 offered by Nanjing Forestry Institute.[10]

Governor Shao wanted his students to grasp their politics thoroughly by way of the social sciences, and the Marxist message was uppermost in the history, economics, and philosophy lessons. All texts had to be cleared for use by the Propaganda Department of the Jiangxi provincial government. Political work assumed that exposure to communist ideas would of itself lead to their adoption in much the same way that the early Protestant educators in China had accepted that the ability of Chinese to read the Bible in their own language opened the gates of heaven. Any student who publicly rejected the political message was suspended or returned home.

Propaganda as such found few apologists inside the university, as it characterized a mode of delivery thought well-suited to the young and less-educated. Party theoreticians generally preferred the force of prescription to analysis, and they were not much excited by debates over ideological critique. Commonly they drew on Soviet philosophizing for Marxist interpretation and understanding. However, they were happiest with the straightforward prose and the forthright expression of their own leaders, which related typically to strategy and action. The absence of intellectual cut and thrust in political discussions can also be attributed to physical danger, an individual accused of deviation from the line fearing public criticism and arrest, or worse.

Despite Shao's enthusiasm — he would take occasional lectures himself — and much busy work, the level of political study at the university never achieved theoretical sophistication. The university did not specialize in the teaching of politics, although staff and students were expected to have a basic knowledge of Marxism, and locals were offered some short courses in 1964. In ordinary lessons, a stack of moral tales was drawn on to illustrate communist morality in an applied fashion, breaking down the weight of generalized propaganda. For example, the story of an exemplary graduate, Leng Baoyu, was told — how he returned to his home village though all his family members were dead or missing, and made the poorest of places independent of loans of money or grain.[11] His story, put forward near graduation, was a means of forewarning students to accept their postings.

Another story praised the talents and attitude of Xie Caiyan, a graduate in veterinary science, who had returned from the Jingdezhen Branch to her production brigade deep in the mountains. Those who jeered at "the girl with the castrating knife"[12] had their words thrown back at them: "Times are different — men and women are equal." Caring for animals in the villages, Xie offered her services while pregnant up to the last, her tours then continuing with the infant strapped to her back. Offered free meals by clients, a traditional payment, the vet opted instead to use her coupons in the brigade's dining room. Of course, such uplifting stories are simplistic, though many of these men and women did undertake public service: the selectiveness and didactic style of the tales may belittle the human subject.

Political action in the field was related to notions of fairness and work output. A pair of students who shirked their duties, cutting and carting only one or two logs compared with their comrades' ten to twenty, were the subject of a team meeting.[13] Another nonperformer received a serious lecture from a farmer-teacher on his attitude to life. In attempts at extending political cohesiveness, instructors organized group competition in field work, teams were recognized as "advanced units," and individuals as "three good" students, possessing moral, intellectual and physical qualities.

That extrinsic rewards were necessary suggests that recruits were not mentally willing to undertake periods of labor or see labor as a lifelong expectation. While students would toil at school, the motivation of many was a nonlaboring job later — a view they shared with other entrants to higher education. This expectation was considered especially strong because the university's students, mainly eighteen and nineteen years old, had been schooled after 1949. Students also feared they would not be in demand as graduates, given the labor component in their courses. The Party Committee of the Main Campus found it necessary to mount regular internal campaigns promoting the virtue of hard work; however, the problem remained throughout: "Resistance to the combination of education and productive labor appeared constantly among students and teachers."[14]

Those appointed to teach politics needed to be reliable men and women of good character prepared to take an interest in the well-being of their students, a significant task being their reconciliation to daily life. Youngsters objected to the constant climbing of mountains in forestry, complained about the blood and dirt in veterinary work, and opposed theoretical studies in agriculture, arguing that they knew enough about farming already. Two groups subject to particular attention were the "born reds," comprising the children of workers and peasants, leading revolutionaries, and revolutionary martyrs, and the Shanghainese cohort of 1961. The behavior of the "born reds" was neither meek nor humble. Regarding themselves as the inheritors of the revolution, aggressive and demanding of privilege, they had to be put in their place. Similarly the Shanghainese were singled out for bringing bad city ways to the countryside.[15]

It was in the nature of the beast that instructors became overly inquisitive about their students, itself part of a lack of privacy in university life.

Instructors advised students on such petty issues as personal grooming — that to comb their hair too often was a waste of time, and that fashion conscious Shanghainese should not to waste hours looking for black trousers to match their blue jackets and red socks to go with their black shoes. "Students must realize that life is not food, clothing, and manners, but the realization of the lofty ideals of communism."[16] Campuses reported back to parents regularly on their children's progress, including the security of female students, regarding the latter as important for the university's public acceptance. For their part, parents were told to view the political instructor as standing in loco parentis.

Morale building, which included turning around negative perceptions, was seen as another political task. A bias against the university had been obvious from the outset when the concept of work-study at tertiary level became the target of cynics who convulsed with laughter or sighed with despair at the very idea. The place was "a labor reform brigade,"[17] its graduates were no better than high school graduates, and expenditure on it an absolute waste of money, the critics maintained. Only the foolish would enroll. Among most savage critics were staff from other universities: "We were offensive in their eyes."[18] Established universities wanted it merged with some respectable place or closed down: "They thought naming us a university detracted from their own standing and dignity." The incompatibility of the demands of the part-work and part-study were at the core of objections.

> It's waste of talent in people if you fritter away their youth laboring with workers and peasants. The best students should go to good universities, and the young and strong to the fields. The losses outweigh the gains. If you want to be self-sufficient you cannot guarantee quality in study; if you want quality in study, you cannot be self-sufficient.[19]

Too much time, critics argued, was spent in production, too little in learning — and learning was what counted.

Early on, Communist Labor University administrators promised coexistence with older universities, but their academic colleagues showed no interest in cooperating or recognizing their students' degree or diploma qualifications. No doubt they were unwilling to give the work-study movement further momentum. Because the university was itself a member the higher education club, its response to faultfinders had to be muted. It singled out the preliberation institutional model, claiming it perpetuated dogma and blind orthodoxy. By contrast, its own learning was relevant to the real world. Nevertheless, incessant harping and snide comments saw patience and good temper run out. It became clear that the university leaders had particular targets in mind and it was inferred that Chinese universities as a whole had failed the peasants and the countryside, a strong indictment indeed.

The squabbling among institutions did little for staff confidence. Newly appointed members were apt to see the hand of ill fortune at work, the university appearing a second-rate career option compared with national or provincial centers: "It is the sign board of a university, not a university," one declared.[20] Students were similarly affected, as Wang Jin Xiang reports:

> Some said a work-study university was a bad idea, others good. The university was not like our Shanghai famous places. Their students attended classes, we labored. Their students had money, we supported ourselves. We had no fine buildings. Our place was not like a university. There were conflicting opinions and some of us didn't want to labor actively.[21]

Political instructors responded with the tried and true — that the Communist Labor University should be judged by proletarian standards. "Although some are against us," they said, "there are many for us." But it was the harder to convince the students and themselves when their graduates were paid less than others or failed to obtain work assignments. When Governor Shao heard these damaging debates were continuing, he had the Main Campus teachers and students assembled. Wang Jin Xiang was there:

> The governor knew we needed a change of attitude so he came to lecture us himself. A large bespectacled man, with a sense of humor, he sat in a big armchair facing 1,000 students. He asked us whether he was handsome. We laughed. "A fat man is different from a thin man. You agree? One university is different from another. Which is better? You cannot compare them. The Communist Labor University has its own characteristics. It will be seen as handsome one day."

Irrespective of the strategies employed, evidence was that many felt the cut of inferiority. When they reached the Bayi River Bridge leading to Nanchang, they pocketed their school badges fearing taunts from the townsfolk, only the fervent wearing the Zhou Enlai insignia with pride.[22]

Nine
On Political Movements

"Combining politics inside with politics outside."

—University saying[1]

The university was no island and reflected in small the many campaigns decreed from above. Some movements, for example, "Take Grain Production as the Key Link," reinforced its own efforts at subsistence agriculture — although the slogan was carried to excess in places through overenthusiastic land clearance and the banning of alternative farming and mixed production. The call "In Industry Learn from Daqing," the oil city, encouraged its factory projects — again this was at a cost, with some ill-planned industrial projects on campus having to be relocated or dismantled. The association of national campaigns with local action was known as "combining politics inside with politics outside."

The longest-lasting campaign, "Learn from Dazhai," spanned more than a decade. The university leadership felt an affinity toward Dazhai, a village in mountainous Xiyang County in Shanxi Province, which became a national pacesetter in rural development. The small community of eighty families turned barren gullies and hillsides into terraced and irrigated farmland. Peasants planted trees, raised silkworms, constructed brick kilns, mined bauxite, and built solid stone houses, and they provided basic education and health care for themselves.² Senior university staff toured the village several times. "Learn from Dazhai" campaigns were attended, the Main Campus holding the accolade "Advanced unit in learning from Dazhai."

Alas, the reputation of Dazhai was systematically destroyed in the Third Plenum days when its production brigade was accused of exaggerated reporting, unauthorized use of army personnel, and making a virtue of physical labor. Serious changes were laid against the leaders, including one of murder. More recently Dazhai has become a tourist attraction, a model village with a socialist history. On balance, though, the series of Dazhai campaigns were rated a positive influence at the Main Campus:

> Dazhai did have the spirit of hard work: it was good all-round and we needed that quality. Surely it had its propaganda side. In Henan they had to build terraces because Dazhai had them. We had to switch from raising cattle in Jiangxi to rearing horses because Dazhai did. We were forced to grow more corn and wheat than we wanted to because the brigade did. Really Mao would never have agreed to these things if he'd known — people took things too far. Still, you could say Dazhai and the Communist Labor University were in the same family. ³

The university would also involve itself in the Four Clean-Ups and in the Socialist Education Movement in 1963-65, when teams of university administrators, teachers, and students were dispatched to check corrupt rural practices, learning of misdemeanors like excessive bride price, beam-raising parties, and extravagant funerals. Engagement in the two movements was thought to give its students backbone in denouncing dishonesty and venality.

> We used it as a form of social investigation to teach students more of how the countryside worked. Not much was turned up except small crimes like Party bosses taking the best food for themselves and their families. Things were not so bad here.

Across China, serious corruption was unearthed, and the Socialist Education Movement then turned to investigate Party activities, a move which entangled it in the power play of the Cultural Revolution and the campaign's eventual termination.

Another movement, "Learn from the People's Liberation Army," launched in the early 1960s, aimed at cementing the power of Lin Biao, the ambitious defense minister and Mao's heir apparent. The PLA was depicted as "a great school" for learning politics, military affairs, culture, and public life. While the university had never organized itself along military lines, staff frequently drew on military language in their teaching: there was talk of battles joined, forces deployed, and enemies vanquished. "Everyone a Soldier" saw military training introduced to the curriculum, students marching to the fields in formation, hoes on shoulders.

University students had to study and carry on production and propaganda work in the same way that the army was undertaking its responsibilities. After the PLA reorganized its political division, the university followed suit in 1964, appointing political advisers and opening a Political Department.[4] The university began to offer outsiders short-term courses in political theory and training, key groups were organized for political study internally, and classes were identified as model platoons. With the death of Lin Biao in 1971, however, the "Learn from the People's Liberation Army" movement was downgraded.

A further army link accommodated the heroes Lei Feng and his disciple, Wang Jie. An orphan, reared by a Party member, Lei claimed a simple ambition — to serve the Party and the people: "To be a cog which does not grow rusty."[5] His was a posthumous glory, having been raised to secular sainthood following a motor accident in 1962. All China was to "Learn from Comrade Lei Feng." Actually, the man was a more popular figure in kindergartens and primary and middle schools than in universities where the attractiveness of the immaculate is apt to diminish with maturity. Adults who valued thinking for themselves thought the heavy propagation of the Lei Feng story an unhealthy call to blind obedience.

The university also celebrated Wang Jie, an avowed follower of Lei. The Jiangsu squad leader had saved lives by throwing himself across exploding ammunition during a training exercise in 1965, being admitted to membership of the Communist Party after death. The same year, the Main Campus began a campaign to emulate his spirit.

Although the university mounted displays on Lei and Wang and students undertook extra duties in their names, lavatories being cleaned and public furniture mended, the leadership would have preferred heroes closer to home. In January 1965, Zhao Guohua and two other students from the 1962 intake of the Forestry Department died in a brushfire. After death the youngsters were promoted as exemplary individuals. "How did they grow up? How did they develop their proletarian world view? They dedicated themselves to the study of Mao's works."[6] Gongda students were called on to wear their laurels.

In the Lin Biao years, study of the writing of Mao Zedong was stepped up and it was decreed that Mao thought be taught across the curriculum in May 1966. Much of the Chairman's prose was straightforward and easy to grasp, stressing as it did the importance of experience and the human spirit. The style fitted the university's own arguments that peasants with work experience already had a valuable educational start, and its opinion that the quality of its equipment and facilities were less important than students' will to achieve.

Historically nurtured on Confucius, the Chinese were well positioned to accept the word of sages, reverence for the written character having existed traditionally where script was attributed magical qualities and characters themselves were works of art. Mao himself was an amateur calligrapher and poet of note. A lover of writing and books, he traveled with a small library packed in wooden cases which held a mix of poetry, reference books, political texts, and novels. His popular recreation was to turn to a book or newspaper.

Modest about his own writing, Mao advised those in his inner circle to read widely when he came on them construing his tracts. But the zealots whose exaggerated claims did his own talents no credit were not reined in. The Chairman's writing had been raised to a status of a creed in the desperate days of the 1940s, and Premier Zhou had been quite comfortable in advising the students in Nanchang in 1961 to follow Mao's advice, that "long-lasting truth."[7] Idolatry reached its peak during the Cultural Revolution when Lin Biao told the Red Guards: "Whatever Chairman Mao says — every sentence is true: one of his equals ten thousand sentences of others." By then the once iconoclastic and irreverent young revolutionary was surrounded by a coterie of bodyguards and sycophants who echoed his thought and words. Alternative commentaries on Chinese economic and social conditions were largely ignored or played down by the subservient media, it being as risky not to credit advances to the Chairman as it was safe to do so. Late in the decade, his books and newspapers were the only literature found in many homes.

The whole university community read the Chairman's utterances. Edited versions of his writing and speeches were available in his *Selected Works* and in pamphlet form, and 1964 saw the publication of *Quotations from Mao Zedong*, known as the "Little Red Book." Much of the history of the Party, as it was understood, was garnered from Mao's edited writing and its explanatory footnotes.

Three prose stories, "Serve the People," "The Foolish Old Man Who Removed the Mountains," and "In Memory of Norman Bethune," were the texts most frequently referred to in classrooms.[8] In the first, Mao exhorted Chinese in leadership positions to care for others: "All people in the revolutionary ranks must care for each other, must love and help each other." "The Foolish Old Man Who Removed the Mountains" told the story of a man's perseverance in removing two mountains in front of his door, little by little, generation by generation, the gods finally taking pity on him lifting his burdens away. "Today, two big mountains lie like a dead weight on the Chinese people. One is imperialism, the other is feudalism," Mao declared; they would be removed only by the united action of the Chinese people.

"In Memory of Norman Bethune" was the Chairman's tribute to Bethune, a Canadian doctor who had served in World War I and the Spanish Civil War. Arriving in Yan'an in 1938, he had set up mobile field hospitals caring for the wounded on the battlefield. In a 69-hour period in early March 1939, the tireless doctor treated 115 cases.[9] Operating under fire the same year, he cut himself, dying of septicemia. Mao wrote: "We must all learn the spirit of absolute selflessness from him."

Mao's three tales were told and retold, their readers and reciters knowing every character by heart. Overexposure began in the earliest classes of elementary school, when the essays were introduced and memorized and students could be reading from the "Little Red Book" by third grade. Mao's ideas on education were among the selections for intense study. Other popular articles dealt with the Jinggangshan and Jiangxi days, improving Party organization, analyzing the social classes, and strengthening the youth movement. The Mao paper "On Practice" (1937) was thought to reflect the university's style: "If you want knowledge, you must take part in the practice of changing reality. If you want to know the taste of a pear, you must transform the pear by eating it yourself."

It was accepted that reading Mao's works in private and public showed people the way, protected them from error, and inspired them to extra effort. The greatest feats of the Communist Labor University were attributed to mass read-ins, for instance, the successful land reclamation and dike building at Nanhu Lake.[10] Finding the soil as hard as iron, students lost confidence and retreated from the task, but after time out to study "The Foolish Old Man Who Removed the Mountains," the once-poor performers achieved the impossible.

It took 100 teachers and students well read in Mao Zedong thought less than six months to build eight li of road at Hualin connecting its three teaching and production bases — experts had estimated would take 500 laborers at least half a year.[11] Many similar examples are on record. Asked to design some new machinery, the Agricultural Machinery Department class of 1962 thought the job too complex.[12] After turning to Mao's texts, however, they renewed their purpose. The key to their eventual success — the adoption of a three-in-one team of teachers, workers, and students — was put down to the Chairman's wisdom.

When one county planned a dam in cooperation with a branch campus which would inundate 800 mu of fertile farmland and the homes of eighty peasants, the families protested strongly. A meeting of villagers was called and a reading of the text "In Memory of Norman Bethune" followed. When the peasants understood the relation between their 800 mu and the 25,000 mu of irrigated land, "they sacrificed their own interests for the interests of all."[13] Helping them move to another location, the local branch did its best to make up the loss.

Mao's words were applied unsparingly across China as motivation and justification. Deeds great and small were paraded under their aegis, whether the labor was well or ill rewarded, or the worker a believer or not. It was a case of — in Mao's name. Reporting the priorities facing the university, instructors saw the same issues that Mao himself had isolated. After the Chairman complained that young people were growing up unused to labor and unable to distinguish between the five grains, its teachers discerned students unable to use their four limbs or recognize China's life-sustaining staples.[14]

Some movements presented particular problems for staff, the "Never Forget Class Struggle" of the mid-1960s being one. Mao had interpreted life as a perpetual struggle for power between antagonistic social groups, with consensus and harmony the superficial manifestations of never-ending contest. His worldview, which promoted the innate virtue of the masses and a corresponding unfitness of professional groups, categorized young people into good and bad elements according to their parents' occupations. This visitation of the sins of the father on the child was a discriminatory and patently unfair practice, however, and university staff were not given to making fine distinctions between the social class backgrounds of their students. Individuals were typically valued for their deeds rather than the contents of their personal files held in the Administration Office. "Yes, we must carry out the class struggle," they said. "We dare not say we cannot carry it out, otherwise we'd be punished. We thought we were 'red flag' anyway, so we didn't take it too seriously."[15]

Wang Jin Xiang has elaborated a similar theme:

> In the "Never Forget Class Struggle" movement, we had some students from Shanghai who came from bad families — they were children of property owners, or of a KMT father, or they had relatives in Hong Kong or Taiwan. Zhang Yuqing, who was not of working-class background himself, was sympathetic to these young people. He'd tell them, "We say it's impossible to choose one's family, but possible to choose one's own path."

Recorded examples of class struggle in the university are petty instances. A young man confessed to failing to draw an ideological line between himself and his parents — his cure was deemed complete when he spurned letters, parcels, and remittances from home. In other cases, a student admitted to undue mother love, a branch justified enrollment of children from exploiting-class families on the grounds of strengthening their reform by separating them from their parents, and administrators confessed to keeping watch on children from non-working-class homes and educating them in their families' history.[16] Students were generally skeptical of any manifestation of class struggle at the university and were not backward about putting their views:

> The classes have disappeared since the landlord has no land, the rich peasant is no longer rich, and the capitalists have no factories of their own. These people labor like us, and they earn their salaries and support themselves by their own toil. We shouldn't call them exploiting classes.[17]

The class struggle may still exist in society, they argued, but it was no longer evident at the Communist Labor University. Individual students went further claiming that their parents had made their money legitimately through hard work.

Usually the class struggle was dealt with as a theoretical principle, instructors contenting themselves with dark hints of the existence of a tortuous and protracted struggle taking a complex and hidden form in society. Admittedly, enemies at home and abroad sought to suborn the young, but their efforts would be frustrated once students learned the nature of the social classes. At the largest centers, a room was dedicated to displays such as the Landlord's Courtyard and further study of the class phenomenon. A minor victory was represented when one branch was praised for returning 100 mu of private plot to the collective.[18] It was a matter of regret, instructors said, that many young people had no knowledge of Marx's social classes, or understanding of exploitation even. The same movement heaped further obloquy on staff already designated rightists: "Yes, they had a harder time then."[19]

In society at large, the class struggle emerged openly in the late 1960s and early 1970s when figures such as China's "number one capitalist roader," Liu Shaoqi, the "traitorous" Lin Biao, and the "slave-owning" Confucius could be safely named and reviled as the people's enemies. In the future these assessments of Liu Shaoqi and Confucius would be overturned and mention made again of Lin Biao's glory days.

Down the years, movements shifted in focus from political themes to social ones. The last engagement for the university was the Socialist Spiritual Civilization movement of 1980, which promoted a conglomerate of qualities — hygiene, manners, morality, ethics, discipline, aesthetics, good language, good behavior, patriotism, and so on — offered as an antidote to the nihilism of the Cultural Revolution. The university was awarded a citation for its effort.

China's political currency became devalued as instructors struggled to justify turnarounds in Party policy. One year students were taught that Liu Shaoqi's instruction about "two education systems,"[20] was the key to balanced rural-urban development; a year later, the same directive was condemned for perpetuating low-grade rural education. Further down the track, it was in favor again. So far as students were concerned, political work too often became a study in rationalization, an activity characterized by admonition, and a chore. There was built-in conflict in the messages they were told to receive. Students were told to put the study of Mao above all else, yet to demonstrate an open mind and come to Marxism of their own free will. A political instructor wrote of this public resistance:

> Although over 90 percent of students joined our mass study periods, results were not satisfactory. Some students lacked proletarian feeling and the consciousness for making revolution. They would not put their study of Mao above their academic and production work, or their social

activities. Students thought that the big issues Mao raised of revolution and international events were properly affairs of state having no real meaning for them.

They failed to study politics hard, especially when teaching and labor loads were heavy. Students said, "If you don't study your courses well, you will have to repeat your work; if you don't labor hard, you will be criticized; if you fail to attend meetings called by the Party organization regularly, you'll be singled out for violating the university's regulations; but if you don't study Chairman Mao, it doesn't matter."[21]

Instructors were not immune to cynicism themselves as major campaigns and leaders of the past were discredited and policies became harder to predict. A falling off in support for political study saw academics on the staff challenge the importance of an instructor's role in the university's mission. Dissidents held that the subjects had always been the domain of the least-educated university staff, those lacking scholarship or technical skills, or who could see no academic promotion ahead. Political teaching was a soft option, a refuge for the least able. Yet ex-instructors maintain the strong belief today that their ministry did give purpose and meaning to the lives of the young people in their charge and that this duty of care has served their students well down the years.

Part IV

Steps Back and Forward

Ten
Famine and Fortitude

"Gongda was dynamic in 1958-59, dull and deadly in 1960-61, closed down in 1962-63."

—Student prediction[1]

False claims of harvest bounty accompanied the hasty collectivization of agriculture during the Great Leap Forward. After the state had requisitioned its share, based on untruthful figures, farmers had little or nothing left to feed themselves and their families. In the years 1959-62, some 30 million men, women, and children starved to death.[2] Especially hard hit were the provinces of Henan and Anhui, where famine stalked: trees were stripped of bark and eaten, and corpses alongside the road were commonplace as unfortunates attempted to cheat death by searching for scraps of food elsewhere.

Both fate and design played out their parts. In Jiangxi, the weather was unseasonably wet and there was periodic flooding; however, the province was comparatively underpopulated and its rural people, poor and conservative, were less given to political enthusiasm than their northern and eastern neighbors. Still they suffered badly. Rations were cut and the surplus food stocks diverted to a central distribution pool on the phoned orders of Mao and Zhou. The province was instructed to try to assist an influx of starving people from Anhui and Jiangsu.

Campuses of the Communist Labor University ran short of food and essentials, as they were not guaranteed the rations other universities received. Agricultural yields also fell back: the 1960 grain harvest, for instance, met about one-third of the Main Campus's requirements.[3] Several branches cut down timber indiscriminately to clear land and earn cash. Wang Jin Xiang comments:

> The leadership of the branches that had gone in for unsustainable agriculture should have known better. They were not clear-minded. We had to step in when we heard branches were hurriedly clearing timber to grow crops. We told them to stop — to cut selected timber only — others could grow and share the grain and vegetables.[4]

Not all branches were convinced. They looked after themselves first of all, a few underestimating their output in attempts to scrounge supplementary grain from better-managed places.

The national agro-politicians made much of their nostrums: give mechanization priority, speed up water conservation, promote cross-species breeding, eradicate sparrows (devourers of precious grain), and introduce new fertilizers.[5] However, the remedies were ill-applied and frequently impractical: deficient strains of plants and animals were introduced, silting and flooding followed poorly conceived conservation projects, plagues of insects descended after the killing of their predators, and erosion and land souring increased.

The university aimed to obfuscate and delay putting ill-considered top-down slogans into practice. They played off the controlling agencies one against the other, the center against the local, the province against the district, and the branch against the Main Campus. "We had a saying: 'Which way does the wind blow? — wait for a change in direction.'"[6] When action became unavoidable, token projects were mounted to meet the letter of the agro-politicians' decrees. Such stratagems enabled the university to avoid entrapment and ultimate catastrophe.

CPC plans to industrialize the countryside had proven little more successful than the agricultural policy. Millions of sweating farmers constructed small steel and iron furnaces which were fed day and night with charcoal, ore, and scrap metal. Fires belched across the countryside and the horizon of the night sky was colored by innumerable flares. Given abundant rivers, lakes, and mineral-bearing ranges, Jiangxi people were among the most enthusiastic ironsmiths. Of course, the university had to set up furnaces of its own, staff and students putting in extra hours and laboring in the red glow careless of burns and injuries.

Lacking quality control, much of the national output of ingots proved useless: left to rust in unwanted piles, it was utilized as filling, while the cutting of timber to fire the furnaces devastated mountain slopes. Local leaders were ready converts of this obsessive drive for the base metal, with senior personnel in a position to know better holding their tongues fearing accusations of want of zeal or worse. By late 1958, the furnace movement was revealed for what it was, and Mao himself had begun to doubt his own certainties. If small furnaces were so efficient, why did the West prefer large steelmaking complexes? Peasants drafted from the land to work these "samovar furnaces," as Khrushchev called them, were no longer available for harvesting. Crops vital for future subsistence rotted in the fields and fresh planting was cut back. The Communist Labor University closed down its smelters after finding there was no market for the product. Across Jiangxi, however, there were some beneficiaries from attempts to industrialize the countryside as small industries did take root in rural areas. The establishment of factories in the countryside was further boosted by Mao's predictions of atomic war and the need for decentralization, the university offering sites for city factories and cooperatives seeking sanctuary.

By 1959, vegetables were in short supply at the Main Campus and Li Chao left for Lushan to plead with Governor Shao for land for vegetable gardens to feed his several thousand teachers and staff. Shao asked if vacant plots were available close by. "'Yes,' reported Li, but it was hilly land and lacked water so vegetables died off in dry weather. It grew only grasses. Shao replied: 'If the land can grow grasses, it can grow vegetables.'" He told Li to give students hoes and buckets and send them to the waste plots. Staff remember Shao's retort and admit that some vegetables did grow, though the relief was temporary and inadequate.

As the famine hit, Jiangxi work units stopped supplying vegetables and other necessities. The university was self-supporting, the farmers claimed, so they owed it no special responsibility. Their rebuttal conveniently ignored the fact that the university had never intended that self-sufficiency apply immediately or cover staff. Even so, Nanchang Municipality informed the Communist Labor University in 1960 that it would no longer supply meat, vegetables, or soybeans. Protests were to no avail, and Li had to call in favors owed him by county authorities in Anyi and Yongxiu to ensure at least a short-term supply of foodstuffs.

The only real solution to the food shortages was more land. Li went to Nanchang again asking for several hundred mu for gardens: once more the municipality was unwilling to help, not least because it wanted to keep the university as its customer when things improved. Instead, it offered to hand over limited supplies. Li reported his failure to Shao, who moved decisively at last, providing the university with allotments in Fengjing County.[7]

The famine years set up new hurdles. The Jiangxi provincial government considered shedding many nonproductive ventures in 1960, and the Communist Labor University appeared vulnerable given that it was funded from the discretionary chest. The problem was the greater because of the sheer size of the university's staff and student population, the equivalent of twenty or more standard institutions. Wang Jin Xiang explains: "Being outside the higher education sector meant we couldn't get money from this budget. This wasn't such a bad thing, as we could never have recruited 10,000 students a year otherwise. Still, our place in the planned economy was not secure."

Despite earlier projections of full employment, the university's first graduates met difficulties when they joined the labor market in 1960-62. Jobs were hard to get, and its ex-students were not paid at standard rates. Protests were met by the rejoinder that they would be tested in the fields and remunerated accordingly — effectively they were on probation. Given the lack of recognition of their qualifications, many graduates moved out of agriculture, the police force being a favored destination.

Ambitious plans were scaled down, and morale fell. Students were in no physical condition to labor and study enthusiastically, their thoughts centering on personal survival. With living standards and graduation prospects falling, complaints about the university were heard openly, including attacks on the academic quality of staff: "Whether a university is any good or not depends upon the quality of the teaching, not on results from production."[8] Graduating with a Communist Labor University degree was likened to "jumping from one basket of rice into another." Several branch campuses compounded the situation by shamelessly exploiting student labor in the hard times, forcing the Main Campus leadership to insist that the predetermined hours be implemented to the letter. Some of the students attempted to re-enroll themselves in other Jiangxi institutions, which also did not help the university's standing.

There was talk of the forced closure of the university on the grounds that its standards were too low. Critics from other universities joined in: "They called for the university to be totally reformed. All should be of one mold. We countered, 'If we followed your way, what's the point of our existence.'"⁹ Given its own deficits, the province could not and dare not give the university special treatment: "President Liu told us privately that he would have found some money for us by scraping the provincial agriculture chest, but he must be seen as even-handed. So we missed out."

By 1961, grain production was still less than half the Main Campus's needs.[10] The amount supplied by the provincial granary had been severely cut, and some branches were harvesting less than a quarter of their usual output. Whereas students at regular universities received 30 jin of grain monthly, only 20 jin went to Communist Labor University youngsters. The province argued that the university had more students than it could feed; the students replied they deserved the extra grain as they labored for their keep. Li Chao and the leadership at the Main Campus rejected the role of supplicant: "No way would we be beggars. We offered a nearby district a sizable labor force for an urgent project, our best fighters. In return they gave us 500,000 jin of grain. We also traded and bartered among our branches to keep ourselves going."[11]

In the spring of 1960, Wang Dongxing heard that Mao, disturbed by recent setbacks, had issued a call to run agriculture in a big way, giving institutions the right to manage substantial farms. Wang, fully aware of the university's food crisis, contacted Li, who phoned Shao asking for a major land grant under the new policy. Yes, came the reply — but Li could only expect waste land unwanted by farmers. Shao told Li to apply for land in Chang Yi County bordering Boyang Lake.

In June 1960, the university heads met the local Guazhou brigade, asking for access to 10,000 mu of their low-lying land. It was agreed that 1,200 mu would be opened up initially for rice, soybeans, and vegetables. After 800 students were deployed at the Guazhou Farm for three months, the first harvest collected 300,000 jin of rice and 40,000 jin of beans before the floods came. By the spring of 1962, an additional 30,000 jin of rapeseed was brought in. Altogether, 8,000 mu of waste land was in cultivation, with roads and storerooms built.[12]

Plans and permissions can change quickly. In 1962, the Provincial Party Committee and People's Congress determined that the university's parcel of land at Guazhou was preventing them establishing a full-scale agriculture project in the district — "so it was eaten up."[13] As compensation, they were given one million yuan for a new holding at Jiangjunzhou. Four thousand staff and students from the Main Campus and other schools cleared 7,000 mu, and built an 18-li dike largely by handcart in some four months.[14]

When Jiangjunzhou came into production in 1963, the immediate food crisis ended. The student ration was raised to 30 jin for students in class, and 38-45 for those doing hard physical labor. Teachers and cadres received a minimum of 36 jin. Some outside the university objected to the size of the new rations: "Li Chao replied, 'Why didn't you say anything when we only got 20 jin and you had 30!'"[15] The physical achievements of students and staff were there to see. Not only were they morale boosters and sources of individual pride, they also provided useful publicity for the university, encouraging new enrollment.

The failures of the Great Leap Forward were blamed officially on bad weather and Soviet Union treachery. In 1959, Mao went into retreat, standing down as chairman of the republic, the post going to Liu Shaoqi, and power shifted to Liu's Beijing administration. Now there were two tigers on the one mountain peak. In dealing with its problems, the university had cause to look over its shoulder. The school foundings of the Great Leap Forward were reassessed as irrational phenomena — part of an extravaganza which had doubled primary school enrollments and tripled higher education institutions in under a year. Yet the percentage of state funds expended on education actually fell between 1957 and 1958.[16] Many of the new masters and mistresses were unskilled and untrained, their classes taught in huts, caves, and abandoned buildings and their enlistments phantom. As the famine bit deeper, commune heads, unable to feed unproductive mouths, reduced the size of schools, returning many students to the fields: "They cut down the students not the branches."

Lu Dingyi, the propaganda chief, among the strongest supporters of work-study in 1958, now played a different tune:

> The pace of growth was too fast and too much power was delegated to the lower echelons; there was too much labor and too few classes; language courses were taught as political classes; the standard has been lowered; chaos prevailed and it has greatly hurt the schools.[17]

The national reconsolidation of 1960 applied the slogan "Adjust, Consolidate, Replenish, and Enhance." Its cadres openly attacked the expansionist policies of the past, linking high enrollments with qualitative decline, political work with intellectual interference, practical work with theoretical emptiness, and critiques by students of their staff with teacher humiliation.

The first target of the national authorities was the work-study school sector, which they saw as having lowered standards and drained scarce funds from regular enterprises. The "red and expert" agricultural middle schools, which had mushroomed in 1958, closed their gates. Most of their teachers had known little of agriculture and were unable to drive a tractor, let alone maintain one, and parents had only supported the schools on the misapprehension they offered their children a second chance for university entry. Once inside the classroom, the pupils probably learned less about agriculture than they would have learned in the commune. In reality the work component was forced labor, which explained the considerable dropout rate. Any institution which hoped to continue now had to meet standards proclaimed by the Liu bureaucracy.

Among university reforms was a loosening of the ideological straitjacket. Courses introduced primarily for political purposes were dropped; individual research was reinstated as a healthy phenomenon, provided the motivation was unselfish; and university and college entrance examinations once again mandated a foreign language. Restrictions on children of non-working-class backgrounds entering university were eased. Foreigners reappeared in Chinese institutions, particularly in the teaching of English, and China's students were sent abroad to study in nonsocialist countries again.

Improvement for some threatened closure for others, a situation recognized in a later admission that "the bourgeoisie inside the Party" had obstructed the university's operations "in every possible way."[18] It was charged with "blooming without bearing fruit." With so many achievements of the Great Leap Forward revealed as phony, the quantitative claims made by the Communist Labor University were suspect, an indication of ill, not good, management. From the perspective of the Ministry of Education, the university was in the camp of the work-study institutions it was busy shutting down. The authorities stereotyped it as a deviant institution, its claims to university status challenging the meaning of the word. It was a "troublesome place,"[19] whose continued existence gave heart to substandard institutions promoted out of political zeal. Being an experimental institution, not a mainstream provider, it appeared the easier to terminate.

In early 1961, the university appeared on a list of twelve full-time provincial institutions marked for closure. Carrying a large deficit, the Jiangxi Education Bureau claimed the province could no longer afford to keep its gates open. Li Chao, questioned by Governor Shao before the crucial meeting expected to confirm things, was asked whether the university could carry on if shorn of its branches. "Yes," Li answered. Shao replied: "I'm not so silly as to say all our branches can last. At the worst, we can claim victory if the Main Campus survives."[20] Shao spoke angrily at the Party meeting as he listed the efforts the university had made towards self-sufficiency and defended it. It was no mendicant, he said. Finally, a consensus decision allowed two of the twelve institutions to continue: the Communist Labor University and Jiangxi Industrial College.

As part of the deal, the university had thirty-four staff from the ten closed institutions "forced on us." It also agreed to cut student numbers and close down branches. Following internal assessment and external consultation, particular branches were singled out. Some had already shed students and were relying on core staff to manage production work. An investigation revealed the work at several was little more than the reclamation of waste land. Some places had a dropout rate of over 50 percent. Having overenrolled at first, they failed to cope with the expansion that resulted as student cohorts moved through the years. Many buildings were substandard, the staff student ratio was too high, and there was not enough land to ensure self-reliance. Branches which relied on a single crop suffered badly if it fell in value.

Some campuses had added bogus cadres to their workforce to justify higher subsidies. Others had failed to apply their student force satisfactorily, under- rather than overworking them. Several branches employed very few skilled teachers, or had nobody with university-level qualifications. Yandi Branch had just one cadre and he was not a Party member,[21] while some of the attached technical schools had no land of their own. Severe pruning followed. In August 1961, the leadership presented a summary to the provincial Party Committee meeting at Lushan which designated particular branches and technical schools. Students from failed ventures were enrolled in other branches or sent home.

During the rationalization, Shangrao District, which had managed twenty-six branches, saw these reduced to eighteen, and then to fourteen, seven senior and seven junior technical schools.[22] One survival device was a reduction of a branch's status. Hualin, which had commenced at college level, was reduced to senior technical, and finally to junior technical status. It also agreed to cut its student load by nearly half.[23]

It became apparent that the Main Campus had been remiss in accepting so many branches in the first place. The rapid buildup of branches, some thirty to forty extra centers a year, meant that little assistance for new enterprises could come from the top, beyond the luster of the name. Main Campus staff were busy with their own projects, leaving smaller branches on their own, and sustained academic input was wanting. Across the branches, there was an acute shortage of human resource skills: a 1961 survey of 131 specialist teachers in 42 centers counted 4 with university qualifications and 117 with some secondary technical training.[24] Who could have predicted the calamities, though? Some branches singled out for closure had insufficient time to prove themselves or benefit from trial-and-error experience. Had they had a longer and more supportive induction, outcomes may have been different. Others had hard work to their credit and were aggrieved at arbitary orders to shut down: they bowed the knee but vowed to restart when economic conditions improved. A few rebelled outright.

Shangyou's time was declared up in 1961. Teachers began leaving, and students class by class. Its properties were handed over to local units. Disgusted by the events and the supineness of a local authority too willing to surrender, a group took matters into its own hands. Led by a hired farm hand turned teacher, Tian Jiecai, himself a former Gongda man, they determined to found Shangyou afresh on Meiling Mountain.[25] The Communist Labor University's name board was wrapped in a piece of red cloth, and the young people climbed to a clearing 1,000 meters above sea level, where a lone peasant family eked out a living. Here they nailed up the board and began to hack out and terrace a tea plantation.

On the mountainside, grass shelters collapsed under ice and snow and students' clothing was frequently soaked. Food was scarce, and the winds blew cold as Tian and his forty-one fellows worked the red soil and read by oil lamp at night. Plots for rice and vegetables were cleared for immediate needs, and wooden dormitories and tea-processing sheds erected. The autumn of 1962 saw large characters carved on blocks of stone on Meiling Mountain: "Climb to the top of Meiling Mountain: Stand firm against wind and rain." Shangyou Branch reopened in 1965.

Deng Xiaoping's Draft Higher Education Sixty Articles, issued in July 1961, confirmed the reconsolidation. It required that universities give priority to teaching again. Curricula were to be laid down nationally and the time for productive labor cut back. After special pleading, however, the Communist Labor University was treated differently. President Liu Junxiu as provincial Party secretary, was able to gain a dispensation by quoting Mao's special instructions, and the university developed its own version of the Sixty Articles at a meeting of the Main Campus and twenty-two branches in September.[26] Regulations were tightened and enforced, teacher training was stepped up, more emphasis was put on examinations and less on field assessments, teachers' academic study and preparation time was raised to 66 percent, and persistently poor performers were failed and excluded. In mid-1963, the university decided it would further consolidate economically and consider a five-year degree structure, part of the ongoing academic upgrading.[27]

Nonetheless, branch numbers dropped rapidly between 1961 and 1964, from ninety-six to forty-six campuses, twenty-three senior technical level and twenty-three junior — and enrollment fell from 39,691 to 11,705.[28] Of the campuses which remained, only seventeen could cover the grain and cash income usually required for their student workforce. New enrollments at the Main Campus fell as low as 554 in 1963.[29]

Still, the university was lasting the distance. In tough times, youth and fitness were good allies. Further, it had capable management and a strong skills base and had been able to shed unproductive branches. When the university worked land, its yields were generally 50 percent above average; it had also introduced crops such as sweet potatoes and encouraged mixed production, with more pork lowering the demand for grain. Larger branches had agricultural machinery departments which raised overall efficiency, and improved farming techniques and pesticides were utilized. Another reason why it triumphed was that it had gained the ear of Mao himself.

Eleven
A Letter from Mao Zedong

"Comrades: What you have been doing has my full support."

—Mao Zedong[1]

Increasingly anxious as to the future, Shao and Liu asked Wang Dongxing if he could persuade Mao to put his known backing of the university in writing, an immense favor to ask. Were this to happen, though, the university would secure a second breath and more. Now a member of Mao's party at Lushan, Wang found an opportunity to bring up the prospect at a meeting on 29 July, when he judiciously inserted further news of Gongda:

> Mao listened and responded cheerfully: "The university is big enough. They have boldness of vision, well done! It seems that what I intended to do thirty years ago has come true in Jiangxi. Education is a cause, an important thing. It is impossible to construct socialism without literacy and scientific knowledge, and without talented people." [2]

Wang pressed on.

> Sensing his good humor, I asked: "August 1 will be the third anniversary of the Communist Labor University of Jiangxi. Please write something to encourage them. Is it possible?" Mao thought yes. "This is a big event. I'd like to write something in appreciation."

But later in the discussion, the Chairman showed signs of changing his mind:

> "You're a leader, you go back and congratulate them." I answered: "I'm in meetings and too busy to leave. Besides, I'm not prepared." "It won't interfere with your work," Mao replied, "You can leave tomorrow and come back the following day. You'd better go back." I agreed. "All right, please write something. I'll take it back for them, shall I?" Mao smiled: "The university is run very well. I'll think what I should write." By the smile, I knew Mao would keep his word.

Clearly the Chairman had proposed Wang pass on his comments orally, but the astute chief of guards extracted his letter.

An hour before daybreak on Sunday, 30 July 1961, Mao Zedong left his bed in the study at No. 1 Lu Lin, Lushan. "I can't sleep," he said, "because I have one more thing to do — to write a few words."[3] Given that the man's biological clock was peculiarly his own, the bodyguard on duty, Zhang Xianpeng, was not surprised by the predawn activity. Spreading out his papers on a nearby desk, the Chairman's brush raced fluently down the page, a letter addressed to the heads of the Communist Labor University of Jiangxi Province unfolded:

> Comrades:
>
> What you have been doing has my full support. A school run on the basis of part-work and part-study, self-supporting through hard work, without having to ask the state for a single cent, a school embracing primary school, middle school, and college courses and functioning mostly in the hilly regions of the province though also on the plains — such a school is a very fine one indeed. Most of the students are young people and there are also some middle-aged cadres. I hope that besides Jiangxi other provinces will set up this kind of school. They should send competent, discerning, and responsible comrades to Jiangxi on a study tour to draw on its experience and give such a school a try on their return. It is better for the enrollment to be small at the beginning and to expand gradually to reach as many as 50,000, as in Jiangxi.
>
> Furthermore, Party, government, and mass organizations [of workers, youth and women] should also set up schools on a part-work, part-study basis. But work and study in these schools should not be the same as in Jiangxi. In Jiangxi, work means farming, forestry, and livestock breeding and study means the study of these subjects. In the case of the

schools run by Party, government and mass organizations, work refers to the work done in these organizations and study refers to acquiring basic knowledge in culture and science and studying current affairs and Marxism-Leninism. Therefore, the two are different.

The offices of the Central Committee have already set up two schools. One is run by the Central Guards Regiment and has been in existence for six or seven years. The soldiers and cadres start with literacy courses in primary school and go on to middle school and college courses. By 1960, they had already reached college level. They were very happy and wrote to me a letter, which will be printed and sent to you. The other school was set up last year [1960] by the Party offices in Zhongnanhai, also on a part-work, part-study basis. Work means the work done in these offices, such as by the personnel handling confidential documents, the service and reception, medical and security staffs, and others. The Guards Regiment is an army unit, which has guard duties, such as keeping guard and standing sentry, that is their work. Besides, they engage in strict military training. In all this their school is different from those run by non-military organizations.

On the occasion of the third anniversary of the Jiangxi Communist Labor University in August 1961, the Comrades in charge asked me to write a few words. It is a matter of importance, so I have written the above at their request.

Mao Zedong
July 30, 1961

The brushwork finished, Mao told Zhang: "I've written a letter to the Communist Labor University because they expected me to. Ring Dongxing and ask him to come over to view it, then give it back. I'll check it again."[4] Wang read the 500-character piece with rising excitement; at best he had expected a few words — the July 30 letter was a massive vote of confidence in the Jiangxi experiment.

On the afternoon of the 30th, Mao reread his letter once more before telling Wang to pass it to the Political Bureau of the Central Party Committee for sighting. Shao, who happened to be in Lushan at the time, received a call letting him know the great news. The governor hurried over to Wang's office where he copied it before returning to the Main Campus. In fact, Wang Dongxing would keep the letter in his care until after Mao's death when he released it for the Central Files.

The Zhongnanhai schools Mao mentioned had been set up by him personally as centers of spare-time study for the Guards Regiment and Central Office administrative staff. The Chairman supplied them with brush, ink, notebooks, dictionaries, and textbooks paid for out of his own pocket, the money drawn mainly from his book royalties. Five subject specialists were invited to teach literature, mathematics, geography, politics, and natural science, and Mao would occasionally check and mark the students' assignments himself. By 1957, about seventy of these men and women had reached middle school standard. One month after Mao sent his letter, Wang Dongxing released ten teachers from the two Zhongnanhai schools for a study tour of the Main Campus of the university and seven of its branches under his vice director.

Mao had written the letter because of his private belief in work-study and his understanding of the university as relayed by Wang and others. After liberation, the Chairman had promised the self-supporting education system of Yan'an would become part of China's education policy. Gongda, in his mind, was akin to the Yan'an institutions of Hongda and Kangda, which he regarded as universities despite objectors who muttered that there really had been no universities in the old liberated areas.

Work-study practices in schools were first introduced on a large scale in China in the Program for Agricultural Development, 1956-57. In the name of agricultural development, tens of thousands of agricultural middle schools opened where pupils learned the junior secondary curriculum along with practical subjects like planting crops, insect control, collecting fertilizer, and tractor maintenance and repair. However, the movement was largely unsuccessful, not least because good quality rural technical education was costly to establish.

The Chairman stepped up his backing for "books without words" during the Great Leap Forward. On 13 August 1958, he stopped to chat with a young girl working a cross-cut lathe in a Tianjin University factory. "How do you like the work-study program?" he asked. "Very, very well," she replied. "Under this program, one learns theory as well as the actual operation of machines."[5] The woman's instructor reassured Mao that those who had feared that work and study would lower academic standards were wrong. — in fact, it improved learning and teaching. This was news Mao liked to hear, although he was upset when he heard that factory staff and students had gone without sleep for 24 hours in an attempt to assemble an automobile before National Day. They must take adequate rest, he insisted.

Off-the-cuff remarks by Mao promoting work-study were widely circulated and applied in the cause. After the Tianjin comments, the Central Committee of the CPC and the State Council ordered that all schools introduce productive labor immediately. In other well-publicized remarks in 1958, the Chairman cited evidence from Chang Ge County, Henan, where students from a primary work-study school had gained more places in middle schools than pupils from conventional classes. Both the Tianjin and Chang Ge comments were cited by Wang Dongxing in support of the university's mission.[6]

Given his commitment to productive labor, it may surprise that Mao's letter achieved only restricted circulation. The reasons were various. When Mao had passed it over to Wang that July afternoon, the told his security chief:

> I have thought things over and decided not to issue it publicly for the time being. If it goes public, everybody will want to visit Jiangxi, and they will have to take care of them for accommodation and other things. It will affect the university's production and teaching. It will increase their burden. A good thing will become a bad thing.[7]

In January 1965, the Propaganda Department of the CPC would release the letter to senior Party leaders and ministers. An accompanying memo noted the congruity between Mao's and Liu's educational ideas, the point being to preempt any suggestion that, by supporting Gongda, Mao was opposing the Liu Shaoqi consolidation. This limited circulation, and some later publicity during 1967, encouraged a movement to found other Communist Labor Universities. However, it would be another ten years before the public would read the letter in the provincial press in extract, and it was not printed in full in the national press until 1977. By then its force was blunted.

A further reason why Mao's letter was not circulated immediately was that its argument was diametrically opposed to the current policies of the Ministry of Education, then busy setting standards once more. Had it been known publicly in 1961, it would have set off a mass movement to found work-study places across the country, and conventional universities could have faced transformation into work-study institutions — such was the power of the recommendation. A teacher reported: "Yes, the traditional universities did fear they'd be changed. That was a reason why they didn't want it published."[8]

Zhou Enlai had no desire to see the letter further circulated either, as he had opposed the educational enthusiasm of 1958. When university staff wanted the letter known, he told them that publicity should wait until more research was forthcoming — after all the university was an experiment. The premier said that Mao agreed with him:

> Why has the Chairman kept the letter out of the press? The Chairman is very prudent. He is afraid that if it were published many would follow suit like a swarm of bees. We are talking about an experiment, but lower levels will follow in a big way as was the case in running public canteens. At first it was small-scale thing, then everybody wanted to join in and it became large. In China, if everybody wants to try something, enormous numbers are involved. [9]

Zhou's comment on public canteens referred back to the earliest days of the Great Leap Forward when some local leaders, believing that communism had been realized at last, practiced the creed as they understood it. Commune heads distributed property according to need, individuals' credits and debits were amalgamated, payment in kind superseded currency, and talk of price, profit, and value was frowned on. Families ate in public canteens, their privately owned woks and cooking utensils melted down for their metal. Each commune strove for self-sufficiency, restricting the transfer of commodities across its boundaries. Although this "communist wind" blew itself out as the most zealous communes bankrupted themselves, it was the worst of beginnings for collectivization.

Whether Mao really had the scruples that Zhou Enlai attributed to him is a moot question. He is on record for the remark: "One Gongda is not enough for the whole of China."[10] Certainly the Chairman wanted China's universities to adopt work-study arrangements comprehensively, but could not carry his wishes. "Mao hoped for the change, but he dared not." Also it seems Mao had learned from the excesses of the Great Leap Forward when he told Wang Dongxing privately that the expansion of work-study should be pursued according to the situation: "Do things gradually, not in a great rush. Gongda can wait ten years or more." Work-study would not become universal in China until the Cultural Revolution opened that particular door.

Even limited knowledge of Mao's letter was sufficient to protect the university from the vociferous critics of the day, ensuring that it was given latitude in interpreting demands for national reconsolidation. As Wang Jin Xiang has remarked:

The letter made it clear that the Communist Labor University belonged to Mao and other Party leaders. Our critics in 1961 abounded. So the support was vital. Even those who had hated the university from its beginning had to accept it. They had no option.

Mao always wanted to see the university for himself and had planned this for his 1961 tour of Jiangxi. Similarly, in 1964, a last minute change in the itinerary saw him send the Party secretary from Hunan, in his place — the man was charged to write up a report for Mao in Beijing. In May 1965, again in Jiangxi, Mao directed central government staff to inspect the Jinggangshan Branch and let him know their evaluation. When the Chairman visited Jiangxi in his special train in February 1975 for the last time, he asked of the university and left a message for staff and students.

Twelve
Good Friends Rally

"I raise both my hands to salute your way."

—Marshal Zhu De[1]

Whereas Mao's commitment to the Communist Labor University was based on its affinity with his own ideas, Zhou Enlai's attachment was a personal one. The premier's early association with work-study programs had begun just after World War I when he joined a Sino-French work-study project near Paris. Not impressed by the opportunity, he thought the French program inadequate as it stood, arguing that Chinese students were physically weak, that they found it difficult to get jobs, and, when they did, their employers overworked them. After a day's labor, the would-be students were too tired to study. Zhou preferred the American part-time work-study arrangement whereby overseas youngsters had a stipend and could generate supplementary income around the campus.

The firstborn son of a prominent gentry family in Jiangsu, Zhou was brought up in the Confucian way. After graduating from the famous Nankai Middle School, student days were spent in Japan before he became active in the May 4 movement. Led by Beijing students initially, the movement protested the Versailles Treaty decision to transfer German-occupied Shandong to Japan after World War I. It soon spread to academic and political circles, bringing calls for Western liberalism and democracy in China. During this time, Zhou moved to France again where he adopted Marxism as an instrument of social analysis and action.[2] In 1925 he married Deng Yingchao, a life-long partnership. Among their common interests was a high valuation of the Jiangxi experiment, and they would prove no fair-weather friends.

The premier's backing of the Communist Labor University came from firsthand observation. On 17 September 1961, Zhou called at the Lushan Branch at the end of the Lushan Party Conference, six weeks after Mao had written his letter. The campus was located on a small clearing in the "Five Old Men Mountains."[3] Leaving his car at the foot of the slope, Zhou joined other leaders in climbing to the site, congratulating the welcoming party along the way on the step-like terraced fields and orderly tea plantations. Ignoring suggestions for a rest, he headed toward the student dormitories, where his old gray uniform was instantly recognized. "It's Premier Zhou!" More than 200 students rushed from dormitory, classroom, and library to sight him, at first standing back wondering if they dared come close. Zhou called to the Party secretary, Yang Cai: "Tell the students to come up. We can talk." Zhou shook hands in the crowd, asking for names and fields of study, wanting to know where they were from, their schooling, and if they missed their families. Young people from sixteen cities and provinces, and from worker, farmer, and professional backgrounds, identified themselves. Most had only elementary school or junior middle qualifications on entry.

A boy in the Animal Husbandry and Veterinary Department, Xiao Li, squeezed to the front. Zhou offered his hand — Xiao hesitated, rubbing his own on his jacket before shaking. He was from Shaoxing, Zhou's hometown and admitted to homesickness. "Your home is across the country now," the premier told him kindly but firmly. "That's where you'll do your revolutionary work." Another student, a young girl, volunteered to tell Zhou of the branch's research activity. Xiao Gao explained how they managed the early germination of rice despite periods of heavy rain, impressing the premier with her earnestness and care.

The day after the Lushan visit, Zhou and Luo Ruiqing, secretary-general of the Military Commission, invited provincial Party and Congress leaders, and a group of ten staff and students from the main campus led by Li Chao and including Wang Jin Xiang, to join them at the Nanchang Hotel. Luo, who graduated from the Whampoa Military Academy, had fought in Jinggangshan with the Fourth Army. A known supporter of the wartime universities of Yan'an, he had served as director of education at the Red Army University before transferring as vice president of Kangda in 1937. Together they walked into the room, Zhou waving and clapping before shaking hands with each representative, holding each for a time. Staff and students were closely questioned and Zhou appeared mostly happy with the answers. "The Communist Labor University has a Communist style — you are doers, not talkers!"[4] Caution was there though. Told that the 1961 harvest was below expectations, yet the future rosy, Zhou retorted:

> That's better, wonderful, yet is it practical? Targets must be reached gradually. If you really have problems, we'll help you out. Yours is a school, it is also a farm and a factory. You are students, but you are also farmers and workers. Marx and Chairman Mao both recommended this.

He had brought good tidings:

> Let me tell you the news. Chairman Mao is greatly interested in you and feels a special concern. Comrade Wang Dongxing has told him about your progress, and Chairman Mao was much impressed and pleased. He understands what you are attempting. While in Lushan he wrote you a letter. This kind of school is excellent and he approves it absolutely.

"Long life to Chairman Mao! Long life to Chairman Mao!" students shouted back.[5] Zhou's goodwill was up front. The university party was invited to stay for lunch and told they should eat up and tell him their stories. Nervous young people were put at ease, Zhou passing food from the large plates to their individual bowls in the way of a good host. The meal over, they sat together on sofas around a table, where the students unburdened themselves, Zhou learning of continued harassment by critics: "They say our place is only the nameboard of a university — it has middle school content — and primary school students."[6] Zhou raised his voice:

> Who are these people? Where do they stand? Don't they know better or do they have some sinister intent? To run a new type university needs a great revolution in education. There can be no calm water. You must expect conflict. If there was none, that would be unimaginable. Stand firm under pressure. What you are attempting today has assaulted and violated the old conventions; their backers will certainly rise up against you.

The premier urged the Jiangxi leaders and students to demonstrate the strength of their experiment in Mao's name: "Under the leadership of Chairman Mao we defeated our enemies, and we established the Communist Labor University. Follow him and we shall be victorious. This is a long-lasting truth." At the same time they should

> examine achievements and shortcomings. It is impossible to reach perfection overnight. Yours is a newborn thing. We should support it, and help it run well. Summarize your experiences, with the positive and negative — these can be promoted to the whole country when the time is right.

The hour was 2:30 p.m. and Zhou's staffers said he was extremely busy, having come directly from Lushan. There was much to do, time was precious. They stood ready to say good-bye, but nobody wanted to leave first. Finally the initiative was taken by Zhou, who suggested a group photo on the ninth floor. This gathering in Nanchang would be especially prized because the Zhou inspection came in 1961, a year of economic devastation.

Zhou's commitment was soon tested. Many of the university's original teachers had been recruited from the cadres sent down to the countryside and guaranteed a salary for three years by the state; however, when the time was up, the university was required to support them. Given the famine years, it was still struggling to feed all its students, and to pay staff from its budget was an impossibility. Already the university had closed sixty-two branches and sent 20,000 students home.[7] There was no way the labor of the remainder could provide for staff and their families. The usual enemies hovered.

> When we asked for funds, the local authorities replied, "You told Chairman Mao you could run yourselves without a single penny from the state." When Li Chao protested at the interpretation, they shot back, "Every word of Chairman Mao's is the truth. Do you disagree?" Actually Mao said people would use his own words against him after death. This was the case — and they did so even when he was alive![8]

Government payments for teachers' salaries were to cease from the beginning of 1964, which meant that the Communist Labor University was unsustainable, in effect bankrupt. What to do? Backing from Mao two years earlier was not sufficient of itself to ensure the university's long-term survival without sympathetic action. Any real hope the university had of extricating itself from its financial black hole depended on allies answering calls for recognition in cash and kind.

When Zhou heard the shock news from Wang Dongxing early in October 1963, he phoned the provincial Party Committee asking that the university report on its situation and present their statement to him personally in Beijing. A draft report was quickly prepared,' with Vice President Li Chao, Director of the Dean's Office Zhang Zhongyu, and Party Secretary Zhang Yuqing chosen to present the case. They left immediately by car for Shanghai, thence by plane to the capital. Wang Dongxing met the party at Beijing airport, the four holding a gathering back at their hotel on how best to prepare for the coming meeting. They agreed to split likely questions among themselves and share in the reporting. Wang then helped them rework several drafts of the original report.

Zhou was extremely busy. On 16 October, he invited the Jiangxi delegation to join a group discussing the relocation of urban youth in the countryside. (Later the university would be asked for its own contribution.) The premier welcomed them afterwards but was unable to meet them privately given a meeting overrun.

The next morning, 17 October, the party was driven to the Ziguange Pavilion in Zhongnanhai where Zhou had put together a formidable group, under his own chairmanship, comprising Vice Premier Tan Zhenlin, the Agricultural Minister in charge of cultivation and reclamation farms, and vice ministers from education, CPC propaganda, finance, forestry, cultivation and reclamation, labor and personnel, and hydro power and fisheries, and office heads from agriculture, water, and forestry.

To settle the visitors down, Zhou asked where they were from, when they had joined the revolution, and their ages. Remembering Li Chao from their earlier meeting, he made a complimentary remark on the characters in Li's name. Moving to serious business, he told the leaders that the meeting had been called because Mao thought the university an important matter. Taking out the Chairman's letter, he read it aloud and explained Mao's educational position. Why had the letter been held back from general publication? Because it would have attracted too many followers. But when the experiment proved itself, Zhou told the meeting, it would be introduced across China.

Turning to his copy of the Communist Labor University Report — covered with red pencil marks — Zhou queried the number of students recorded by Mao: "In the letter there were 50,000 people. Why are there only 40,000 shown in your report?"[10] He was told that those at lower levels in the university had exaggerated enrollments in order to gain more state funding. Wang Dongxing had been given an incorrect count, which he had passed to Mao. "Future generations will learn this and will see it as reflecting badly on the university's leadership. But we can't blame the Chairman or Comrade Wang, or those below them — the bureaucratic work style is at fault." The premier told the heads that they must accept the blame for making it necessary to exaggerate enrollments, and a note should be added to Mao's letter to explain the overcounting.

> "We must respect facts; people should tell the truth; achievements cannot be exaggerated; and a problem ought not be hidden. Your statement, although well written and argued, gives insufficient space to an analysis of your own shortcomings. Only ten lines. It is quite impossible that there should be so few of them. The Communist Labor University is still in its initial stage. A truthful account would have covered the negative as well as the positive."

> "Our shortcomings are interspersed in the text."

> "They had better be discussed separately, highlighting key problems. Will you meet your target of 12 million jin of grain this year?"

> "I'm afraid we can't. There was drought in the second half of the year."

> "If you can't reach that amount, don't suggest that you can. How many family members do you have in addition to your staff?"

> "Twenty-five to twenty-six thousand in all, including over 5,000 dependents."

> "They should be noted in the report. There are 25,000 people each consuming 600 jin of grain a year, so you need 15 million jin for support. If your population is stable, can you reach self-sufficiency by 1965-66?"

> "It depends on the availability of land."

> "How much land have you?"

> "Forty-five thousand mu."

> "With 40,000 in grain, and 5,000 in cash crops, and a per-mu yield of 400 jin, you should have 16 million jin."

> "Four hundred jin is not attainable, I'm afraid. The average is 200 jin per mu."

"That's too low."

Zhou asked his vice agricultural minister the average per-mu of the Jiangxi acreage set by the State Plan.

> "Eight hundred jin." Zhou told the university people that their project had great potential. "Could they try for 400 jin?" "It's a bit high," Li Chao said. "I'm not saying you should reach the target in one year," Zhou replied. "You can do it step by step. You can reach 400 first, then 600. Anyway you must aim for self-sufficiency. The average yield of 400 is not so high." "I'm afraid that would be difficult," Li Chao answered the premier. "If you can't do it by 1965 or 1966, we can alter the target and put it off until 1967. Is that OK?" "That should be all right," said Li Chao. Then Zhang Yuqing interrupted: "Most of our branches are in the mountainous areas. There are different priorities for farmland and forest. It's impossible for some schools to obtain self-sufficiency in grain."

Zhou agreed: "A balance must be achieved. It is imperative that we not destroy the forest to open up new land." He thought the point should have been brought up in the university's report:

> Make sure that there is no soil erosion or we shall be criticized by our descendants a hundred or a thousand years on. If that happens, what is this communism that we talk about? To emphasize grain without considering conditions is no good. Production must go hand in hand with water and soil conservation, which is of primary importance. When a factory is badly run, it can be closed, but when soil erosion happens, the problem cannot be resolved in a few years, but will require a hundred years.

Zhou asked about the cash crops, Li Chao answering, "Peanuts, cotton, tea, and fruit trees." Zhou advised them to plant more fruit trees for cash cropping. Li Chao then returned to the forestry issue: "We used to have afforestation money. Nowadays the government invests only in those projects utilizing timber. Other projects will not be funded. They say this is the policy from the central government." Zhou spoke to Vice Premier Tan: "You are the boss. Is there such a policy?" Tan replied, "There's no such policy. I've told the provincial leadership that colleges which carry out afforestation can have some money." When Zhou asked about the possibility of planting more oil-bearing trees that could earn cash, he was told these took three to five years to mature. The premier continued:

> Why don't you plant some. Afforestation must have long-term plans. Forestry and farming are really closely related. We must pay attention to water and soil conservation. China is a big country with vast lands, deep forests, and abundant resources. But there are two things in which we are far from rich — they are mountain forests and farmland, which are out of balance with the population.
>
> I was once asked to write a few words for the Communist Labor University. I thought of the combination of communism and labor. Communism means spirit — while labor is a material force. Gongda must have the communist spirit. It must protect the forests not destroy them to open new land.
>
> We must educate people with political consciousness, basic literacy, and strong health. Students must be equipped with these three components. Four hundred to 500 graduates of the university can be put in the general distribution scheme for employment. However, the length of their courses should not be short, since yours is a half-study and half-work program. Three years is not enough. It should be longer. The ministry of education should make decisions on the length of your courses, and theoretical and technical standards. You can ask them for some equipment.
>
> Other provinces should learn from Gongda's experience and you can give some quota of enrollments to other provinces. The enrollment for the diploma course [normally three years] is sixty students, and for the certificate course [normally two years], 100 to 150 students. Don't expand before 1967.

Then Zhou asked Li Chao how much money the university needed. Li responded:

> One and a half million yuan for staff salaries, one million for teaching and administration, half a million for capital costs and equipment purchases, and one million yuan for circulating funds and supplementary funds for branch schools not yet self-sufficient. Four million yuan altogether.

The finance head, Vice Minister Shen, replied that the university had been allocated two million in the budget, and that four million was difficult. Li suggested that if the central government agencies agreed to two million, could the province provide two million? Shen responded, "The provincial reserve is short of money, too, and it would be difficult to appropriate a separate two million."

Shen moved to stop the haggling:

> "The central government will provide three million, and the provincial government, one million. But can you cut down the amount you need after 1967?" Li replied, "Yes, we can reduce by one million then." "All right. Before 1967 it is four million a year; after 1967, the support will be cut to three million."

Zhang Zhongyu raised the question of his graduates' salaries — all should be paid the same across the country. He received the reply that the issue would be treated according to government regulations — in effect, no change. Zhou spoke to Mao's letter again at the conclusion:

> The passage, "operated without government funding," really means that the students meet their own living expenses. Are the schools run by the central government in Zhongnanhai equivalent to a university qualification? I have an assistant who is now a third-year student of history, but he has learned only history and doesn't know even fractions in mathematics. How can he be counted as a university student?
>
> Basic courses are necessary. Students must learn the essentials. A university student needs comprehensive knowledge and this cannot be assessed through one subject only. Here a note should be added to the Chairman's letter, otherwise people will think that all the staff in Zhongnanhai are university graduates.

Finally Zhou directed Jiang Yizhen, a vice minister of cultivation and reclamation, to produce a summary of the discussion. The meeting ended at noon.

Li Chao and party were invited to lunch with the premier and the secretary-general of the State Council. The dishes were Chinese cabbage and pork, bean cake, cold meat, and pickled vegetables, which Zhou especially enjoyed. No wine was served with the simple fare. Over lunch the Premier told them a little of his upcoming diplomacy in Africa. The meal ended at 2:00 p.m., when the premier was called to meet a foreign delegation. In the evening, the Jiangxi visitors saw a revolutionary opera, *The Young Generation*, about educated youth; it made mention of the Communist Labor University.

On the 18th, Jiang Yizhen chaired a small group which produced a summary of the meeting of the 17th for approval. Included in their determinations was the agreement over the budget. University staff were delighted: they had argued hard that they were cadres of the state and that the state should support them like a regular institution. Now they would receive the same welfare and medical benefits and be eligible for the same disability and retirement benefits as full-time university staff. However, in the event, only two million yuan of the promised four million would be paid out.[11]

It was also decided that the university would be listed as a provincial institution under the Provincial Party and People's Congress, with assistance forthcoming from the various education, agriculture, forestry, and reclamation divisions, who were to help in the recruitment of teachers and in the provision of trucks, tractors, and other specialized equipment. National enrollment and assignment was permitted, but most students should still return to their commune or machinery station. In addition to the obvious gains, Zhou Enlai sent the university trio home with a gesture of goodwill — fifty Liberation lorries for use in mountainous regions. This munificence was at a price: an urgent and comprehensive upgrading of the university's teaching plans and standards.

Thirteen
"The Golden Years"

—Chen Ping, Dean of Studies, Communist Labor University[1]

When Zhou Enlai refinanced the university in late 1963, the reforms demanded went beyond those the institution had imposed on itself in 1961. It was agreed the institution would adopt Jiangxi as part of its name, becoming the Jiangxi Communist Labor University. The move was not unpopular on campus as some confusion had arisen with the appearance of copy-cat institutions. Other reforms standardized entry requirements across campuses and demanded more recognition for middle school qualifications. The number of courses on offer was reduced more hours were allowed for catch-up studies, and test material would thereafter be drawn from the national syllabus. Time for productive labor was cut back. Fresh teaching plans and some new texts were to be in place for the 1965 intake, and other material upgraded by the 1968-69 academic year. Wang Jin Xiang commented:

> When some courses were canceled, we had to rewrite our texts. We must also think how to integrate our two-year and four-year courses. Sometimes our students did the right things, and got the right answers, but they didn't know why. After 1964, we had to consider whether

we'd been neglecting basic theory, and we looked again at the national texts.²

While staff members were proud that Zhou had rescued their institution and had a vision for its future, they were aware too that the premier wanted to raise China's educational standards. Chen Ping, the dean of studies, later admitted: "We thought Zhou right to be strict and emphasize quality."³ However, some feared the reforms of the early 1960s had emasculated their prime objective. By moving the university away from its original purpose, the Main Campus had become a *de facto* orthodox institution. A dissenter made the point: "The emphasis was wrongly put on the regulation of the university. We tried to compete with other places in classroom hours, courses, books, and subjects taught, neglecting our own character."⁴ The introduction of a five-year course, said to equal four years' study in a conventional university, was a loss of face considering the university's earlier claims about its degree, as was the downgrading of the four-year course to diploma status and the demand that more time be allocated to catch-up studies. Higher entry standards appeared to curb its unique mission for peasants and workers and it made the enrollment of minority nationalities more difficult, while a decision to cap the number of branches and student numbers at 12,000 was disappointing given earlier ambitions.⁵

Mao had not been happy when told of the upgrading: "No matter whether Liu admits it or not, you should make your own decisions. Remember to enroll more poor and lower middle peasants' children. Those with literacy and primary school level should have access to the Communist Labor University."⁶ Nevertheless, the university continued to follow Zhou. Branches were directed to set aside at least one to three mu per student place, depending on the speciality of the branch; their land was to be consolidated geographically, and each campus would maintain a farm, processing factory, plantation, and horse and wagon or truck.⁷ The number of factories was increased overall to raise more income and provide employment for the children of staff. In 1965 an Education Research Office was opened to encourage teachers to raise academic skills and performance.

After permission was received to recruit students from the national pool under the unified enrollment plan, 250 newcomers joined from Beijing, Wuhan, Tianjin, Shanghai, and Changsha.⁸ Those recruited nationally were assigned by the state, others from branches under provincial or prefecture control were placed at district level, and those from county-run branches normally returned to their home units. In a significant recognition of the university's potential, postgraduate students were allowed in agriculture and forestry, again drawing from the national pool. Fifty postgraduate places were approved, twenty allocated by Jiangxi Province, twenty by the Ministries of Agriculture and Forestry, and ten by the university.[9] However, the latter recommendation stayed on paper because of the Cultural Revolution.

The Zhou reorganization had created a three-level structure: the Main Campus (four- or five-year university level), provincial and prefecture (three- and four-year secondary and technical level), and county (two-and three-year lower technical level). Longer courses were to ensure that national curriculum standards were met. To the extent that the university maintained nurseries and kindergartens and had primary, junior technical, and senior middle schools and cadre training classes, it operated a comprehensive complex.

With administrative and curriculum reforms in hand, momentum was regained; branches reached 107 in 1965, with more than 26,000 students enrolled.[10] The time is described in the university annals as the "golden years." Grain output exceeded 4.6 million jin at the Main Campus, which achieved self-sufficiency and sold 300,000 jin to the state. Across the university, 10 million jin of rice was harvested.

The university's new policies were tied to the fortunes of the Liu Shaoqi administration. Although moves by Liu to invigorate the economy had been reasonably successful, Mao, watching from the sidelines, remained wary of moves he thought influenced by backsliding, capitalist-minded Party members. Keeping a special watch on the education sector, he revealed his fears to a delegation from Nepal in August 1964: "I advise you not to entertain any blind faith in the Chinese educational system. Do not regard it as a good system. Any drastic change is difficult, many people would oppose it."[11] Earlier, he had told a Party gathering: "There are many things which cannot be learned merely from books; one must learn from producers, workers, and the poor and lower-middle peasants."[12] Particularly teachers must learn from their students.

In Hangzhou in 1965, Mao reiterated his faith in the place of productive labor in any education worthy of the name. Today's students knew nothing of the cultivation of rice and other grains, he complained, so his son was told: "You go down to the countryside and tell the poor and lower-middle peasants, 'My dad says that after studying a few years we become more and more stupid. Please, uncles and aunts, brothers and sisters, be my teachers, I want to learn from you.'"[13]

According to Mao, university students aiming at the arts should labor for two years before entry and during their degrees, while comrades who studied philosophy needed to take up political activity: "If you don't engage in class struggle, then what is this philosophy you're engaged in?"[14] All staff and students should learn about agriculture and work in fields and factories. "Going down won't kill people. All they'll do is catch a cold, and if they just put on a few extra suits of clothes, it'll be all right." His conscientious and proper niece, Wang Hairong, was told that her teachers should let their students read fiction and take a nap in class, and that she herself should lead in rebelling against institutional rules and regulations. When Hairong protested, Mao called her "too metaphysical."[15]

Unrehearsed comment by Mao had an impact throughout the education sector. The Beijing authorities found it necessary to advise teachers not to invoke Mao's name rashly. When educational leaders did have recourse to Mao's views, it was to quote the advice that students "dig" into study.[16] Though ministries were bound to investigate issues raised by the Chairman, such as the proportion of workers and peasants entering higher education, the optimum period for productive labor, and the need for rest by students, they did so in their own time and insisted on well-designed plans.

The kinds of research the Ministry of Education preferred were schemes for greater specialization in studies and quick promotion for the able. Officials were keen to protect the regular education sector from further interruption and disruption. Although they had few reservations about the rebirth of initiatives like the winter classes movement, or national conferences on the "public help, people-run" schools, or even a second look at agricultural middle schools, they feared that the wholesale reintroduction of productive work and other radical practices would infiltrate the regular schools. If this happened, idealistic, well-qualified, young people could miss out on academic study.

Even so, middle schools began to report renewed interest in work-study, and technical and vocational schools tried out part-time employment. Earlier practices, which the ministry considered antipathetic to quality education, such as reducing the length of schooling, open-book examinations, the admission of older entrants, and more time in the curriculum for the study of Marxism, reappeared. Some universities initiated a separate work-study stream — "two systems, one university."[17] Setting their own example, Mao, Zhou, and Zhu were photographed in the press pushing wheelbarrows and wielding hoes. As part of this renewal of spirit, there were accounts of teachers and students abandoning their classrooms to bring in the harvest.

At Gongda the advantages of the recommendation, "from the commune to the commune," were pressed again as the best means of ensuring enrollment and attracting good students. In part, this was a response to improving economic conditions, with communes seeking to retain young workers. For all these initiatives, Mao still thought the pace of school change too slow and threatened to set up his own Ministry of Education unless the pace of reform hastened.

Liu Shaoqi carried the blame for attacking revolutionary innovations and restoring conventional solutions. It was claimed that the Communist Labor University was singled out for attention, its students either removed to regular colleges or sent home. "They basically negated it and even stopped paying the teachers and staff members and cut off the supply of food for teachers and students."[18] There is no evidence though that Liu showed any personal animus. Early in 1957 the man had toured five provinces in the central and southwest, learning firsthand the difficulties the authorities had in coping with educational demand in the countryside. As a step forward, Liu argued for the recognition of part-work, part-study education in rural areas as an approved and legitimate alternative under the "two-track" education scheme, which accepted that rural education could differ from urban. His two tracks helped open the way for experimental institutions and Governor Shao was hailed as a leader in implementing Communist educational policy by following the Liu model. Opinion inside the university generally favored Liu's position.

> Most staff agreed with the "two-track system," though we recognized it was untested. It was unclear how far rural education could be improved without state funds. If Liu's system had been developed, it could have achieved more. But it became a slogan in the struggle between Mao and Liu. It was depicted as the "straw shoes versus leather shoes" debate. Yes, there was hatred between Mao and Liu — yet both agreed on Gongda.[19]

Liu's interest in work-study was made public when he advocated his own type of school/factory institution in an article in the *People's Daily* of 30 September 1957:

> In the old days, schools had their own policies, while factories had theirs. They were quite separate from each other without any links. Now we can join the two together. To open a new factory is to open a new school. The enrollment can be jointly made by the Labor Department and the Education Department, so a new worker is a new student as well.
>
> After three to four months' training, students will begin to operate machines. They will be employed for four or six hours a day; in addition, they will study for four hours or three and a half hours a day. In this work-and-study system, they can study at a junior middle school level and eventually become university graduates.

China's president was on record as approving the way American students worked at part-time jobs during their college years, making the point that China should consider introducing a trial of the U.S. practice.[20] The Central Committee held a working meeting to promote Liu's system in May 1964, and, in a report to the Committee on 1 August, Liu cited the experiences of the Jiangxi experiment. Later that year he reported that the university had "done the right thing."[21] Representatives of the university, including the dean of studies, Chen Ping, along with members of the Bayi Reclamation Farm University, were received by President Liu during a Beijing conference on work-study in higher education in July 1965. Like the Communist Labor University, the Bayi institution had been founded in 1958, after Wang Zhen, minister of state farms and land reclamation, had led 100,000 PLA into remote Heilongjiang.[22]

For all its tensions, the mood of the mid-sixties was buoyant. While there was conflict over policy in education, there was an accompanying excitement. A uniquely Chinese system of education was in the making, and the Communist Labor University was contributing to the national debate. Its progress had demonstrated how a university could live with both the Beijing government's consolidation policy and the radical ideas of Mao. Seeking to straddle two worlds, it had gained the right to follow a revised work-study arrangement and take a share of national enrollments.

Zhou Enlai kept his word that the university would eventually be promoted as a model enterprise, telling Wang Dongxing that national publicity could commence in August 1964. An investigation team from various central ministries, led by Education and Agriculture, inspected in November, the university passing cum laude. Selected as China's major center for training teachers in work-study principles, it arranged a program taking in eighty-seven staff from thirty-six regular universities and colleges.[23] The following year, the provincial Party Committee affirmed that part-work and part-study was the "cardinal system" for China,[24] and its members refurbished or created sixty extra branches out of agricultural schools and cadre training centers.[25] As part of its mission, the university established model branches for activities such as forestry and horticulture.

Self-publicity was stepped up. President Liu Junxiu was invited to address the First Plenary Session of the Third National People's Congress at a meeting on 20 December, and the paper was published. The following year, staff and graduates produced the illustrated book *Training New Type Personnel through Half-Work and Half-Study*, which recorded its diverse achievements. In the summer of 1964, university leaders had joined a meeting of forestry institutes called by a vice minister at the Nanjing Forestry Institute to discuss their experiences. Some of the representatives were skeptical of the Communist Labor University experiment, others sympathetic. In 1965 the leaders attended a second work conference of forestry institutes in Beijing, this time chaired by Vice Minister Tan. Materials circulated about the university were generally well received, though several participants thought the labor component too demanding.[26]

The Jiangxi experiment became a magnet for local and Chinese visitors. Among the first was a group from Beijing Agricultural University, China's top agricultural institution, and Pu Yi, the last emperor and his wife. Anna Louise Strong, an American correspondent, toured Yunshan Branch in 1960, and Rewi Alley, Damaoshan, the following year. On 3 January 1966, Wang Dongxing took an opportunity to revisit his spiritual home with a group from the General Office of the CPC, and Lu Dingyi, the propaganda chief, visited two months later.

The community was conscious of its own success. "It was unique in the world. The peasants said that our students were an 'Everlasting Friend,' not a 'Flying Pigeon' [The names of two Chinese bicycles]."[27] Following the establishment of a Foreign Affairs Office in 1962, groups of foreign visitors were accepted — among the observers, a hundred delegates from the an Afro-Asian Writers' Emergency Meeting held in Beijing. Groups of British and European journalists also inspected the Main Campus and branches. "The arrival of the world at our door took our fame a step further. We were significant not just in China."

Part V

Cycle of Revolution

Fourteen
Cultural Wars

"The tree prefers calm but the wind will not die."

—"Mao's Brilliant Directive."

Wang Jin Xiang's first taste of the Cultural Revolution came on 1 June 1966. In Nanchang on business, he was stopped in the street and asked which line he supported — Mao's or Liu's?

> By the time I returned to university, students were "connecting" with each other. No one cared about the harvest or production work. The young students were out of control, so we used teachers and workers in the fields. Soon the young teachers went to the Party Committee of the university. They accused the leadership of putting production before revolution: "Which should come first?" Things were becoming chaotic so Li Chao gave a few lectures to straighten things out. But no one listened. Who knew the future?[1]

The rationale for the Cultural Revolution was that the country had socialized its industry through nationalization and its agriculture through the establishment of communes, but its educational and cultural sector remained unreformed. This was the first of a series of upheavels, Mao predicted, which would lead to the end of class distinction in China.

Fearing a waning of revolutionary drive among his veterans, Mao produced a big character poster of his own, urging young and old to "Bombard the Headquarters" and assail enemies within the Party.² The language fed the passions of the day. It was each individual's challenge to grasp the revolution — "ignite it, fan it up," and risk the burning. "Fear," Mao urged, must give way to "dare."³ While the draft set of guidelines issued for the Cultural Revolution had "Wage peaceful, not violent struggles" added, well publicized statements by Mao justified the use of force.⁴

School students from Tsinghua University Middle School started the Red Guards, a movement commended by Mao in August 1966: "I am fully behind you."⁵ These young people demanded obeisance to the Chairman's name. They took at face value the maxims "Destruction before construction," "Strike down all vermin, freaks, ghosts, and monsters," and "Obliterate the four 'olds' — old ideas, culture, customs, and habits," in attempts to enforce a literal interpretation of his word.

Private homes were invaded and ransacked for illegal gold and antiques and for evidence of things Western like letters and photographs. Among the suspects were boys from Rewi Alley's Sandan, allegedly graduates of a nest of imperialist spies. History books and popular fiction were collected and burned, ancient monuments defaced and bones scattered, and stone grave markers pulled over with ropes and smashed at Confucius's tomb where a road was cut through the cemetery. Ceremonial parades were required to move from the west to the east, the revolutionary direction.

The Red Guards' prime targets included their own educational institutions, those "little treasure house pagodas" devoted to the "sons and grandsons of dragons."⁶ The Ministries of Education and Higher Education were dissolved, and the presidents and Party secretaries of the nation's universities and colleges denounced at mass meetings in their own institutions and local towns. Statistics were publicized claiming that children from exploiting-class families were overrepresented in higher education: few peasants' children entered and few of these attended the best universities. If a handful did gain places, they were discriminated against. Senior staff at the Communist Labor University were accused of shutting out peasant students under the Zhou reforms by raising entry standards in 1964.

On 6 June, the Cultural Revolution Office opened on the Main Campus, its first task, organizing the 2,000 students and young staff who planned to desert the university for two weeks or more in September and October, their destination Beijing, where literally millions of Red Guards were swarming in the squares and lane ways.[7] An enormous logistical feat brought them to the capital by train, bus, steamer, and foot, utilizing makeshift accommodation and designated "kitchens." From August to November 1966, Mao greeted about 11 million Red Guards and their teachers in eight receptions for the rebels in the capital. The exposure was eye-opening for the young who had limited experience of life and seldom strayed far from home. Excitement, new friends, and original ideas had a liberating effect on those who still cherish their day in China's history.

The university's students took advantage of their stay in Beijing to attend a National Conference on Part-Work Colleges, designed to attack the two-track proposal of Liu Shaoqi. Hearing that its first-year students were likely out of control, the leadership feared they could be swayed against their own institution, so they dispatched a party to Beijing to put its side to the conference. They found a capital in chaos.[8] Calling in at the Agricultural Ministry first, they discovered officials more worried about protecting themselves than succoring the Jiangxi people. Eventually the group succeeded in locating the conference, speaking for a short time before the microphone plug was pulled on them. Accused of sabotaging the meeting, they were pursued by Red Guards, finally finding sanctuary at a friendly institution in an underground room that carried the overwhelming smell of formalin from its use for the dissection of animals. For several days they dared not go out, at last escaping to Nanchang by train. Unhappily, Beijing Red Guards were on the platform to greet them, having arrived earlier by air.

The Jiangxi contingent was put in a truck with derogatory characters painted on the side. Each had a high cardboard hat with characters painted on it accusing the wearer of defending the capitalist line, which they were told to keep upright. Bricks were strung on a wire around their necks, and they were put on show in the city and nearby towns, where children were encouraged to abuse and stone them.

While Jiangxi students were moving to Beijing, urban Red Guards were moving into the Jiangxi countryside. The city students and young staff aimed at retracing the footsteps of the revolutionaries of the 1930s, raising the political consciousness of their rural comrades along the way. Over a million young people visited Jinggangshan. A young teacher from Beijing recalls:

In September 1966, students answered Mao's call to retrace the steps of the revolution. Shortly afterwards, young teachers were called to join them. I was among the most eager of teachers to leave Beijing University. To go to Ciping in Jinggangshan was a great adventure, and anything was better than staying on campus. My friends and I walked the distance through the frosty countryside under snow-laden trees. When we arrived in Ciping, 30,000 kilos of rice were required to feed the visitors. There was not this food in the town, so supplies had to be dropped by helicopter to keep us alive. A great shock awaited me. A telegram was nailed up at the Ciping post office. I was instucted to return to Beijing immediately for interrogation. When I did, I was put in solitary confinement.

Among the visitors to Jinggangshan in these early days of the Cultural Revolution was the educator Rewi Alley. He observed:

> Now, in the midst of the Cultural Revolution, classes and study courses have mostly stopped. The students rise at six. Until breakfast they do morning exercises and study Chairman Mao's works. Then all the morning is spent on military training, while two and a half hours in the afternoon are for practical work, whatever department they are in. Two hours in the evening is used for more study of Chairman Mao's works. [9]

Little by way of learning was taking place at Jinggangshan, its 500-odd students, including eighty-seven females, being caught up in political homage, army training and labor. The branch closed not long after Alley's visit, victim of the social disorder and fighting of the times, its students dispersed to various state farms and mines or taken home.

The Jiangxi events echoed those in China at large. Degrading treatment for academics was standard, with staff set to cleaning toilets and pigsties. Paraded wearing placards listing their sins, they were made to write strings of confessions, which never proved acceptable. A mother was charged five cents for the bullet that killed her "reactionary" student daughter; an aged woman professor killed herself when deprived of her helper; teachers were hanged in their school grounds; and parents were condemned as political deviates by their children.

With the Chairman's knowledge, the luckless head of state, Mao's personal rival Liu Shaoqi, was denounced as the number one follower of the capitalist road. Deprived of medicine, adequate food, and suitable bedding and clothes, he died on a cell floor in Henan in 1969, his thin body a pitiful sight, his hair and beard uncut for several months. Another of those purged was Luo Ruiqing, who had joined Zhou Enlai in hosting the 1961 meeting with the university in Nanchang. Luo attempted suicide early in 1966. Deng Xiaoping himself was removed from all posts and put under house arrest near Nanchang, where he labored in a tractor repair shop.

In 1967, the Red Guards turned on Gongda's special friend, Zhu De, that "big war lord who wormed his way into the Party."[10] The marshal was accused of opposing Mao's policy of rural collectivization and of preferring Soviet military reforms over the Chairman's theory of people's war. On the cultural front, he was attacked for trying to find a publisher for his *Selected Poems* and a hobby of collecting over 1,000 orchids in pots rather than growing humble and useful vegetables. Zhu's wife, Kang Keqing, was also labeled for keeping a flock of rabbits. The Red Guards demanded Zhu surrender himself or be "destroyed." Already an octogenarian, the marshal would last out the public assaults.

Different Red Guard factions sprang up at the Main Campus. The university had its "Red Flag Headquarters," manned by the rebels, who would ultimately triumph. Then there were "The Red Flag General Headquarters," "The Graduates of the Gongda Revolution," and "The Red Family." Wang Jin Xiang aligned himself with the conservatives and "The Red Family."[11] The radical leadership in Beijing had senior Jiangxi staff brought to the capital where they were charged with running an inferior rural institution approved by Liu Shaoqi. Even when it had admitted peasants, its best courses were reserved for students with high marks came the accusations. The staff responded: "We said that Mao and Zhou supported the university. Although Liu had mentioned us occasionally in his talks, we were always a place for all students."

The university's enrollment of peasants and workers, and its known attachment to Mao's philosophy of education, were points in its favor: it was the conventional agricultural universities, the Gongda staff insisted, that had poisoned the attitudes of their students, encouraging them to leave agricultural work on graduation. At worst Gongda could be said to have been influenced in isolated ways by Liu Shaoqi. Red Guards were unimpressed, insisting that students there had enrolled "for the sake of throwing away the hoe." Their lecturers taught that basic theory came first and insisted they attach importance only to knowledge gained in the classroom. Staff and students actually looked down on the proletariat.

> The university was "Black Flag," a place where students labored without gaining knowledge, and which had never actually supported itself. Our president, Liu Junxiu, who was a specialist in growing cotton, was condemned as "Black Gang, the cotton President".

In January 1967 the Red Guards took full control of the Main Campus and, in July, PLA Unit 6012 invaded in support of the leftist faction. The various parties were designated and labeled by a management group — Red Flag, Black Flag, Gray Flag, and so on. Wang Jin Xiang's group was Black Flag. Paradoxically, many of the rebels were themselves from Black families, and conservatives like Wang, whose father had worked in a rice milling factory, had Red antecedents.

At the provincial level, Liu Junxiu and most of the one-time Shao Shiping administration were condemned as followers of Liu Shaoqi. The university's great founder, Shao, was spared indignities and torture, having died on 24 March 1965 at Nanchang, after a long illness. By January 1967, the rebel faction held unchallenged sway on campus and, in September that year, the university published the *Journal on Educational Revolution*, which included an article, "Smash Old Gongda and Construct a New One." Leading conservatives such as Liu Junxiu, Zhang Yuqing, and Li Chao were paraded through the streets together, and another thirty, including Wang Jin Xiang, were on regular public display.

> We were made to line up in front of Mao's portrait and confess ourselves. We chanted:
>
>> "I am a snake, a cow, a ghost.
>> I am guilty.
>> I have to bow my head and accept punishment.
>> If I don't admit my mistakes, send me to prison.
>> I am guilty."
>
> We did this twice a day.

Several staff being investigated refused to eat as a form of protest. Liu gave up his beloved cigarettes and, under the constant humiliations of the time, his health deteriorated. Finally a call came from Beijing: at Zhou Enlai's order, the veteran revolutionary was escorted to the capital, a move which saved his life. Li Chao was forced to look after cattle. His son, who had just graduated, asked the father what career he should choose. "Never become a cadre," the father replied. (The young man would become a leader in a television station.) Another constantly attacked was Yang Weiyi, the university's most senior professor, and the one-time president of Jiangxi Agricultural College and head of the Jiangxi Branch of the China Academy of Science. He died on 21 February 1972 "from the persecution of the 'Gang of Four.'"[12]

The secretary of the Party Committee of the university, Zhang Yuqing, was put under constant interrogation and lost his physical orientation. Wang Jin Xiang tells the story:

> He knocked on our family window. "Oh," he said, "it's your home. I thought it was the dining room." I invited him to eat, my wife making him noodles and putting in an egg. "It's so nice, just the flavor from my home town." Zhang always remembered this little kindness; later he would ask my wife to call in on him whenever they met.[13]

Many less-senior people were harshly treated too. The vice president of a university factory took time off to go home to repair his father's tomb. Severely criticized, he was labeled and put under constant supervision in the fields. When Li Chao regained some authority, he asked what the man's crime was. "That happened too long ago," Li said, and the Revolutionary Committee was persuaded to release him.

About half the student body had armed itself, many students carrying rifles given out by PLA units. Machine guns were mounted at the campus, and pistols worn on belts. Much practice firing took place, with buildings damaged and defaced. The rebels threatened to "wash the Communist Labor University clean with blood." Staff and students fought and killed each other in factional warfare, and a chemistry teacher was killed when the bomb he was constructing exploded prematurely. There were also gun accidents involving those unused to carrying arms, who shot themselves in the side or foot or killed their own friends. Guns were also used for suicides.

Wang Jin Xiang's own trials worsened:

> I had the hardest life. Every morning I listened for the loud speaker. It relayed our tasks. "Wang Jin Xiang, go to the road." My five-year-old daughter picked up my hat for me. I had to work on my knees. My wife made cloth padding for my legs. When I returned, she would wash the blood from the knees very gently and softly. My wife and daughter waited up late at night for my return, and they always saw me out in the morning. Their care kept me alive. The worst time for me was October 1966 to July 1967.

Released from the road torture in 1968, Wang was released to the newly founded Reception Office the following year where an initial group of nineteen visitors awaited. For all his pain and suffering thoughout, he did not lose faith in the Communist revolution: "I never believed I was a rightist."

Political struggle split homes asunder, child against parent. Some conservative students left their parents' university apartments to continue their fight in the mountains of Jinggangshan. There was also grim humor. One teacher tells how his young children were influenced by the events around them: "Families all around us were being moved further into the countryside to live. One day my children came to me to see if we too could volunteer to go down!"

In December 1968, Mao had urged intellectuals to move to the countryside, where they were to settle down permanently and start families. Agricultural colleges and departments located in the cities and townships were expected to lead the way by moving to remote regions. Beijing Agricultural University, for example, set itself up in Yan'an. There were few more-enthusiastic followers of this policy than General Cheng Shiqing, a backer of Lin Biao and chairman of the Jiangxi Provincial Revolutionary Committee (1966-71), who effectively dismantled Jiangxi's higher education system by moving its three best urban universities and colleges to Huanggangshan, Yunshan, and the Silkworm Factory, respectively. "We had to accommodate them. If the Provincial Revolutionary Committee said, 'We welcome it,' the university said, 'We welcome it.'" Other institutions, like the Arts Institute and Jiangxi Technology University, were sent to remote countries and locations. In the dismemberment, irreplaceable equipment was lost, laboratories and facilities destroyed, and library collections built up over the years dispersed or dumped in pits. By 1970 there were only five higher-education institutions in Jiangxi, including the Communist Labor University.

In September 1969, Jiangxi Agricultural College, located in a Nanchang suburb, heard the news that it must answer the call for institutions to go down to the countryside. It was to abandon its convenient location and amalgamate with the university's Main Campus.

The premier agricultural institution in Jiangxi, the college had once been part of the National Zhongzheng University. After 1949, the college associated with Nanchang University, but this arrangement was terminated in the reforms of 1952. Granted its independence, Jiangxi Agricultural

College had taken over the veterinary science faculties of agricultural colleges in Guangxi, Henan, and Hunan provinces.

The merging of the academically respectable Jiangxi Agricultural College with the Communist Labor University, famed for its practical agenda, was portrayed as the best way of serving the province's poor peasants. It was bitterly opposed by many Jiangxi Agricultural College staff who must leave their homes and be yoked to an inferior institution, losing their own name in the process. Nevertheless, they had no choice other than to accept. Gongda staff though were more sanguine:

> We were pleased to hear they were joining us: they would bring equipment and expertise. Their teaching levels were much higher than ours, especially in veterinary science and animal husbandry. Unfortunately, nearly all their equipment had been smashed or stolen and the book collection destroyed. The gates of their campus were closed in the Cultural Revolution and their campus buildings vandalized.
>
> Many of their staff had been sent to the countryside and, when they eventually returned, our campus became overcrowded, for we had two secondary schools with us as well. Including ourselves, four institutions now occupied the Main Campus. The living standards of all fell. If we had applied our different strengths, we would have improved quickly. This was not to be.

Another General Cheng decision had ordered two Nanchang middle schools, No. 2 and No. 22, to the Main Campus as part of a relocation of 128 urban and vocational schools, of which a further 14 were relocated at branch campuses.[14] The schools were to "take the road of the Communist Labor University."

> On the surface, the move was very revolutionary; in reality, it wasn't at all. The schoolchildren could only run down our facilities, not add anything to them. Really the move destroyed the middle schools and hurt us. One of our staff said wryly, "If they don't destroy everything around here, we've done well."[15]

Those who watched the children arrive by truck were surprised at how little they had with them. "These teenagers were pathetic, really. They were too young to work hard and they had no parents to worry about them." As was the case with the Jiangxi Agricultural College, the two middle schools had already lost much of their equipment and most of their books. A teacher reported: "I visited one of their Nanchang campuses. It was like it had been through a war — it was completely looted."

Later, when delivery trucks arrived at the campus, the children would climb aboard to try to get back to Nanchang and their homes. Vehicles leaving the campus had to be searched and stowaways persuaded to climb down and try for a leave pass. The schoolchildren also committed the cardinal sin of wasting food. "They shared big bowls when they ate, frequently spilling the food, even playing with it. They wasted rice and vegetables, a terrible sight."

The earlier predictions about their disruptiveness proved well founded: "The children didn't care. We couldn't organize them to work outside, or in the classroom. When they became homesick, they threw desks and chairs out of the second-floor windows."

Wang Jin Xiang was brought in to lecture the unruly boys and girls. He told the youngsters stories of how the university's students had constructed the desks and chairs themselves and of how they usually walked the 18 li each way to Nanchang city. He also took them on a tour of the university campus, pointing out the tombs of students who had been killed in building the university. "These secondary school students are now in their thirties. Sometimes I see them in Nanchang. They still remember the stories I told them."

A further direction from General Cheng in mid-1968 severed the branches from the Main Campus. All but three branch campuses were detached from the mother institution and put under the charge of the Revolutionary Committees of their sponsoring districts, counties, or work units. There was an accompanying expectation that they would support themselves without any cross-subsidies. Linkage with the central government ministries was broken at the same time: "We no longer had help from the Jiangxi Party Committee and People's Congress — our working system was destroyed."[16]

In effect, the policy change meant turning the branches into independent institutions, although most kept their old and familiar name of Communist Labor University, adding their location name as a prefix, e.g., Ji'an Communist Labor University. With few students enrolled in 1966-70, the available labor force of branches was depleted, and good students could no longer be retained for teaching functions as most graduates from the Main Campus and large branches were assigned to army units or army farms.

Eighteen branches were rationalized out of existence in 1968 or closed because civil war made their continuance dangerous. The shutdowns led to scenes similar to those experienced a decade earlier as eighteen branches were shut down, their production bases surrendered.[17] Several resisted the order to padlock their gates. For example, when the local power brokers drove up to Donggushan Branch, angry scenes ensued. With little progress made, the invaders changed their strategy. Knowing that the teachers and students would leave to join their families for Chinese New Year, a convoy of trucks was sent over the holiday to load up the books, desks, chairs, movable items, and cooking utensils. They were only prevented from taking away the branch's name board after a standoff.[18] The same staff refused to surrender the seal of office; otherwise, everything usable was found and taken away, including the school's grain supply and thousands of yuan deposited in its bank account. Somehow the Donggushan leaders would manage to keep the doors open: "The cold winds cannot stop the spring returning."

The campuses of the university experienced the events of their time, each in its own way. An ex-student reports:

> After graduating from a junior middle school in 1966, I was assigned to study at the province-run Huanggangshan Branch. Since the Cultural Revolution had begun, the unified entrance examination was canceled. School graduates who had bad family backgrounds, the *Heiwulei*, the Black Five, were told to go up to the mountains or down to the countryside. Others of us were placed in further education according to our family backgrounds, social connections, and sometimes our academic performance.
>
> I entered Huanggangshan in October 1966 and left in January 1970. There were four classes — agriculture, forestry, medicine, and accounting. Because of the Cultural Revolution, we learned hardly anything except for loads of Chairman Mao's quotations.[19]

The young enrollee left the Huanggangshan branch with some friends at the end of 1966, joining other Jiangxi Red Guard contingents traveling in China. Some three months later, he and his friends returned to campus life:

> We came back to the branch one after another and began to establish all kinds of Red Guard organizations. The Red Guards in Jiangxi were divided into two major factions which either supported or opposed the deputy Party secretary of the Province. Most of us were his supporters

and most peasants opposed him. The split deteriorated into armed fighting by June and July. People began to seize weapons from local troops — rifles and machine guns. During the years 1967 and 1968, we didn't give up farming but feared going into the mountains to transport bamboo, which caused financial problems. As a result, our food allowance was cut down to 8 yuan a month.

Bereft of its campuses, the university was a shadow of its former self: "We were an institution full of misfortune."[20] The devastating results of separation were further compounded by leadership changes.

The leadership of the various Party Committees was weakened. It could no longer lead the branch Party committees or those of the reclamation farm campuses. They received no attention. As time went on, leading comrades at all levels who knew about and supported the Communist Labor University were transferred to other jobs and places. The new leaders didn't know much about the university and had no direct interest in it. They dare not and did not put their heart into the university's work. Some of the replacements knew nothing at all about education.

Several branch campuses were unhappy over their enforced separation and petitioned to rejoin the Main Campus. On 30 June 1971, an office was opened at the Meiling location to help the newly independent branches arrange teaching and research programs, the latter having been abandoned altogether in many places. Fifteen months later, the university was called on to exercise a more direct supervisory role and an Office of Inspection was established. However the easy cooperation of Main Campus and branch, characteristic of the early years, never returned.

On 7 May 1966, Mao had passed a major instruction to Lin Biao: "The length of schooling should be cut short, education should be revolutionized, the phenomenon of bourgeois intellectuals reigning over our schools can no longer be allowed to continue." The Chairman called for teachers and other state functionaries to undertake industrial work, military training, and farming. Two years on, convoys of trucks began shipping university and college staff to May 7 Cadre Schools in the countryside where they would live and labor like peasants. They were expected to read the works of Mao and Marx in their recreational time and it was uncertain when, if ever, they would return to academic life. Although Gongda's Main Campus was sited in the countryside, 428 of its 522 teachers and cadres were sent deeper into rural Jiangxi to toil.[21] Being poor and rural,

Jiangxi Province was a favored site for these May 7 campuses. The time individuals spent in one depended on their class background and behavior. Because of the university's special political standing, people from other parts of China came to regard it as some kind of giant May 7 school itself — no flattering image, for the camps had been designed for re-education.

Another institution of the Cultural Revolution, the July 21 Workers' University, opened in larger factories where it aimed at strengthening in-house technical training. Like the cadre schools, its beginning was a directive from Mao:

> It is essential to shorten the length of schooling, revolutionize education, put proletarian politics in command, and take the road of the Shanghai Machine Tools Plant in training technicians from among the workers. Students should be selected from among workers and peasants with practical experience, and they should return to production after a few years' study.[22]

The Shanghai Machine Tools Plant enrolled workers with a junior middle school qualification and five years' work experience in two- to three-year full-time courses in fields such as grinding machine design and manufacture, mechanical drawing, hydraulics, and foreign languages. The factory also ran spare-time courses for less-qualified workers. Similar-style workers' universities opened across China, ranging from full-time, well-organized institutions, with good quality training programs, to the odd classroom or two put aside for after-hours learning. The new-style factory cum school was seen as a kind of urban equivalent of the Communist Labor University. It was a force to be reckoned with, not least because it was publicized as the socialist university of the future.

As the Communist Labor University had its own factories, and these were largely integrated into its activities, it was not thought necessary to set up a July 21 Workers' University. However, senior staff were called to Shanghai in June 1975 by the heads of education and the First Machinery Ministry to learn more of the workers' university movement. Gongda's own factories, reassessed for their contribution to training and production, did not emerge unscathed, their managers accused of an obsession with moneymaking.

> Instead of taking up the work of agriculture, forestry, and stockraising, these people ran gift factories and soap plants and even restaurants. It was really a case of "whether a white cat or a black cat," — it was a good one as long as it could make money. As a result, the students'

work was divorced from local realities and the guideline of combining education with productive labor could not be properly implemented.

> The masses had this to say in criticism: "They have grasped money but lost the line." Students trained this way often are contaminated by the idea of attaching greater importance to industry or side occupations than to agriculture. How can they become backbone forces in building a socialist new countryside?[23]

Not all in the ranks of the Communist Labor University were browbeaten: "What's wrong with an umbrella or soap factory? They're useful, aren't they?"[24] Such objections proved counterproductive and the offending factories were quickly closed. One of the approved workshops that opened in their place was a factory for pharmaceuticals and traditional products, part of a resurgence of interest in indigenous medicine as an alternative to Western drugs. An associated movement for the widespread teaching of acupuncture, promoted by the PLA, swept the country.

The mass migration of youth in late 1966, Communist Labor University students among them, led to serious economic effects nationally, interrupting the flow of essential raw materials for factories. Large towns began to run short of food. Late in 1966, Mao had told an audience, "We should let the chaos go on for a few months."[25] But early the following year, the country was experiencing civil war. His own words were now echoing from Red Guard lips: "Doubt everything and overthrow everything" and "The world is ours." Mao complained that he could not remember having coined all the catch phrases.

Rising anarchy across the country was blamed on the young people he himself had stirred up. Having singled them out as the new revolutionaries, Mao now believed that his Red Guards had let him down by factionalizing. It followed that only the masses were fit to lead: in effect, this meant intervention by the PLA to restore stability and the dispersal of the Red Guard hordes ordered back to their home districts to make revolution.

The first call from the State Council to return to school and university, variously heeded, came on 14 October 1967, and the Red Guard movement was broken up over the next eighteen months. Across the country, university students received graduation certificates despite broken schooling and lack of academic attainment. An estimated 10 million urban Red Guards and other educated youth were eventually relocated in the countryside, bands of young people pledged to rural assignment, leaving in trucks and trains decorated with slogans and flying red flags. Although communes were exhorted to care for them until their work output was on par with the average, life for many was isolated and desperate. Red Guards, who had enjoyed the fermenting of trouble and the infliction of pain on others, would survive to bewail lost opportunities. They felt betrayed and disillusioned by events and from having been denied education and careers so close to their grasp.

The effects on China's higher education of the standstill of the mid-sixties, and the limited restoration of classes of the early seventies, were catastrophic. There was a sixteen-year break in the graduation of postgraduate students. The university's own attempt to enroll postgraduates early in 1966 had been abandoned altogether, and the nation counted 1.5 million specialists lost. Further, 200,000 teachers, scientists, and educational staff were recognized as having been illegally persecuted.[26] Revolutionary idealism was at a discount, and many university teachers remained frightened and fearful of stepping out of line.

> Yet our university survived. We did get our harvests in. We did have students. We never closed our gates. As to forgiving those who persecuted us at the time, you must see it in perspective. Many of them just wanted to show their love of Mao — they didn't know any better. When Li Chao returned, he was quick to put aside what happened. The rebel students eventually met their fate by being sent down.[27]

During the Cultural Revolution, decisionmaking at the national center was capricious, and the university leadership was uncertain of its standing from month to month. In one sign of favor, the July 30 letter was published in 1967, one of a confidential set of reference materials for senior cadres endorsed by Lin Biao. However, the university had been forced into a shotgun marriage with Jiangxi Agricultural College. It had lost its branch network and, as the seventies unfolded, new exemplars emerged which challenged its status as favored revolutionary son.

1. Main Campus, Communist Labor University.

2. Eighty-five percent of students claim worker or peasant origins; new enrollees, 1964.

3. First-year students in the classroom, Department of Agricultural Economics, c. 1965.

4. *Early buildings, Damaoshan Branch.*

5. *Administration building, Taihe Branch.*

6. *Meeting hall, Taihe Branch.*

7. *Jiangxi brick kiln.*

8. Wang Dongxing speaking at the opening of the Main Campus of the Communist Labor University, 1 August 1958.

9. Liu Junxiu teaching cotton planting at his experimental plot, Main Campus, 1965.

10. Shao Shiping lecturing at the university, 1959.

11. Party Secretary of the Communist Labor University, Zhang Yuqing, talks on teaching reform, 8 December 1964.

12. Zhou Enlai meets representatives of the Communist Labor University at the Nanchang Hotel, 18 September 1961. From front row, left: Luo Ruiqing (Secretary General of the Military Commission), Yang Shangkui (First Party Secretary, Jiangxi Provincial Committee), Zhou Enlai, Liu Junxiu, Shao Shiping, Fang Zhichun (Party Secretary, Jiangxi Province), Peng Mengyu (Vice Governor, Jiangxi Province), Li Chao, and Wang Jin Xiang.

13. Zhou Enlai's inscription, Communist Labor University, August 1959.

14. Zhou Enlai chats with Xiao Gao, a student from Shaoxing, Zhou's hometown.

15. At Lushan Branch on 17 September 1961, Zhou Enlai talks with Yang Shangkui, fourth from left, Yang's wife, Shui Jing, and Yang Cai, Party Secretary, Lushan Branch.

16. A student forestry class from Damaoshan Branch.

17. Silkworm factory students gathering cultivated mulberry leaves.

18. Carting logs, Damao mountains, c. 1972.

19. Animal husbandry students from Taihe Branch examine domestic animals for common diseases.

20. Worker-peasant-soldier students return from the countryside under the Zhou arch, c. 1973.

21. Yunshan Branch student musicians, c. 1965.

22. Zhu De sits alongside Dai Shuirong in a mathematics class at Yunshan Branch, 12 March 1962.

23. Zhu Min (center) visits and talks on her father's concern for the university following his death. From left: Zhu Jingshu, Zhu De's nephew and Gongda graduate; far right: Wang Jin Xiang.

24. Wang Jin Xiang orientates new students to university life in the Main Campus exhibition hall, 1960s.

25. Graduates of Nancheng Branch return to the commune.

26. Shao Shiping's inscription congratulates the Communist Labor University on its first anniversary: "Persist in carrying out the principle of combining education with productive labor and open up the road for all those seeking to enter university."

27. Zhu De's title for the magazine of the Communist Labor University: "Furnace of Jingganshan."

28. Mao Zedong's study, No. 1 Lu Lin, Lushan.

29. July 30 letter by Mao Zedong to comrades of the Communist Labor University, 1961.

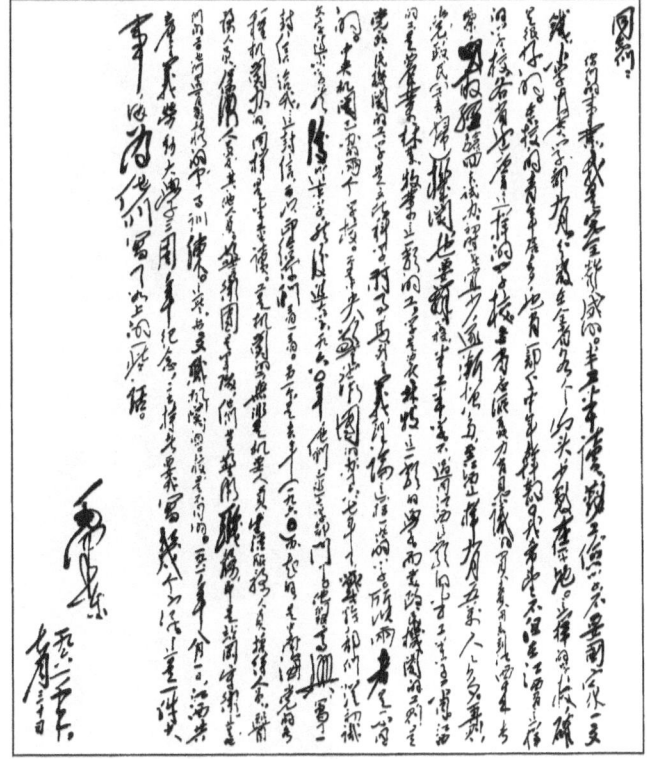

30. *"Knees as desks": Mao lecturing at the wartime institution, Lu Xun Academy of Arts, Yan'an, 1938.*

31. *Mao at the construction site of a Ming Tombs reservoir, 1958.*

32. Slogan on the wall of the main teaching building, Main Campus: "Three key issues in university administration: i) Party leadership, ii) mass line, iii) the combination of education and productive labor."

33. Students from Taihe Branch listen to veteran Zhou Wenkai at Mao's stone seat outside his former residence at Ciping.

34. Students of Yunshan Branch listen to a peasant's story of his family's "bitter past."

35. Scene from The Break. Principal Long holds up the hand of the blacksmith, Jiang Danian: "To enter our Communist Labor University, the first qualification is to be a laborer. The thick callus on the hand is the qualification!"

36. Cinema, Taihe Branch.

37. Living room: peasant home, mountainous region, Southern Jiangxi.

38. Kitchen: peasant home, mountainous region, Southern Jiangxi.

39. External: peasant home, mountainous region, Southern Jiangxi.

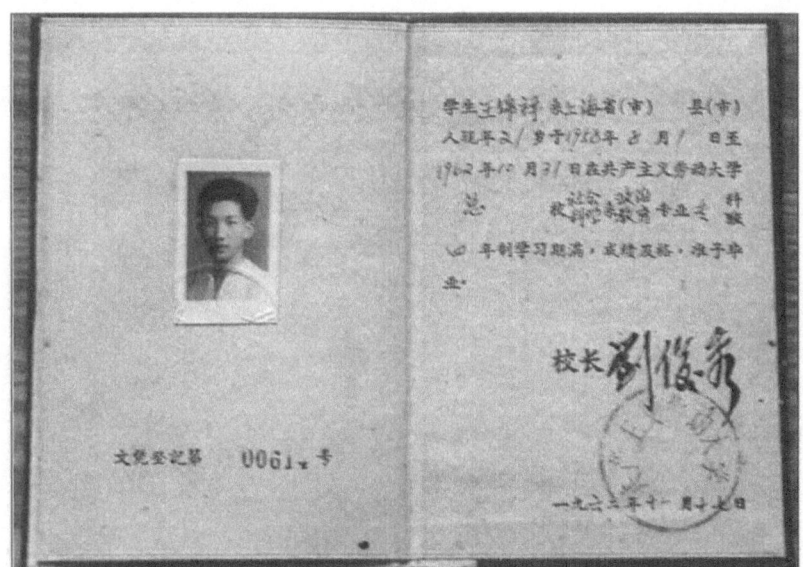

40. Graduation certificate of twenty-one-year-old, Wang Jin Xiang, who studied at the Communist Labor University from 1 August 1958 until 31 October 1962, majoring in political education in the Department of Social Sciences. Signed, Liu Junxiu, president, 17 November 1962. Seal of the Communist Labor University.

41. Wang Dongxing with author (center), and, from left, Wang Xiaoyan, his third daughter; Wang Yanqun, second daughter; Du Li, Beijing Agricultural College; Liu Guimin, secretary; and Xu Xiangyang, third son-in-law; Beijing, October 1998.

42. Administration building, Jiangxi Agricultural University.

Fifteen
An Open Door

"In primary school dead serious about reading books. In secondary school read dead books seriously. In university seriously read books to death!"

—Cultural Revolution saying[1]

China's civil armies deployed tanks, cannon, and planes in their internal wars until intervention by the PLA reimposed a form of government in 1967 by establishing a network of Revolutionary Committees representative of the army and worker and peasant groups. Somewhat grudgingly, Mao moved to legitimate the existence of universities in the new order: "It is still necessary to have universities; here I refer mainly to colleges of science and engineering."[2]

The Main Campus of the Communist Labor University set up its own Revolutionary Committee in April 1968, the whole placed under the Jiangxi's Agricultural Group of the Command Post for Grasping Revolution and Promoting Production. An uneasy peace settled as these revolutionary organs introduced social reforms for which no historical precedent existed. Applying the slogan "Open Door Schooling," enrollments were massively increased, courses cut savagely in length and heavily politicized in content, and young learners taught to challenge and confront teachers in class and outside.

The Revolutionary Committees displaced the Red Guards in authority. The last of the Red Guards to hold out were in the large city universities; divided into antagonistic parties, they controlled mini-kingdoms on campuses, making teaching activity impossible. In July 1968 Mao told them he was sending Mao Zedong Thought Propaganda Teams onto campus to assume leadership. The first of the teams, predominantly Xinhua Printing Plant workers, was sent to Tsinghua University, where it was received by rounds of gunfire. Many were killed or wounded. In a gesture of reconciliation, Mao gave a five-hour audience to the Red Guard's leaders, then sent the workers a plate of mangoes urging them to unite peaceably with the students.

Propaganda teams entered the Communist Labor University in the second half of 1968; the first to arrive, from the Nanchang Railway Bureau, stayed for two months, and the second, from the Nanchang Power Plant, remained until the end of 1969. Another group, the Nanchang Machine Tools Factory, left in 1976. The newcomers immediately involved themselves in major and minor decisionmaking. All syllabuses and textbooks required their prior approval, even if its members had no understanding of the technical content. A team led by seven peasants at the Nancheng Branch advised on matters academic, and lectured staff and students on how the Jiangxi soldiers had repelled the KMT's attacks on a near-starvation diet of pumpkin soup, wild grasses, and unpolished rice. Once the novelty of proletarian opinion had worn off, the team members' anecdotes, political admonitions, and academic censorship were resented. Staff and students objected to their power and interference and the time-wasting. They were useful, though, when they assisted the university in making links with local work units, raising the output of campus factories and helping sell products.

The Mao Zedong Thought Propaganda Team from the Nanchang Power Plant arrived as the Main Campus was settling in the boys and girls of No. 22 Middle School. The teenagers were proving a handful. "You could say the team became babysitters. I remember that when one of the Power Plant people made an overlong speech, they fired paper darts at him. 'Just wait till I finish,' he shouted plaintively."[3] Another of the Mao teams at Meiling was notably politically active:

> They decorated a room with patterns of red hearts and sunflowers and collected together numerous badges and portraits of the Chairman.

> Altogether 1,000 yuan was spent on this "loyalty room." When the team leader asked the vice principal, Wan Jianhai, for more money, he replied unceremoniously, "What's this? One decorated room — or a hole without a bottom!" They needed the extra money to make patterns of flower hearts for all campus windows, and they wanted the university painted red so it could be seen from afar. Wan was characteristically forthright: "What are you doing here? This is not a nursery or a kindergarten!" The team leader, not impressed with our vice principal's reply, called him "a class enemy," and threatened to "beat this dog's head into pieces."

Propaganda teams on the larger campuses usually included units of the PLA. "When the PLA marched, the road was red; where they bivouacked, the district was red." The first army team members joined the university's Revolutionary Committee in 1968. On taking charge, they began to plan for the recommencement of classes, releasing a few middle level leaders — Li Chao being freed late in 1968 at the favor of Wang Dongxing, who had come to exercise extraordinary powers in Beijing. The guards' chief said Li's attitude was friendly, noncombative, and Maoist.

> Asked for an opinion on the return of Li, Wang replied: "He mixed all his views together — he can be restored." Only a year earlier the university students had been shouting, "Down with Li Chao!" By releasing him, and others, the university could start again.

Li would eventually take the leadership of the Revolutionary Committee.

Enrollment at the Main Campus fell from 1,600 in 1965 to 100 short-course enrollees in 1966.[4] No students were taken in during 1967, and the only enrollments in 1968 were the 2,300 high school students. A fresh intake was planned for 1970, but this did not happen until 1971, when a spring enrollment was permitted. Some 1,100 students at the Main Campus were shown as admitted and graduated in the same year. Rewi Alley was among those to inspect the revived Main Campus classes:

> They may be graduates of middle or primary school, or even illiterate, and their age varies from the earliest 'teens to the late twenties. The youngest I met told me he was 14. But the majority appeared to be in their late 'teens or early twenties. They study intensively for a year in six subjects that are of the greatest use to them, the first, of course, being politics and the remainder technical.[5]

Teachers sent down were returned to their campuses. The length of the qualification was raised to two years in 1972, and entry ages were fixed in the ranges 18-25 for the Main Campus and 16-20 for the branches. Course lengths for undergraduate and senior specialists were increased to three years as of 1973. The same year, the Main Campus was commissioned to manage an eighteen-month course for scientific workers destined for Africa, with the support of Zhou Enlai. The last of the high school students sent by General Cheng were returned to Nanchang in December 1971, to the relief of all.

Worker-peasant-soldier students, as they were now known, were no longer admitted directly from school: they needed to have a minimum of two years work experience; be selected by the masses — that is, enrolled through their work or army unit; gain approval from the authorities at a higher level and from the host institution; and be in good health. Married women would be admitted. Most new enrollees had some years at middle school or equivalent and had applied for entry themselves.

In getting the schools and colleges moving again, the Jiangxi provincial powers spoke out against a widespread opinion that service as a teacher was "dangerous."[6] Lecturers were also told to undergo re-education and welcome workers, peasants, and soldiers as fellow teachers. Women would now make up at least 20 percent of the student body.[7] Nationally it was stipulated that more women would be admitted to higher education and selected for membership of major committees — actions supported by Mao's wife, Jiang Qing.

Encouraged by free tuition, food, accommodation, medical treatment, and pocket money, open-door schooling saw some of the poorest, least prepared students placed in university, including those from the minority regions. Able and highly motivated men and women, albeit with minimal qualifications, also entered higher education this way, studying hard to justify the faith put in them. Understandably a number of the ill-educated, for all their commitment and dedication, failed to cope with the academic demands put on them; facing difficulties in the classroom and frequently homesick, they were moved into truncated courses, graduating after a few months.

The new system's social purpose became corrupted as individuals learned to manipulate it for private benefit. Students were selected because they were relatives of the Party secretary or a member of the Revolutionary Committee, or in return for payment, gift, or sexual favor. Throughout the early 1970s, the weight of government opinion was that these worker-peasant-soldier students should return to their work units, a move said to raise grass roots expertise in the countryside and prevent airs and graces, and, if all returned home after training, their units could be expected to help with on-course expenses. The most meritorious graduates, according to the radicals, were those willing to return to work as peasants and draw "work points," a means of payment based on labor targets set by local production brigades. Men and women who chose a peasant's life were praised during gatherings of university staff, students, and visitors, especially those who sought assignment in border regions and Tibet. In 1975 the stipulation that all new students return to their production brigades was written into enrollment papers.

The introduction of the Revolutionary Committees and the Mao teams diminished the authority of the university itself. Deans and their departments were consolidated into four groupings: politics, teaching, production, and administration. Staff were required to discuss their courses with rural clients. Typically the production brigade leaders wanted a year or two of study for their students at most, improved literacy and numeracy skills, and a capacity to contribute immediately to field work. Commune heads took a broader perspective, wanting trained people amenable to rural life who understood mechanization, electrification, accounts, and the use of farm chemicals and fertilizer.

Campus courses were pared back to essentials, subjects were dropped or amalgamated, and production was favored. Geometry and algebra were excluded from school mathematics and replaced by lessons on the use of the abacus, and Chinese literature was removed from the curriculum, the released hours given over to preparing notices, writing letters and receipts, and reading official documents.

Writing teams were revived in 1964-66, part of the call for stronger theoretical underpinnings. In 1967 the Cultural Revolution leaders rejected these latter reworkings, wanting shorter books which summarized main points, emphasized local conditions, and found more space for political exhortation. Texts, it was determined, should abandon the spiral theory of curriculum development from near to far in favor of direct relevance.

Where general knowledge was included in textbooks, it returned to the earlier university practice of drawing on the local scene as much as possible. "Our textbooks were supposed to be compiled in the light of local practice. However, we tried to include some general knowledge about the country."[8] Neighboring river systems where natural conditions were similar to those in Jiangxi were investigated. "In this way specific knowledge of Jiangxi Province and the country are brought together, and essential knowledge and a broadening of outlook combined." A good deal of teachers' time was spent on the textbooks, which included a period of compilation in the field. Again this was in line with an earlier practice where lecturers had written textbooks, "utilizing peasant knowledge and experience in local production."[9]

Finally, staff had to obtain permission from the Revolutionary Committee and the Mao Zedong Thought Propaganda Teams to use these revised texts. By 1973, core texts in agriculture, forestry, and animal husbandry had been approved. Printed locally, the textbooks appeared as sets of notes on rough paper stapled together and headed "Draft", a precaution against failure by the writers to interpret correctly directions from above. Some in the university argued that the concentration on short-term objectives and politics was self-defeating, but the views were whispered.

Should a student fail to keep pace with his or her fellows, it was thought to be due to lack of opportunity, poor teaching, or physical disability, an assessment of individual difference in line with the Marxist argument that it was the environment which mattered in learning, not genes. The university's philosophy accepted that human mental capacity was sui generis, that is, the same for all. Belief in this justified the existence of a common curriculum for students, the Party dismissing any theorizing about different or unique qualities of an individual as metaphysical thought.

Proponents of the open door targeted the traditional habits of rote learning and an overreliance on the words of the lecturer and examination results. Although the university was known for its frank relationship between teacher and learner, youngsters were now encouraged to stand in class and criticize their teachers' social background, lesson content, and methods. When brawling erupted, staff were afraid of controlling students and exerting influence. Zhang Chunqiao, the propaganda chief, named such fighting courageous, likening the smashing of school windows and desks to the actions of the Luddites, the eighteenth-century destroyers of machinery.

Statements of the day constantly put down teachers and their professionalism: "One who acquires professional competency forgets the dictatorship of the proletariat."[10] Others were anti-intellectual in thrust: "We'd rather read a couple of books less than allow the bourgeoisie to influence our younger generation."[11] Mao's saying that "The problem of educational reform is primarily a problem of teachers"[12] was eagerly seized on, with teachers named the "stinking ninth category," bottom of a list of malefactors headed by landlords, rich peasants, and counterrevolutionaries.

Cries that "to read too many books is harmful"[13] and "the more they read the stupider they become" were echoed in the university's advice to students to reject the assumption that the more reading they did, the more knowledge they would absorb. The radicals' slogans were uncompromising: "Study is useless"[14]; the young can "make revolution just as well without being literate"[15]; and "It would be better for the intellectuals to forget everything they had learned from primary school to college."[16]

Still, some staff could agree with the increased importance now put on problem-solving strategies. "Cramming the duck" must end: "Students have received 10/10 in the past but are not good at observing and analyzing problems; some get 5/10 today but are better at analyzing — they are better than the first group."[17] To introduce more individual student involvement in learning, the "one talker" method was replaced by "mass talking," youngsters moving to the dais to state their views.

University examination practices also bowed to the radical policy-makers, Mao leading the assault with a declaration that exams were a device designed to exclude workers' children from higher education. He particularly queried the validity of the unseen question:

> If your answer is good and I copy it, then mine should be counted as good. Whispering in other people's ears and taking examinations in other people's names used to be done secretly. Let it now be done openly. If I can't do something and you write down the answer, which I then copy, this is all right. Let's give it a try.[18]

Mao's was a deliberately offensive attack on an ingrained belief in examinations which emperors of yore had applied to select men to rule the empire. The imperial civil service exam system had been abolished in the Chairman's lifetime, yet the credibility of the external examination remained high. This willing public acceptance of selectivity through assessment was said to mask the need to make education more accessible, an objective of the left-minded reformers.

University entrance examinations were banned and internal examining stopped. When testing was again allowed in 1973, it took a modified form, with prior discussion of questions, textbooks to hand, and answers discussed in class. Students and teacher would join together in an agreed assessment, the new procedures stressing collective effort. No marks were published. Repeating a class was regarded as a form of educational discrimination. With progression automatic through the grades, it was assumed that students would teach each other, making sure nobody fell seriously behind.

Following political shifts at the national level, a "cultural test" on entry was reintroduced at the Communist Labor University in 1975. The system of enrolling students sent by units had not worked particularly well: students' academic levels overall were regarded as too low and could not be raised adequately given the time required for labor. It was made clear, though, that this test was not the prime criterion for entry.

Productive labor was enforced across the country, an antidote to unnatural bookish habits. Physical labor was depicted as the best means of achieving national self-reliance, vocational training, and character building. Labor classes began in kindergarten where small fingers pasted brown paper to make shoe bags, sorted and tested flashlight bulbs, and folded cardboard boxes for miniature padlocks. In primary school, children wired transformers, assembled light switches, and made wooden toys for export. In secondary school, youngsters operated lathes, spun cable for trucks, and hammered out homemade tools such as pincers and awls from cast-off machinery. Universities produced pesticides, synthesized drugs, and manufactured furniture and automated machinery. Local factories helped supply raw materials in cooperative arrangements with schools and colleges and fixed contract rates for payment.

Here, Jiangxi Communist Labor University was very much in its element. Its work-study program had been actively promoted, and its factories had restructured themselves according to the latest policies. The time given over to productive labor relative to teaching was increased again. One spectacular project was underway at the Main Campus. "What they are perhaps most proud of at the moment is their industrial side, in which students under worker leadership have turned out fifteen large-sized jeeps during the past year and have now made all preparations to produce 150 this year."[19]

Noting that Jiangxi Province had no car industry, the university's Agricultural Machinery Department and its associated factories had decided to follow the example of some national universities by setting up a car plant. Wang Dongxing was enlisted to collect the scarce machinery in Beijing. In October 1969, the Agricultural Machinery Department was transformed into the Automobile Production Factory, its objective an assembly line of 5,000 "Shuang Mashi" jeeps annually.

> Unfortunately the prototype jeeps were not well made — indeed only a few could move. In 1971, the university determined to return to its prime function as an agricultural institution, and its machine tools were parceled out among five Jiangxi factories. Although these factories were supposed to combine in producing a Jiangxi vehicle, this never happened.[20]

The educational reforms of the day were carried out in a highly charged ideological atmosphere which began in kindergarten. Children no longer played with tea sets, learning instead how auntie and uncle worker had shaped clay under the harshest of conditions before liberation. The rich treasury of Chinese folktales was banned and replaced by stories of ordinary men and women performing superhuman feats of toil and military service. On campus, students sang songs about the Chairman's virtues, praising him in chants at morning ceremonies, their copies of the Little Red Book held over their hearts. They were told that the thought of Mao was "the acme of Marxism-Leninism in the present era — a weapon more powerful than the atom bomb."

Courses inside the university such as Chinese and the humanities were heavily politicized. Students were "to take society for their factory," and lecturers accompanied students on tours of local factories and farms, where they talked with workers and peasants, writing down their biographies and bitter tales. The university's leaders, attesting their continued faith in hard work and self-reliance, sent themselves on a tour of Dazhai.

All staff were to imprint the "consciousness of the theory of continuous revolution" on their students. It was his clear knowledge of the class struggle learned at university that enabled one graduate, Li Dehou, to recognize his work unit was on the wrong political track. Discerning "a capitalist tendency,"[21] he re-educated his fellows at night school. The university had to constantly affirm such benefits from its graduates, fearing the charge that the best of them abandoned the countryside for posts in towns and East Coast cities. The university's growing fame saw its name inscribed on an exclusive ideological listing of the 1970s, along with Tsinghua University's Water Conservation Department, where staff taught "at the first line of harnessing the Yellow River" at Sanmen Gorge;

the May 7 Agricultural College at Yuetan, Henan, whose students had passed "the three hard tests in ideology, labor, and technology"; and the evergreen Dazhai.[22]

With the Cultural Revolution stabilized through the intervention of the PLA, military men increased their influence. The downfall of Liu Shaoqi saw the political star of a defense minister Lin Biao rise, and the army became increasingly represented in educational decisions. A directive in 1967 required that all students above lower primary school receive military training and army discipline; it followed naturally that Communist Labor University students involve themselves in reading sessions and discussions and military lectures and drill. Army influence lessened after Lin was killed in the crash of a Trident jet in 1971, although the PLA retained a presence on the campus. Two years later, the Communist Labor University was put under a leading cadre in the provincial Party Committee, and it was agreed that the university's management become an item on the Party agenda again. As the Party reasserted its authority, professional groups in education and farms, forestry, and reclamation resumed their say in its affairs.

Machinery taken from branches in the late 1960s was now to be restored to them. The university's resources were further enhanced by a successful water supply project at Long Quan Dam and heartened by a guarantee of a grain ration from the Provincial Grain Authority. In 1971, the Political Department of the Provincial Revolutionary Committee announced plans to celebrate the tenth anniversary of Mao's letter by book, exhibition, song, and film. The following year, Liu Xiyao, head of the Science and Education Group, which had replaced for the Ministries of Education and Higher Education, inspected the Hualin campus.

Such official goodwill added to Gongda's revolutionary status, and clones of the university began opening across China. Henan had 100 Gongda institutions, the best-known being Yishen; Heilongjiang had Tieli; and Hubei had Yingchen. Beijing, Guangzhou, Yan'an, Hunan, Anhui, and Shandong all managed well-known counterparts. Beijing Gongda, for example, became the base for Beijing Agricultural College. Wang Jin Xiang was known to appear at these various foundings, where he was publicized as "Chairman Mao's representative."[23] Some of these Gongdas were ill-considered failures. In Henan Province one regular college had directed a convoy of its staff and students virtually into the unknown:

After we climbed down from our lorry we had more than two days' walk before coming to a river. Here we were put on barges and ferried to a remote island. This was the site of our Communist Labor University. Nothing was provided for us. We had to use the plastic sheeting we brought to keep out the elements — we nearly froze to death! Then we nearly starved to death! Fortunately some staff knew how to make oil from plants, which we sold to local peasants. So we hung on to life until they let us return to our home campus. The name, Gongda, was bad news.

With so many units asking permission to tour the university, the reception center became increasingly active. Wang Jin Xiang was managing it because of his reliability, wide experience of the campus, presentable manner, and a capacity to explain. It was said, "Dazhai has its iron man, the university its iron mouth."

By the early 1970s, the university was catering to hundreds of visitors weekly from universities, districts, schools, factories, kindergartens, and overseas. The provincial government paid 10 fen a day in subsidies for its guests who were accommodated free on campus or, for higher status visitors, a local hotel was booked, which they paid for themselves. Lectures were given twice a day by the reception teams — unlike some other famous revolutionary shrines, taped addresses were not used. Wang Jin Xiang tells of the work:

> So many visitors were a real burden and disruption. But we did our best for them. When they arrived, they found a new kind of university. We didn't take them to our laboratories because these were not our strength. They went to the animal farms, orchards, or fields. Visitors liked to be photographed with our students. Some of the barefoot teachers were embarrassed — our students were not well dressed and they carried axes and hoes — they were not like students.
>
> When foreigners came, we fed them in a special dining room. They didn't like this: they wanted to eat with the students. So we sent groups of twenty to the department which was to provide them lunch. If there was no meat that day, the cooks could kill a rabbit for them. Some Japanese students asked if they could come back and teach, and a Frenchman wrote an article on our use of fruit by-products. Several of these visitors keep in touch today. Over these years, we gave out thousands of badges and booklets about ourselves, a costly business. Things were busy in reception. We worked 18-20 hours a day — even our own children didn't see us as they grew up.

After a group of Africans returned home, they wrote to Wang Jin Xiang inviting him to visit the continent to set up and manage a Communist Labor University, an offer not taken up.

University staff and students had come to their own accommodation with the reforms of open-door education. By 1975, the Communist Labor University held just over 31,000 students across the Main Campus and 108 associated branches.[24] While its leaders argued that they had preempted the important open-door reforms, privately they had little stomach for the dogmatic quality of many of them. Some educational requirements of the early 1970s were embraced enthusiastically and creatively; others were pushed forward unthinkingly or with a view to short-term political gain. The radical reforms failed across the country because they appeared on the scene too suddenly to be assimilated through persuasion. Applied comprehensively and inflexibly, they became just another part of a wider frame of arbitrary government and fear.

Sixteen
Trial by Media

"*The Break* is the battle song of proletarian education."

—Chu Lan, Reviewer[1]

"A movie damned a reputation."

—Wang Jin Xiang[2]

A two-hour color film, *The Break*, completed in the Beijing Film Studios late in 1975, portrayed the university's break with the traditions of school orthodoxy. Unlike the various short documentaries made on the university to date, this was a major national film production. Distributed at a time when few feature films were available, an audience of hundreds of millions would watch its story line unfold, some seeing it as many as ten times over.

The Break's opening shot tracks a man in a faded army uniform steering a bamboo raft down white-water rapids into the calm of a smoothly flowing tributary. Long Guozheng, an ex-PLA officer and head of a reclamation farm, secures his raft and crosses a bustling roadway past trucks decorated with red flags and placards extolling the Great Leap Forward movement. The secretary of the district Party Committee greets him at headquarters and gets straight to the point: "We've been liberated for nine years but haven't transformed our universities yet."³ He wants Long to form the Sungshan Branch of a Communist Labor University in the mountains.

Together, the two overrule a recalcitrant vice president, Cao Zhonghe, who wants the university built on the river flats close to the township available only to qualified senior middle school graduates. The conservative elder watches horrified as Long implements the open door, enrolling a blacksmith on the strength of his callused hands, a pig farmer of low educational background, and a child bride whose literacy level is limited to the characters "Chairman Mao is our liberator."

Principal Long and his students construct their own classrooms and dormitories on a mountain plateau, sawing, splitting, thatching, and rock pounding. Working alongside them on the roof of a near, complete dormitory, the soldier reminisces on his days at Kangda when he learned his lessons squatting on a knapsack. The few doubters and backsliders among the new enrollees are patiently brought around by Long and an enthusiastic learning community.

The principal's academic rule begins with an attack on the appropriateness of the teaching plan he should follow: "The syllabus does not accord with the seasons in this part of China; the forestry content is about white birch not bamboo; and the study of soil deals with the black soil of Siberia not the red soil of Jiangxi." An amusing sketch follows as the sanctimonious dean of studies, Sun Ziqing, who fills his teaching hours describing the features of the Mongolian horse, points to a large model of the animal and talks on "the function of a horse's tail." He smartly shooes away a deferential peasant who enters the classroom wanting treatment for a sick water buffalo.

Efforts to add more local material to the college's textbooks and work-study practices are derided at the District Educational Office as examples of Long's "wartime thinking." The unsound man is sent off on a tour of the big agricultural colleges for an academic re-schooling, where he spies careless seniors who trample and waste grain in completing their graduation exercises and postgraduate ingrates who spurn their mothers' gifts of peasant-spun clothes and homemade shoes. Aristocratic professors attend their experimental plots under handheld canopies. Small wonder the enforced inspection merely confirms the wisdom underlying Sungshan.

The implementation of the open door soon flushes out opponents on campus, in particular Long's vice president, who springs an examination on the classes and fails several peasants outright. When complaints are investigated, the principal discovers a girl who had abandoned the class test to join a field team spraying a sudden plague of insects. By contrast, the vice president's top student, a boy, had turned down local villagers asking for help. "Which one is the better?" Of course the girl is reinstated, and Long acknowledges the woman's strength in "standing firm against the absolute authority of the teacher."

Affairs at the branch campus deteriorate. Rightists get the upper hand and news is posted that the branch must close. Students and staff stare disbelievingly at an order nailed to the notice board: those speaking out against this travesty of justice are banished or threatened with prison terms. Long returns from the re-education tour and calls a mass meeting of a sullen student body. A shock is in store. Moving to a lectern, Long opens an impressive red and gold folder and reads aloud from Mao's July 30 letter: "What you have been doing has my full support." The audience erupts — and Long, in heroic prose, attests to the commitment of the Sungshan community to carry the revolution in education through to the end.

The idea of a film chronicling the university's achievements was not new. Within years of its founding, the documentary "Spring at Damaoshan" was completed, and this was followed by a short documentary about the university as a whole, "Charting a New Path," which was screened in October 1965. A more ambitious film, "Jiangxi's New Seedlings," promoting the principle of work-study, was prepared by two Jiangxi writers who knew the university well. Its male and female leads toured the campus for preparation before shooting began just prior to the Cultural Revolution. The project was restarted in 1966-67, with fresh actors hired, and the title changed to, "Creating a New Way." Now it would concentrate on the story of the university's graduates, but again little progress was made. A third rewriting, aimed this time at celebrating open-door schooling followed in 1971, the chief actors spending time at Meiling gathering local color.

While the eventual product, *The Break*, caught the atmosphere of the Great Leap Forward when little appeared beyond human grasp, it also put politics above history, suggesting that an idealized film account was a documentary feature. As the *Jiangxi Daily* of 25 January 1976 explained, "*The Break* is lively teaching material promoting the debate over the revolution in education." However, viewers were encouraged to equate the artifice of film with the reality of university life. Whether the film was a fair representation or not was a question unlikely to have entered the heads of its audiences — to them the Communist Labor University and Sungshan Branch were one and the same place. Indeed visitors to the Main Campus were known to ask for a tour of the imaginary branch!

When a national review of the film first appeared in the *People's Daily* on 7 January 1976, a surprise omission was any mention of its denouement, the July 30 letter, which suggested that the cultural affairs men in Beijing wanted to play down the university's political standing. Whether the Mao letter should have been written into the film had proved contentious during the making, the cultural chief, Zhang Chunqiao, arguing for its omission and Chi Qun, the army man and political boss who reviewed the film prior to its release, also wanting it cut out.[4] Hearing of the likely mutilation, the university sent a senior Party member to the Beijing location to insist that the letter provide the film's unifying theme. Eventually, shooting went ahead, but only the opening lines of the July 30 letter were permitted. Mao was affronted when he saw the picture: "My letter to Gongda was quite long. Why is only a sentence or two left?" The Jiangxi Province Party Committee agreed and would later commission a contemporary drama, "Declaration of War," in which the Mao letter was projected on stage in the concluding scene.[5]

For all the infighting at political headquarters, *The Break* proved hugely popular with audiences. Its scenic footage, including material taken from earlier filmings, was a joy to the eye. Similarly its stand for more educational access for farming families touched a sympathetic chord, local audiences applauding the heroes and booing the villains. Two scenes remained in the memory: Principal Long holding up the young blacksmith's hand and saying, "To enter our Communist Labor University, the first qualification is to be a laborer. The thick callus on the hand is the qualification!"; and his dean of studies teaching the function of a horse's tail. Viewers of *The Break* today will enjoy the scenery and the sly humor of the Jiangxi peasants, and pass over the predictable propaganda of the story line.

Furious charges and countercharges followed the film's release. Although university personnel had seen the early material and had attended many shootings, its leaders were worried about the fictional content that related to the propaganda of open door education. This was not how the university operated. Their opinions, put in writing during the shooting, had little result. When the film was finally shown in the hall of the Main Campus on 29 December 1975, some staff thought it would bring them prominence and international fame; the more sophisticated were less impressed, a teacher in veterinary science being the first to say the film denigrated their institution. Looking back, opinion holds that *The Break* did the university real harm.

> *The Break* has been shown all over China for a prolonged period of time as propaganda. It had a devastating effect on the reputation of Jiangxi Communist Labor University and Jiangxi Agricultural University. Furthermore it changed people's attitudes towards agriculture.[6]

Much that people remember about the Communist Labor University comes from the film. When the weathercock swung away from revolutionary-style education, the university found itself laughed at to an extent that some staff sought a name change. Even graduates of its successor, Jiangxi Agricultural University, have faced sarcastic jibes, "Do your teachers still talk of the functions of the horse's tail?" That scenes from the film are not easily buried and forgotten was evident in a Beijing television commercial in 1995 in which a researcher said he had given up teaching the function of the horse's tail in favor of producing a scientifically nutritious health drink. The incident has passed into popular culture.

Unforeseen political consequences followed the showing. Among other charges, university leaders accused the film of slandering a leading comrade and showing posters attacking others.[7] Then the film's main spokesman for the revisionist line, short in stature and long in reactionary rhetoric, was likened to the disgraced leader Deng Xiaoping. Although Deng had been restored to important posts by Mao in 1973-74, a hostile campaign two years later saw him labeled an "arch unrepentant capitalist roader." Students were to seek out the manifestation of Deng in the film and write essays criticizing revisionism. "When Deng himself saw the film, he said, '*The Break* is about Gongda, and Gongda is against me.'"[8] If it was bad for the film to have spread false stories about the university and its staff, it was worse to have blackened the reputation of China's paramount leader-to-be. *The Break* was withdrawn from public distribution after 1977, and it remains on the not-to-be-released list.

There was a further twist to the film story. It would be revealed that its two scriptwriters had been directed to spend several months at Chaoyang Agricultural College to learn from a truly revolutionary place. Chaoyang had appeared in the early 1970s as a pretender to Gongda's standing as chief pacesetter in agriculture.[9] Its beginnings can be traced back to September 1968, when the Mao Zedong Propaganda Team of Shenyang Agricultural College, enforcing Mao's instruction that agricultural institutes relocate in the countryside, led a party of its teachers and students on a 250-kilometer journey by foot to the southern borders of Liaoning Province. Despite a friendly welcome from 2,000 local peasants with drum and dance, few of the newcomers were content to settle, most of the contingent slipping home when opportunity arose.

In January 1970, a larger Shenyang party, this time with families, was directed to a commune in the north of Chaoyang County. Obeying Mao's order that education be scattered among the mountains, the core group split into six isolated branches where the teachers worked the fields and taught. Eventually the district Party Committee relented and agreed to reunite them in a valley several dozen li from Chaoyang town, where they founded a college known as the May 7 Agricultural Science and Technology University. Following an amalgamation with Chaoyang's own agriculture, water, and agricultural machinery institutes, the whole was renamed Chaoyang Agricultural College.

Back at the Shenyang Agricultural College, recruitment drives to staff Chaoyang began. Party members and cadres led the way, mounting the rostrum in turn, volunteering their services, and taking the Chaoyang Communist Labor University oath. The less enthusiastic had no choice other than to be won over. The first major Shenyang division to relocate was the Water Conservation Department, the district being notoriously short of water and suffering badly from windstorms and scouring: "When rain comes, mountain torrents are wild beasts; when water passes, there is a tract of stones and rocks."

Chaoyang offered long- and short-term courses in water conservation and programs in agriculture and localized research. It also managed a spare-time university providing literacy classes, scientific farming, and politics to local commune members, and its cultural troop was active in singing the songs of the revolutionary theater, "The White Haired Girl" and "The Red Lantern Brigade."

Before any student places were taken up, Chaoyang's recruiting teams would visit peasant applicants in their homes where they studied Mao's works together and with the families. In the college's orientation period, enrollees were required to pledge to dedicate themselves to agriculture, each standing to make an affirmation to return to their commune on graduation. A motivational talk on the achievements of Kangda and the Communist Labor University of Jiangxi followed. Finally, each young person received a gift of works by Marx, Lenin, and Mao, a hoe, and a set of carry poles and buckets.

Chaoyang dispatched its administrators and teachers on a tour of several national work-study projects to expand their thinking. Dazhai, "the best agricultural university," was the first call; the Communist Labor University, "that new type university established in accord with Chairman Mao's idea," the last. On the group's return, characters were carved on a rock face of Eagle's Mouth Mountain: "Vow to turn the agricultural college into a Communist Labor University."

The new college faced its own setbacks. The leadership professed astonishment when the graduates of its first twenty-month experimental class of 1970-71 sought assignment by the state, a move totally opposed to the college's philosophy. To prevent this happening again, the leadership introduced the "several ups and several downs" program, requiring that trainees attend a first year of classroom study and labor, with the second and third years taught mainly in the home brigade. After further specialties were allowed in 1973, including water conservation, students took heart to ask for state assignment again at least within the province, calling for a system of "walking on two legs" —one leg "from the commune, to the commune," the other, "from the commune, to the state." Officials opposed received poison pen letters and the Party Committee was forced to launch an internal rectification campaign.

The Chaoyang experiment came out of Liaoning Province, which boasted its own tie with Mao Zedong, as the vice chairman of its provincial Revolutionary Committee was Mao Yuanxin, the Chairman's nephew. Born in jail after his father was executed in Xinjiang, Yuanxin was brought to Zhongnanhai by Mao for protection. During Yuanxin's time at Harbin Polytechnic, the Chairman advised him to combine his reading with practical work and criticized his lecturers' reliance on others' books and sets of notes: "Why don't they distribute their lecture notes to you and study problems together with you?"[10] Liaoning would become a leading center for his uncle's philosophy. In the late sixties, with the Cultural Revolution well underway, Yuanxin sided with the Jiang Qing faction, and his Chaoyang experiment was backed by them. Claiming that many post-liberation teachers were rightists, Yuanxin charged that China's schools had "brought up year after year, group after group of these people — bourgeois intellectuals who had to be remolded again after graduation."[11] Over time the young man came to exercise considerable power: when Mao was too ill to attend Politburo meetings in 1975, the nephew attended in a liaison role.

The college's ideological peak was attained late in December 1974, when the Science and Education Group of the State Council initiated the "On-the-Spot Meeting to Study Chaoyang Agricultural College's Experience in Educational Revolution." And the following May, university staff had to join a provincial meeting on applying the "spirit of Chaoyang."[12] By 1976 Chaoyang had recruited 2,000 worker-peasant-soldier students from across China and maintained 420 teachers and staff. Its courses covered agriculture, horticulture, animal husbandry, veterinary science, farm machinery, water conservation, and land hydrology.[13] Although graduate output was small as yet, the leadership contrasted them with 17,000 graduates from Shenyang Agricultural College, who had not returned to work the fields.

Inside the Communist Labor University, there was grudging admiration for some of the college's projects (said to have been copied from them) and, in November 1975, staff welcomed the principal of Chaoyang, Xie Ming, and thirty-eight colleagues. Wang Jin Xiang reported on the relationship:

> Altogether we helped them solve problems three times. Ming had a special interest in fruit tree cultivation. They put no limits on the ages of students, and they linked their research with orchard work through their production brigades. They did some good things, but they were used by the "Gang of Four," who said, "Chaoyang did everything against the capitalist system." Can you believe it — fifty reporters were stationed there to publicize it nationally?[14]

The university would later disavow any connection with the college beyond the offerings of inspiration and free technical advice. The place, they argued, was in the pocket of the Liaoning radicals and no true disciple of theirs.

> The "Gang of Four" promoted the kind of open education portrayed in *The Break*. This was really a characteristic of Chaoyang, not us. Why, the lead male in the film had a physical likeness to its principal! The

four did not praise us directly: they really wanted to support Chaoyang. They used the flag of the Communist Labor University. In fact it didn't learn our spirit, it only learned how to grasp class struggle.

Later the two scriptwriters of *The Break* were charged with writing an account of Chaoyang Agricultural College and disguising it as the Communist Labor University because the latter was so well known.

Seventeen
Attacked by Left and Right

"The university was attacked not for what it was, but for what people thought it was."

—Wang Jin Xiang[1]

That the university was in the sights of the radical clique was obvious to all at the National Conference on Educational Work held in July 1971, a gathering which met periodically to set educational policy for the next four or five years. Li Chao, the Gongda representative, moved that the July 30 letter be written into the proceedings as a statement of communist educational principle; however, no mention was made of the letter when the Conference draft was released. Chi Qun, head of the Mass Criticism Group of Beijing and Tsinghua, presented the apologia: "Some people believed that the July 30 document should have been written in. We didn't do this. They were unhappy."[2]

Fortunately for Li, more powerful allies prevailed. Zhou Enlai invited Li and others to attend an expanded meeting of the Politburo on 15 April 1971, called to receive the results of the same national conference. Although nonvoting delegates, they were treated as honored guests, being seated at the front of the hall. The Politburo overturned the Science and Education Group's rejection, ordering that the letter be noted, a decision

Mao ratified. A follow-up conference celebrating the event was held in Jiangxi in August.

The early 1970s brought a growing boldness from critics of the university, led by a failed student from Liaoning Province, Zhang Tiesheng, who queried its credentials. Zhang had risen to fame as the "blank paper man." Unable to answer questions in an entrance examination set by his provincial college in 1973, he had handed in a blank paper, a critique appended. "To be frank, I am not impressed by, but rather resent, those bookworms who just fooled around and did not do any useful work in the past seven years."[3]

In August 1973, Zhang's stand for open-door education appeared on the front page of the *People's Daily,* where he was named a hero, a man daring to swim against the tide. Disliked by most teachers, not least for his accusation that the majority had been happier under the KMT leader, Chiang Kaishek, Zhang was one of the main promoters of Chaoyang Agricultural College. Never timid with an opinion, he was the author of the "black letter" informing the university that its revolutionary ardor had waned: "The Communist Labor University is like an oil lamp, bright outside, but dark inside. It is not as good as people think it is because it has not grasped class struggle. It has sided with Liu Shaoqi."[4]

The army man, Chi Qun, entered the fray in December 1974, when he elaborated on a new slogan, "Fight against the Seventeen Black Years," at a Chaoyang meeting. Chi insisted that Mao's philosophy had been ignored between 1949 and 1966, when China's schools were controlled by reactionaries whose practices replicated Liu Shaoqi's direction that "the old system of education be followed." No genuinely socialist model had emerged prior to the Cultural Revolution. A charismatic speaker, Chi had the Chaoyang audience on side. However, the substance of his argument threatened the university's representatives, a substantial part of whose history fell in the nominated "black years." It also reflected on their great supporters, Zhou Enlai, Zhu De, and Wang Dongxing, and on their graduates who must be considered as trained in a revisionist period.

Chi was said to harbor a particular hatred for the Jiangxi university: "It is no longer advanced — the old revolutionary tradition has passed away. The university has been left behind." University staff who attended the December meeting were not called on to speak and the material they had brought for distribution went uncirculated. The Chaoyang conference was followed up by a regional meeting for the exchange of educational experience in work-study. When several participants asked to hear from Jiangxi staff, their requests were denied, though Chi found the time to present the latest Chaoyang advances. The next day, the Hunan representatives left the hall, meeting up with the Jiangxi men and women privately. On their return home, the Hunan people organized a series of ten-day training classes for their cadres based on Gongda-style practice.

The university faced public humiliation again in 1975. Along with Chaoyang Agricultural College, it had been invited to submit a paper for publication in the first issue of the Party theoretical journal, *Red Flag*, in 1976. Sending the article back for revision five times, *Red Flag*'s editors declared themselves unhappy about the tone, particularly its optimism, which they put down to a reluctance to admit the existence of class struggle inside the community: "Given that the class struggle is real, how can the university's future be certain? Circumstances are beyond your own efforts." The university had overemphasized its own strengths they argued, and failed to recognize the importance of the Party in decisionmaking. Eventually the article was dropped, a decision galling for the university as the piece had already been approved by the Jiangxi Provincial Party Committee.

Still the university retained its channels of influence. In 1975-76, two booklets were published on the deeds and activities of graduates; a set of news pictures was circulated; the regular campus journal resumed publication; and *Liberation Army Daily*, *Historical Research*, *Nationalities Pictorial*, and *PLA Pictorial* accepted its articles. Another short documentary, "The Communist Labor University Marches Ahead," was released, and a Yugoslav film crew was given permission to shoot on campus over four days.

The decision not to publish Mao's letter in 1961 had unforeseen consequences. While it may have prevented a stampede to found like institutions, its secret status led to rumors about its authenticity — indeed, that it was a forgery. Two years after it was first circulated to Party heads, the letter was republished in a set of restricted documents, *Long Live Chairman Mao's Educational Thought*, which contained two minor changes compared with the original, probably printing errors. Later, the radical Yao Wenyuan would be accused of attempting a garbled version of his own.

A signal victory came on the 13 August 1975. The Jiangxi Provincial Party Committee received permission from the CPC Central Committee to publish an extract from Mao's letter in the *Jiangxi Daily*, and the provincial Party Committee called on readers to study the Chairman's letter and consider its relevance in their own lives. However, a proposed national printing was opposed by Zhang Chunqiao, the culture head, who thwarted attempts to have it carried in the *People's Daily*, then instituted an inquiry into who had been behind the Jiangxi printing. Nonetheless, popular Jiangxi demand insisted that the university be known as the July 30 Institution.

Publication of the extract was part of the university's reply to its enemies. Wang Dongxing, who had become increasingly alarmed at the ferocity of the assaults, asked Mao to intervene. The Chairman refused:

> Whenever a new thing appears, there will be differing views — we must learn how to live with criticism and analyze it. It's not necessary to fight back immediately. You should listen and try to overcome the problem. In the CPC its not necessary to have only one opinion. Remember Gongda is doing something different. [5]

In 1973, Mao had moved to balance his political team by reinstating Deng Xiaoping, and the moderate Zhou Rongxin was appointed to a rehabilitated Ministry of Education. The restored bureaucrats bravely targeted the open-door reforms. With Zhou Enlai's support, radicals were forced to accept testing in universities, students in disciplines such as mathematics were allowed entry straight from school again, and graduate assignment permitted more state positions.

Zhou Rongxin and senior Tsinghua University staff went further, petitioning Mao in August and October 1975 asking that the open-door policy be abandoned so far as higher education went. They wanted the influence of powerful, nonacademic leaders such as Chi Qun curbed and obvious anti-intellectual practices ended.

> "Colleges and universities must cultivate scientists and specialists. Poor and lower middle peasants may be invited to teach. They can help everybody remember the bitter old days and make sure no one forgets his roots. They can also teach you to tell leeks from wheat and to apply the ashes of grass and wood to alkaline soil. But if you give them litmus paper they will be at a loss. If China's agriculture is to end its backward stage we must train new scientists, grow new species and strive for scientific application. You certainly can't say that we can train students properly by just having peasants as lecturers." [6]

Mao referred the petitions back to the universities for mass debate. As these were centers of radical influence and power, staff and students roundly rejected Zhou Rongxin's opinions out of hand. An aggressive counterattack against the "right deviationist wind" followed. University staff and students, who had already joined in the denunciations of the Anti-Lin Biao, Anti-Confucius Campaign (obliquely directed at Zhou Enlai), entered the Great Education Debate enthusiastically backing the open-door reforms.

The annual July 30 letter celebration fell on 28 July in 1976. In a sign of the times, and to the surprise of many guests, the Nanchang gathering was greeted by a demonstration, opponents of the Jiangxi Province Party Committee protesting its "questionable" political composition.[7] They broke into the meeting at the Nanchang Hotel, "kidnapping" individuals in broad daylight. After order was restored, the 1,000 teachers, students, and army personnel and 347 graduates began the program, which this year lauded its 180,000 graduates who had dutifully returned to work the land.[8] The company joined in song praising the university's achievements and, at the breakup, a small group of representatives remained behind to write a letter to Mao reaffirming the worth of the Jiangxi experiment.

The year 1976 was a momentous one. On 8 January, Zhou Enlai died of stomach cancer. The news hit hard, the *Jiangxi Daily* expressing the feeling: "Zhou Enlai's heart and the heart of the Communist Labor University beat as one." Staff and students set up a funeral room where they signed a memorial book and bowed respectfully to a portrait, and leaders talked with the students about the special relationship. On 6 July, the university learned of the death of another good friend, Zhu De. Soon afterwards, Zhu's daughter, Zhu Min, visited the Main Campus where she talked with students about the friendship between Zhou, Mao, and her father. On 9 September, Mao Zedong himself died, the mourning in Jiangxi befitting the god-emperor.

Political change followed swiftly. On the night of 6 October, Mao's widow, Jiang Qing, and her three main lieutenants were arrested by a headquarters group led by Wang Dongxing and Marshal Ye Jianying. Among those quickly rounded up were the leading radicals in education, Chi Qun and Zhang Tiesheng. The dead Chairman's nephew, Mao Yuanxin, was also arrested and gaoled. Their educational policies would follow them to oblivion.

Although the university was suddenly bereft of its three great allies, fears for the future were calmed when news came of Wang Dongxing's active involvement in the day's events. More happiness followed the appointment of Premier Hua Guofeng in 1977, who would succeed Mao as chairman of the Central Committee of the CPC and chairman of the Military Commission. Hua supported Mao's policies and was a close ally of their friend Wang Dongxing. "This was the beginning of a new life. We were very confident."[9]

A graduate of a county vocational school, Hua had risen to Party secretary of Xiangtan District in Hunan. During his twenty-two years in the province, he paid special attention to Shaoshan, Mao's hometown, where he had the family home rebuilt. He had rail and irrigation projects constructed, a factory built to make Mao badges, and an exhibition hall opened. Promoted to director of the provincial Cultural and Educational Bureau, Hua took a special interest in literacy campaigns and small-scale rural research;[10] another of his projects was to reopen the First Provincial Normal School which Mao attended in 1913.

Hua knew of Mao's attachment to the Communist Labor University, having sent Hunan cadres there between 1961-65. The new chairman had also joined Mao during his 1965 visit to Jiangxi, afterwards instituting a "Learn from Gongda" campaign, with 150 Gongda-inspired colleges opening in Hunan. In 1973, Hua awarded certificates personally to fourteen of the best of them[11] — one of the most famous was at Youxian. In 1975 Hua became vice premier in charge of science and technology under Deng Xiaoping.

The new chairman could rely on the backing of Gongda. Staff and students understood that "wise leader Hua" was on their side, and they joined enthusiastically in his first national campaign advocating rapid economic progress. They noted attempts to promote the man's educational credentials when he was praised for sending his daughter Xiaoli to labor in the Xu Jiawu Brigade outside Beijing, although the girl had been entitled to stay home. On her visits back, he would question her on Marx, Lenin, Engels, and Mao thought and inspect her hands for calluses.[12] Hua and the recently appointed minister of education, Liu Xiyao (Zhou Rongxin had died suddenly), would move quickly to label Chi Qun's assertion of "seventeen black years since 1949" a fallacy, reassessing the post-liberation period as a time of solid socialist gains.

It was Hua who gave approval for the publication of the full text of Mao's letter in the national press on 30 July 1977, and education personnel were called on to study the letter conscientiously and value its practical message. One peasant leader from Yecheng Branch assembled a propaganda team with a repertoire of six speeches and twenty short items that toured eighteen local communes and handed out 10,000 copies.[13] The long-sought happening was recognized by a mass rally of 5,000 in Nanchang, and various provincial newspaper editorials opined on how the Gang of Four had attempted to strangle newborn things.

Further good news came on 18 February 1978 with the State Council's approval of the addition of Jiangxi Communist Labor University to a list of key national universities, a select grouping singled out for priority funding from the government. The attached middle and elementary schools of the Main Campus were named key provincial-level schools. Research activities had restarted in 1971, and, as a mark of its standing, the university was permitted to enroll seventeen master's degree students in 1978. Now student numbers were above 35,000, and 106 branches were in association.[14]

The university had weathered the early 1970s, following the reforms of open-door education and the moderate policies from the center as it suited them. By the 1978 anniversary, Jiangxi's Party secretary, Yang Shangkui, could speak of the university's "great achievements and experience, technicians trained and wealth earned."[15] Wang Jin Xiang echoed the theme: "We had everything — people, resources, products, money, and an international reputation."[16] The Communist Labor University was well positioned to become one of the great agricultural schools of China. However, scores awaited settling: "Why didn't the university go forward when things looked so good? This was a puzzle for us and for China."

Unlike Mao, whose word had defined Party policy, Hua was politically vulnerable. Making the mistake of espousing overambitious economic plans that later had to be abandoned, he lost backing within the Party and confidence in his leadership faltered. Criticism of his role in the Cultural Revolution appeared, posters on Beijing's Democracy Wall attacking his actions as minister of public security. Powerful critics of the Cultural Revolution and Maoist economics such as Deng Xiaoping were emboldened. Hua responded by looking back for guidance: at Politburo meetings he was said to pull out pieces of paper and quote written instructions left him by the late Chairman. The infuriated Deng retorted: "How many more written directions have you left!"

Among the responsibilities which had fallen to Deng in July 1977 was education. Higher education especially was in a parlous state. By the end of the Cultural Revolution, enrollment in higher education stood at only 565,000, or 16 percent below the figure of ten years before,[17] and the attainments of its teachers and student body were commonly regarded as substandard. Deng aimed first to return higher education to pre-1966 standards, then to open it up by introducing world best practice in research. His restoration policy was in evidence when the National Tertiary Entrance Examination commenced again in 1977, with candidates allowed direct from senior middle school. Some young people sat for their first competitive exam ever; nurses were on hand at large centers to help students cope, and a number of examinees who failed suicided. Throughout the regular school system, exams spread like wildfire.

Newly released from bondage, Ministry of Education officials returned to the "quality" argument and set about undoing the open-door reforms. Now under Jiang Nanxiang, himself a victim of the Cultural Revolution, Revolutionary Committees were disbanded, members of Mao Zedong Thought Propaganda Teams were sent back to their factories and fields, and advocates of productive labor and unorthodox teaching and learning procedures were labeled "ultra left" and their voices silenced. Any institution clinging to the reforms of the open education days had its administration and teaching staff changed.

The Communist Labor University was slow to recognize the climate change. Immediately after the overthrow of the Jiang Qing, meetings had been held at the Main Campus to condemn her influence, staff promising to maintain the principle of part-work, part-study; continue their unique program of teaching, production, and research; and carry forward the revolution in education to the end. They disputed the claim of the Gang of Four to have invented the strategy "from the commune to the commune," arguing that this had been their long-time practice — as late as July 1978 the university was affirming the principle of returning students to the communes. It is likely the delay in second-guessing new government policy was not appreciated by the Deng government, which had acted promptly in reintroducing state assignment and had demanded that staff with qualifications be appropriately employed. The university had been on the ideological treadmill so long that it was hard to step off.

The university's own publicity continued unchecked. In 1978 Shanghai Education Press published an illustrated set of essays, recounting Gongda's history and achievements. Although the book included recent setbacks under the radical educators, *The Red Sun Shines over the Journey* came too early to capture the academic mood sweeping the country. By hailing old rather than new priorities, it proved a negative in the realignment underway.

By 1978 the direction of change was undeniable. On 18 March, the National Science Conference was held in Beijing, and the Fifth Educational Work Conference followed in April. Li Chao and Zhang Shimei represented the university, hearing Deng's forthright address to scientists in which he promised that science and technology would rest in the hands of the professionally competent in future. Science was deemed a productive force; scientists were told they belonged to the proletariat, and administrators were directed to learn some science, "for persons in the dark cannot light the way for others."[18] Deng's audience was told that China had fallen ten to twenty years behind the rest of the world. Deng was followed by Guo Moruo, the famous literary figure and head of the Chinese Academy of Science, who predicted a springtime for science, when giants would stride once more on China's soil. The Communist Labor University was among the institutions to receive an award for research, the project being undertaken by Professor Zhang Shimei.

Gradually the university abandoned its backing for the radical reforms. After 1977, the practice of "from the commune to the commune" was discarded for senior graduates, who were instead assigned to specialist jobs. Courses requiring national examination entry were reintroduced; the university established an Academic Committee giving senior staff a greater role in its governance; and model teachers were selected for achievement awards, part of a government campaign recognizing them as "engineers of the human soul," "the fragrant third" alongside workers and peasants. Lecturers were told to spend no more than a sixth of their time at politics or labor. Cultural Revolution textbooks were pulped and new books and materials sent for printing.

Though the university was now applying the national directives, there were still signs of trouble ahead. The university had received no extra funds for development in spite of its listing as a key national institution, suggesting that the Ministry of Education would do things its way. No less worrying were the attacks on Hua himself.

After the celebrated Third Plenary Session of the Eleventh Party Congress in December 1978, Deng Xiaoping emerged as indisputably the most powerful figure in China. Exposed to a typical classics' schooling himself, Deng had had a brief period in a county middle school in Sichuan before entering Chongqing Preparatory School at age fifteen, graduating a year later when he joined a work-study program France.[19] Though the family sold rice fields to keep him alive overseas, the going was tough, the young man laboring in an iron foundry pulling steel bars, then working long hours in an artificial flower factory. Deng reported his five-year stint in France as unsatisfactory and exploitative before moving on to Moscow where he studied at Sun Yat-sen University of the Toilers of China for less than a year. Mao, only too well aware of his comrade's unhappy experiences in France, had a joke at his expense when he once suggested Deng drop in on Paris for a few days during an overseas trip to investigate the latest in work-study.

Deng had learned of the activities of the Communist Labor University as early as 1960, having attended the National Representative Conference of Advanced Workers in Socialist Culture and Education held in Beijing on 1 June at which Vice President Lin Zhong gave a major address. But he was no supporter of it. Exiled in Jiangxi Province during the Cultural Revolution, he was an object of the university's propaganda and ridiculed through the film, *The Break*.

Among Deng's political enemies was Wang Dongxing. Despite Wang's part in overthrowing Deng's bitter enemy, Mao's widow, Jiang Qing, the new Party leader remembered past actions from Wang's office when he was on Mao's wrong side. Now Wang stood accused with Hua as a person still indiscriminately loyal to Mao's ideas, and one who had delayed moves to reinstate Deng. Wang would fall with Hua, being removed from his official posts in February 1980, a massive blow to Gongda. "With Hua and Wang in power, the Communist Labor University was safe. With Wang gone, and Hua deep in trouble, we were afraid."[20]

Part VI

Life and Legend

Eighteen
Decision Point

"A policy dies along with its proponent."

—Chinese saying

Higher education under Deng Xiaoping required that any institutions claiming degree and diploma status enter the academic mainstream; therefore discussion over the future of the Communist Labor University began in earnest in 1977-78. The Jiangxi Province government passed on instructions received from the national authorities that the university adjust its work-study experimentation in the spring and summer of 1979. The first stage saw no more worker-peasant-soldier students admitted once the present two- and three-year cohorts had worked through the system; instead, full-time, four-year undergraduates would be enrolled in revised courses. Even so, these students were expected to labor for three months of the year, and university staff to engage in labor and political activity for one-sixth of their time.[1]

When this first generation of full-time students entered the gates, products of a nationwide examination system, they were upset to learn they would have to undertake physical labor two afternoons a week. "We animal science students were repairing the roads in front of the department."[2] Claiming they were being exploited for cheap labor, the youngsters argued that the university's administrators had shown they were reluctant to abandon old ways, and the physical labor component was dropped after the first semester.

The second stage of the reorganization began on 18 May 1980, when the provincial Party Committee authorized the university to implement the national unified teaching plan for its agriculture and forestry courses over the next two years.[3] Control of the Main Campus was handed over to the provincial Agricultural Bureau, its ideological work was put under the Propaganda Department, and its educational management passed to the provincial Education Bureau. The campus dropped its Main Campus appellation and became known as the Jiangxi Communist Labor University.

With the university committed to a full-time, four-year program, the appropriateness of any networking with academically inferior branches also upset the provincial leaders, who determined the campuses be placed under an appropriate provincial, district, or county office and given new names. Action was sudden. In the period 1980-85, all associated branch campuses were turned into separate technical and vocational colleges, provincial forestry schools, teacher training institutes, senior technical training schools, or vocational middle schools. Nancheng Branch, for example, was restructured and renamed Fuzhou Vocational and Technical College; Damaoshan became a provincial forestry school; and Jinggangshan, a provincial middle agricultural school. A few places were authorized to maintain variants of their old titles, for example, Huanggangshan Branch became Yifeng County Communist Labor University.

As branches were transferred, an undignified scramble for assets took place, with large quantities of land, buildings, and equipment seized by local power brokers. The plunder was resented:

> The farmers of Jiangxi were sorry to see us dismantled. We'd helped them set up electricity plants, cultivate their fields and, open clinics. But local people in China won't rebel. They just obey and mind their own business. We no longer followed the "mass line" — if we had, the university would still be there.[4]

In May 1980, the Meiling office in charge of assisting the branches closed its doors for good — twenty years of network association had come to an abrupt end.

Main Campus staff, who regarded their past teaching as eminently useful, had to hand over to others land and property that they and their students had salvaged, in many cases damaging their own health in so doing. The university was permitted to retain a few bases close to the Main Campus for teaching and research and some land for agricultural production under the newly introduced contract system that operated after the communes were broken up. Many of the original staff were moved out of teaching positions and into administrative work, or else transferred.

The third stage of the remaking saw the authorities move against the all-important name. In rapidly changing times, the once-proud title Communist Labor University appeared a liability. "Communist" consigned it to the camp of those politically run institutions that had distorted the meaning of scholarship; "Labor" associated the university with failed left-wing projects that had put physical work above learning and discounted science and technology; and "University" was thought a misnomer, for much of the work had not been of tertiary standard. On 25 September 1980, the Party Committee of the Main Campus issued its report on the matter, and the Jiangxi Provincial Party Committee and the Provincial People's Congress approved the change from Jiangxi Communist Labor University to Jiangxi Agricultural University on 20 November.

Original staff said they would have lived with a different title, provided they could have met what they saw as the important needs of the Jiangxi countryside; however, it appeared to them that these could not be addressed by a conventional university. The new name, they said, implied a philosophical redirection. Their case was not carried, though, given the purpose of the reorganization — which was to terminate, not resurrect, experiments.

Opponents of work-study within the university were not satisfied with the new name either. They regarded the retitling as a regrettable compromise. In their opinion, the Communist Labor University should have been closed down, then reopened under a distinctively different title. That way, the new university would have denied any association with the past.

> The JCLU and the film *Break* have been resented so much, they have been a pain as well as a shame to ex-JAC staff and the new generation of students. It would better to have announced the death of the JCLU instead of the change of name.[5]

However, this "fresh beginning" solution was unacceptable to the Jiangxi authorities, who were after a relatively noncontentious amalgamation and upgrading.

Staff from the one-time Jiangxi Agricultural College proposed a third option. They would break away from the existing institution and re-establish themselves in their previous Nanchang home. It was a common complaint that ill use had been made of their academic talent, the Communist Labor University having carried out little high-level teaching or scientific research activity. Jiangxi Agricultural College graduates, they claimed, had been superior in quality to those from the Communist Labor University, and were more likely to be found in senior technical positions in the province and outside. Gongda's research was no more than agricultural extension which could have been provided for just as well by lower-level institutions. For their part, founding staff of the university shed no tears at this suggested breakaway, regarding the academic ethos of the college as inimical to their educational principles.

The provincial government turned down the Jiangxi Agricultural College suggestion on grounds that their Nanchang institution had been insufficiently comprehensive in teaching and had lacked a forestry division. Another constraint was that its city site was occupied by others. Nor did the relocation make economic sense, as the province could not afford this institutional dichotomy. Staff from the Communist Labor University and Jiangxi Agricultural College would have to accept the compromise of living with a new name in lieu of old titles, and be prepared to settle long-term at the Main Campus.

As can be anticipated, emotion equally with reason was to the fore in the change of status and the beloved name.

> They asked us to pull down the characters "Communist Labor University" over the main gate. They would be replaced by "Jiangxi Agricultural University." No one could be found to do it, so Zhou's characters were destroyed by outsiders at night. Staff cried at the vandalism — the university was built through their toil. Mao and Zhou would not have wanted it to end like this. They are not feeling good about it in their graves.[6]

The visitor to Jiangxi Agricultural University gates today can still see the shadowing left by the one-time Zhou calligraphy.

Various reasons have been put forward as to why the Communist Labor University experiment was terminated. The first sees it as just deserts. Because the university was founded during the Great Leap Forward, one of Mao's biggest failures, it remained an uncorrected reminder of his folly.

While the Great Leap Forward could not be undone, its products could be cast off and forgotten.

Allied with this assessment was the opinion that the university was a tool of the political left and that it had served out its usefulness. It had only flourished because it existed in an atmosphere that destroyed normal educational services; and it had only retained its position because of powerful friends. The university was a Utopian experiment that diverted educational resources from the more-effective mainstream. Now that its big-name protectors Mao Zedong, Zhou Enlai and Zhu De were gone and Hua Guofeng had lost power and influence, it was fair game.

Others think the Communist Labor University was sacrificed to shut out the influence of the one-time secretary of its Party Committee, Wang Dongxing. Forced to stand down from his official positions for his opposition to Deng, Wang had to go and all his works with him. "One might hate Wang," a complainant said, "but was he bigger than Mao Zedong?"

There were educational arguments, too, supporting closure. Changes in enrollment procedures in 1977 gave top students across China the opportunity to select their own universities — thus the importance of an institution's reputation. Gongda's standing had been damaged by *The Break*, which downplayed the importance of agricultural science and lowered the professional standing of agricultural students and graduates. In the popular view, the university was a place where physical work ruled, a stereotype thought certain to lower student intake levels. The university would become noncompetitive in the marketplace over time.

As General Cheng had destroyed much of the tertiary education sector in Jiangxi during the Cultural Revolution, there was no agricultural university in the province other than the Communist Labor University. It was inconceivable that there should not be a lead institution devoted to agricultural teaching and research in Jiangxi. The university had built up substantial facilities and resources at the Main Campus, and dropping its experimental status appeared a suitable first step toward earning an orthodox reputation.

Failings of the past were admitted. The university had fallen out of step with the national ideology, old strengths had become failings. Self-reliance was no longer regarded as desirable of itself; theory was now valued above practice, and classroom learning above field work and labor. By overemphasizing "learning through doing," the university had paid insufficient attention to agricultural science and had fallen behind acceptable standards. Opinion was: "We should have strengthened the teaching of basic theory and introduced more science and modern technology."[7]

Even after the decision to regularize the university, powerful backing for its continuance remained. The Communist Labor University still had big-name supporters, including Kang Keqing and Deng Yingchao, the widows of Zhu De and Zhou Enlai. Some at the top were taken aback by the decision to close. Between 1968 and 1980, more than 55,000 Chinese, and 7,500 foreigners had toured Gongda.[8] That it was supported by senior leaders was well known in China and outside — it would be difficult to explain the change credibly. A high-level investigation was called by the Ministry of Education's Vocational Education Division. However, memories were more than twenty years long, and those in power were among the original objectors to the experiment. The province offered a compromise to have the name and function of the original university transferred to a senior branch, Yunshan. This was refused, perhaps too summarily. "Yes, we were offered a compromise. But the mood was aggressive: 'If it's not wrong, why shut it?'"[9] The final decision to terminate was passed from the minister of education, Jiang Nanxiang, to Deng Xiaoping. Without Deng's agreement, no one dared pull down the Zhou characters.

Whatever the feelings of participants, the decision to terminate came from above. Paradoxically, the university had survived by imperial edict and was closed by same. The best original staff were able to extract by way of a future was an agreement that their former history be known and taught positively to Jiangxi Agricultural University students. The unfairness of it rankled. Its ex-director of studies, Chen Ping, expressed a common view: "I was at the Communist Labor University for eight years. It had its merits and demerits, but its merits dominated."[10] Wang Jin Xiang was no less sure: "While Gongda had its mistakes, its purpose was right, its achievements demonstrable, and its experiences deserving promotion. Therefore the decision to change its name and the dismissal of its branches were wrong."[11] Of course, the accounting should be weighed against its problems: the community had suffered through schistosomiasis; students were subject to unorthodox learning modes and too much labor; and its mission was distorted by ill-judged political interference.

On the credit side, the university represented change in agriculture in Jiangxi, where it valued the skills and experience of the locals. It spoke the language of rural people. At best the propagation of new ideas was accompanied though a bonding of staff and students working alongside each other, sharing the hard as well as the easier duties. Staff needed to communicate with the farmers and discern how best to motivate them, and farmers discovered the advantages of basic scientific agriculture for themselves — allowing attitudinal change to occur. By enrolling students at various educational levels and ages in purposeful study, the university demonstrated that lack of a formal education was not a bar to self-improvement. "We learned experiences on how to run education well in poor rural areas. The Communist Labor University set people thinking."

Nineteen
Life after Death

"Let the people of the next generation judge whether we were right or not."

—Wang Jin Xiang [1]

Termination of the Communist Labor University experiment was not just the result of another internal restructuring in higher education — rather, it represented the passing of a vision of one kind of Chinese society and future. A university which had served Mao's communist objective was redesigned to match Deng's social and economic pragmatism. Yet individual staff and friends of the defeated university never recanted their faith. An early but futile attempt was made by ex-Gongda staff to reintroduce short-term senior cadre training in agriculture in their reorganized home.

> However, we had to stop halfway. There was a shortage of funds at provincial level and, because we had no money of our own anymore, we couldn't supplement the budget. The heads of the units were unwilling to come to Jiangxi Agricultural University for three to six months. They feared losing their positions while in training. This actually happened. We also had difficulties getting the right kind of staff to train them.

The pot was further stirred by a visit by cadres from Hunan and Jiangsu Provinces sent there at the close to learn more of work-study practice, the Jiangsu inspection being part of plans to revamp its vocational school sector currently expanding to meet the demand of the newly introduced township enterprises. "Yet we ourselves were given no credit or future. Through neglect Jiangxi abjectly surrendered its lead on part-work part-study to Jiangsu."[2]

Dr. Suzanne Pepper, researching a project on the impact of post-Mao enrollment policy,[3] was another caller at the death, visiting the Main Campus and the Nancheng County Communist Labor University between 24 October and 2 November 1980. Alarmed by her lengthy questionnaire, the administration had at first attempted to enlist help from two of the province's best English-language interpreters, the American visitor's fluency in the Chinese language quieted this worry.[4] According to their report on the visit,[5] Dr. Pepper's train was met by Professor Zhang Shimei, Qiu Chaodong, and Wang Jin Xiang, who also arranged a shift in accommodation from the Jiangxi Hotel to the campus. Among the initial university group to greet her was the female vice director of the Revolutionary Committee, Ma Chaomang, whose own incumbency would end the following month.

Pepper's hosts were impressed by her diligent attack on her task and, particularly, her critical faculty. Presenting her with the names of past and present senior leaders, they had deliberately left out that of Wang Dongxing, an omission she brought to their attention. During these discussions at Gongda, the university admitted to replying to her questions "according to fact and according to policy." Nonetheless, the researcher estimated the state of the university, and its authorities were surprised that a foreigner would openly voice their own private fears.

From the Main Campus, Pepper was taken to Nancheng Branch, after the university received a permit from the military enabling her to enter a district normally closed to foreigners. At the conclusion of the stay, she was photographed with Li Chao, and she said that she had lived at Gongda as she had in her own home. Such moral support from an international figure was valued personally by individuals who knew the end was nigh. "She pointed out that Gongda's combination of half-work and half-study was very important and creative in the sense that it was complementary to the functions of an ordinary university and suited to the Chinese reality."[6] The report on her visit went back to the Beijing ministry and, eventually, the provincial government would read her research findings.

Further support came after Secretary of the CPC Hu Yaobang's inspection of Jiangxi Province at the end of 1984. Hu knew Jiangxi well, having joined Mao's band in Jinggangshan as a fourteen-year-old. Rising to political prominence as secretary of the Communist Youth League, he maintained a personal interest in Gong Qing city, the Communist youth colony in Jiangxi near the Nanhu Farm site, where his ashes would one day rest.

> The Communist Labor University was negated and I do not think this was necessary. Chairman Mao once wrote a letter of approval. This university played a major role in opening up the mountainous areas of Jiangxi. The problem is how to improve its functions. I trust you can study and solve the problem.[7]

Alas, Hu would eventually lose Deng's confidence and his own position in 1987. Many old hands, though, agreed with Hu's point, insisting that a redeveloped Communist Labor University would benefit the province. Of an annual output of 80,000 graduates from senior secondary school in Jiangxi in the mid-1980s, only 11,000, including some students from other parts of the country, could be admitted to higher education. Less than half of Jiangxi's 310,000 junior secondary graduates were able to enter further training, the rest having to return home as farmers. Though literate, they lacked sufficient knowledge to engage in the cash economy. Regrettably, it was pointed out, no institution was there to upgrade them.

Plans were unveiled for another Main Campus, which would offer courses for the emerging rural industries and agricultural upgrading. Eleven districts and towns promised to open branches, and others were expected to follow. "The beautiful flower of the Communist Labor University will bud and bear fruit again." Backers of this revived university invoked the late Chairman's letter of 30 July and claimed that the leaders of the Central Committee of the CPC approved. But the proposition was rejected. Things were too far down the existing track. The provincial Educational Bureau declared that China's needs had changed from those of twenty years earlier: by adopting full-time study and regular courses, it was responding to a new stage of China's cultural and economic development. Remoter areas would be better served by conventional extension activities.

Jiangxi Agricultural University did take up some of the lesser burdens of its predecessor, though. In the early 1980s the Ministry of Education insisted that at least 50 percent of China's middle schools be vocationally oriented. In Jiangxi the number of these schools jumped from 51 to 322 between 1980 and 1989, and enrollments grew from 5,100 to 106,000, yet most of their teachers lacked essential skills.[8]

The required ratio of specialized to nonspecialized teachers in vocational schools in 1989 was 1:1, but the ratio in Jiangxi was 1:2.3. The ratio of specialized teachers to students should have been 1:40, but the Jiangxi ratio was 1:89. Just 11.5 percent of Jiangxi's specialized teachers had tertiary qualifications.

The low level of teachers' attainment in Jiangxi correlated with a high dropout rate — some 45 percent across the vocational schools in the nine years to 1989. The existing network of vocational schools, many of which were run by work units, lacked unified and efficient organization, and there was little integration across the levels of vocational, general, higher, and adult education.

Professional training was reintroduced at Jiangxi Agricultural University in 1983, in response to the needs of vocational schooling. The program was upgraded to departmental status in 1990, and then to faculty standing. While the initiative of the new faculty of Professional Education is not portrayed as directly related to an older tradition, many staff from earlier days had sympathy for the work.

Wang Jin Xiang has looked back at the transformation of an unorthodox institution:

> Of course, our university departments today have different leadership and different ideas on the meaning of the spirit of the Communist Labor University. How do we carry this forward? Its essence and hard work, our Party Committee has declared, will be an inspiration for our teaching.
>
> Students who came after 1979 should never forget the students who built the classrooms around them. We had a museum which held tools from the labor of those days. It no longer exists, but ex-staff and alumni will tell you of that time.[9]

In truth, students at Jiangxi Agricultural University learn little of the Communist Labor University or indeed of Jiangxi Agricultural College. What they do know is received as a story of another time and place. The origins of the university appear to have no relevance for present lives and study. One American teacher who taught there for over a year in the late

1980s told me he had no knowledge that he and his colleagues were employed at the one-time Main Campus of the famed Communist Labor University.

Talks with Jiangxi Agricultural University students confirm that its antecedents are very much history. Yesterday's labor and communal effort have been replaced by a mission of individual motivation and professional purpose. This is not to challenge the public-spirited ethos of the young student, although he or she cannot be imagined rallying to the austere call for "the 'mass line' work style, and plain living and hard struggle"[10] of Zhang Yuqing, a previous Party leader. The ambitions of the educated young reflect the more mundane priority of earning a living utilizing high skill levels in an increasingly market-oriented economy. "The future is high technology in our field. We must learn education and technology from other countries."[11] One graduate of Jiangxi Agricultural University has written:

> Most people would like to forget the history of Jiangxi Communist Labor University. The recent comeback of the university would probably be a reflection of current change in China's political situation. The propaganda used in the 1960s revived in the last couple of years. This instantly reminds old staff of Jiangxi Communist Labor University that their past was not completely denied. [12]

It was no easy task for ex-Communist Labor University staff to accommodate the demands of the new Jiangxi Agricultural University. Old loyalties and prejudices linger. In 1984, the enlightened president of Jiangxi Agricultural University, Professor Ou Yangliang, attempted to found an alumni association. A teacher relates what happened:

> The whole thing was not well handled. It was difficult to decide who should be invited — No. 22 Middle School for example? Anyway too few exstaff were asked. Many people were offended. When I visited the Ministry of Agriculture in Beijing, I was not so welcome. "Now you want something from me, you know me — but you didn't know me when you were contacting your important alumni before." Instead of Jiangxi Agricultural University doing the invitations, they should have asked the Ministry of Agriculture to organize it. Why did invitations go out to the Main Campus people but not to ex-branches? [13]

Only one get-together was held. The failure of the alumni association did the university no credit, for it was rumored that the difficulties had arisen because ex-Jiangxi Agricultural College staff and staff newly appointed to Jiangxi Agricultural University did not wish to mix with the original Communist Labor University contingent.

Of the current staff, about two-thirds have some experience of the years 1958-80, the balance coming later. Marriages have taken place across the university divide, and grandchildren presage a new generation. Death too has been a leveler — the old leaders and chief protagonists have passed on. Liu Junxiu, its first president, died in 1985, Li Chao and Chen Ping in 1994, and Zhang Yuqing in 1995. Of the triumvirate of 1958, only Wang Dongxing continues alert into old age; talk of the Communist Labor University still excites him, the closure of the university and his special Silkworm Factory Branch being much felt and regretted. Today Wang regards the twenty-two years of its experimentation as an example of socialism with Chinese characteristics:

> Education is the foundation of a country. It follows that our prosperity depends on it. Part-work, part-study has proven itself at Gongda — it has demonstrated its potential — and its merits should continue to serve China.[14]

The case for listing the Communist Labor University in the ranks of the experiments of world educational history deserves an assessment. Plans for work-study in Europe go back at least to Thomas More's *Utopia* of 1516. The eighteenth-century German educator J. B. Basedow taught his boys skills such as carpentry and wood turning; the Swiss educator Rousseau spoke up for the talents of the practically minded Robinson Crusoe; and the gentle Pestalozzi advocated the combination of agricultural and industrial work and basic learning, a philosophy which inspired the founding of the farm school Fellenberg's Hofwyl in Switzerland in 1800. The European progressives influenced American educators, including men like Joseph Neef and William McClure, who attempted schemes combining farming and industrial work with study. The USA also sponsored the Morrell Act of 1862, which funded colleges of agriculture and the mechanical arts "in order to promote the liberal and practical education of the industrial classes in the several pursuits and professions of life."

Many individual farm projects have risen and fallen in the West since that time. Like the Communist Labor University, the projects typically aimed at a high level of self-sufficiency. The man who established the most famous farm school in Australia, Kingsley Fairbridge, has aptly expressed the expectations of generations of farm educators:

> Agriculture is the very foundation of civilization. The farmer is the producer of all that is absolutely necessary; he is primary while all others are secondary. Properly to pursue his calling he should have no slight knowledge of a dozen callings — from meteorology to mycology, from engineering to plumbing, from financial organization to digging post-holes with a spade. Moreover he seeks his bread and butter not on another man's plate, but on the very lap of the gods. [15]

"Agriculture," insisted Fairbridge, "must be learned." With agricultural learning came steadiness, knowledge, competence, and morality. The Party Committee of the Communist Labor University would have taken his point.

Various innovative schemes for rural education in China were precursors of the Communist Labor University. They were led by educators like Yan Yangchu, who founded the National Association for the Promotion of Mass Education; Liang Shuming, whose Shandong Rural Reconstruction Institute at Zouping County influenced leaders in the Danish Folk High School Movement in the 1930s; and the Chinese progressive Tao Xingzhi, who managed the Xiaozhuang Experimental Normal School outside Nanjing. For all their efforts, agricultural education in China has seldom been preferred by parents and students. Attempts by individual educators to break away from the dominance of the mind-body dichotomy beloved of Confucian and Greek disciples alike have failed to materialize.

Was the university just another failed social experiment? Certainly it had been slow to adjust to changing circumstances, although the situations were not of its own making. Early achievements were blighted by the famine years of the 1960s, efforts to upgrade and restructure were reversed by the Cultural Revolution, a radical clique usurped its promise in the 1970s, and a false dawn was experienced in the late 1970s. Little latitude was allowed it by the Ministry of Education. Yet demonstrable achievements were there to support the another side:

> We saw vast tracts of garden-like paddy fields, countless plots planted to oil tree, fir and bamboo, orchard and tea gardens, granaries filled to the brim with five kinds of grains, and packed with cattle and pigs. It was really a bustling and thriving scene. Some students were experimenting on a high yield hybrid rice variety, others were trying out new breeding methods in the pig sties. Who could imagine that over ten years ago there was nothing here but a dilapidated temple or this was an uninhabited area with barren hills? [16]

It could be accepted that the networking and impact of the branches in their communities was its greatest triumph. Further, the renamed technical, vocational and professional colleges could be said to owe their existence to Gongda.

The political adventures the university was drawn into worked for it at first but damned it later. The task of networking, given the number of branches and the funding and materials required, was overwhelming. Nor was the institution as well resourced as smaller regular colleges. Perhaps its road would have been easier had the university's claims been less encompassing and more modest? But this was no recipe of its time. The eventual reversion of its curriculum to a conventional form, along with the introduction of full-time study, was recognition that a weightier tradition had prevailed and that the day of innovation had ended.

Of the various Chinese institutions to engage in farm education, the Communist Labor University was the most influential and renowned. It had a philosophy. Labor was the creator of human wealth and rural labor the key to China's prosperity; agricultural education would promote human learning and material well-being by blending theoretical and practical knowledge; and a university education was a moral experience based on communist principle. Furthermore, it had been a catalyst for other agricultural learning centers across China.

It can be claimed that the university was the less well-known internationally for having been created in Asia, not in Europe or America. It was also a venture of the closed China of Mao Zedong's time, with its strengths and problems not accessible for weighing in a realistic accounting. Its standing in the company of the world's great educational experiments awaits estimation. In Wang Jin Xiang's words: "Let the people of the next generation judge whether we were right or not."[17]

In 1988, at the thirtieth anniversary of the founding, a meeting was held at an ex-branch that reaffirmed its experiences in promoting modern agriculture in twentieth-century China. Again, at an international conference on work experience held in Jiangxi in 1996, participants noted the earlier efforts of the Communist Labor University in agriculture.

Rural ignorance continues to be a deep-seated and intractable problem. In 1995, the country counted 35 million illiterates between fifteen and forty-five years of age, considered the period of prime productivity for rural workers, and one-third of women were illiterate, the vast majority of them in the countryside.[18] The agricultural workforce remains the most poorly educated segment of the population, and the disparity between city and country continues to widen. Less than 12 percent of the country's agricultural extension employees holds a specialized certificate.[19]

Low investment and the low social evaluation put on the agricultural sector in China have inhibited the development of modern agriculture. While universities have begun to offer extension science as a subject, many agricultural students continue to look outside agriculture for their careers. Difficulties are faced securing opportunities for practical work in these institutions, much of which is not genuinely educational, as agricultural universities have to negotiate for field placements with the numerous small units which replaced the commune and production brigade of the 1960s and 1970s.

These days, volunteers from regular universities are recruited to teach literacy and practical knowledge to isolated farming families, an echo of earlier times. For all such efforts and the activities of motivated staff and students in the nation's agricultural universities and groups like the Association of Science and Technology and the All-China Women's Federation, no certain remedy exists for overcoming the lack of opportunities for rural schooling in situations of small-scale agriculture, isolation, and poverty. Although two decades have passed since the Communist Labor University experiment was abandoned, its educational object remains unalleviated.

In its time, the university recorded 270,000 graduates, of whom 10,000 men and women were at first-degree level, and 60,000 skilled technical personnel. Estimates put its farms' produce at over 500 million jin of grain and other products, valued at above 460 million yuan.[20] Seventy percent of its graduates returned to work directly in agricultural production in Jiangxi: for instance, in Nancheng County by the late 1980s, 80 percent of agricultural technicians were trained at the Communist Labor University.[21]

Those in search of the bygone university can visit some of the ex-branches which retain rooms for memorabilia going back to 1958. A senior technical school at Wuyuan has kept the title Zhanggongshan Communist Labor University on its name board for more than thirty-four years, though no formal link can exist. The school retains its production base with chickens and ducks; a pig farm which once held 1,200 pigs is now used for breeding purposes. It also maintains forest land and small factories, including a winery. Many parents of students are themselves graduates of the one-time branch. Its principal spoke in 1992:

> Our graduates are welcomed by the peasants. People are practical here. They want to earn a living. We have had no request from them to drop the name: many wouldn't want to drop it from the school's title, but the top will decide this. Our name reflects the warmth of our links with ex-Gongda staff and its graduates and philosophy. All of us wish to display our tribute. Mao Zedong's educational philosophy was correct.

Certainly the old university name still arouses sentiment in Jiangxi:

> When we see a truck with Communist Labor University still on the panel, we touch and stroke the name. One driver carried a message to me from staff of the ex-branch to staff of the ex-Main Campus: "Thanks to the Main Campus — we still remember you!"

The spirit lives on in Jiangxi's countryside, as well. Late in 1994, a group of alumni of the Huanggangshan Branch held a reunion in Pingxiang County. "Most of us are now middle-level cadres in factories or government institutions — many have become new stars in politics or business."[22] The gathering was an occasion to recall good times and bad, and the humor of their university days. Lusty singing of the school song preceded a nostalgic breakup.

> Gongda is good! Gongda is good!
> Jiangxi Communist Labor University is really good!
> We learn to be hard-working;
> To learn to be courageous;
> To create a socialist life;
> And learn to make revolution;
> We are heart and soul with the laboring people;
> Good steel is tempered thousands of times;
> True gold is never afraid of burning fire;
> Our newborn university is great!

Afterword

Unraveling the story of the Communist Labor University has been made possible by access to records and accounts from graduates, ex-teachers, and administrators. Among them is Wang Jin Xiang, who contributed to the experiment through its lifetime, and his experiences present an individual's understanding of the progress of the institution from the founding to the death throes. Wang himself undertook the heaviest field work in salvaging land and cutting bamboo, and endured the most degrading physical torture during the Cultural Revolution. Joining the Communist Party in 1973, he has never lost faith in the early mission, unlike many who lived through the Mao era. Despite his own misfortunes along the way, he is no cynic or disillusioned believer.

Mao Bingjie, the courageous female student of 1958, matched his own passion for life. She struggled as hard as her husband in the desperate years to keep him and the two girls alive, overcoming the years of famine and revolutionary abuse. Characteristically she put herself second, her meager income as language teacher mostly going to her aged parents in Shanghai. Brought a woolen dress by one daughter, it was worn only twice, the last time at her funeral. She died on 2 August 1995, aged 55, her memorial ceremony one of the largest such gatherings seen on campus. The university's drivers brought extra mourners to the hall of commemoration in a gesture of their own. Like her husband, Mao Bingjie was committed to the life of the university, the route from the campus hospital being lined with its families.

As recorded in *Jiangxi Nongda Bao*, 20 June 1997, Wang Jin Xiang became the longest-serving cadre in Foreign Affairs Offices in agricultural colleges, having thirty years to his credit and 848 foreign groups received. While the achievement was recognized by flowers, phone calls, visitors, and a commendation award, of more importance to the man has been the growing rehabilitation of the university's reputation. He himself has become one of the tellers, the latest accounts from him appearing in the recent publication *The Road of China's Rural Education*. The work contains a foreword written by an old friend, an octogenarian and one-time Party secretary of the university, Wang Dongxing, who served Mao Zedong for over three decades and backed the university wholeheartedly throughout its life.

Wang Dongxing returned to Jiangxi Province in September 1999, experiencing afresh "the revolutionary route" of his youth, a tour that included mounting the remnants of the city wall of Nanchang. A site of great interest was the Jiangxi Agricultural University, the successor of Gongda, and the scene of the educational adventure of 1958. Wang had a photograph taken with his surviving colleagues in front of the one-time administrative building of the Communist Labor University, where he made a short speech in favor of the application of research findings in production. He also toured the pharmaceutical factory founded in the Cultural Revolution which now makes antibiotics for animal use and export. During this tour he returned to his home village, a place still poor. Returning to Beijing to celebrate the 50th year of the formation of the People's Republic of China, Wang stood in the first line of dignitaries at the eastern end of the Tiananmen rostrum.

At the final stage of completing *In the Lap of Tigers*, Wang Jin Xiang sent the author a note:

> I believe the direction of the Communist Labor University was right. I love the Communist Labor University with all my heart. I experienced thirty-eight years' trials and hardships, walked a long distance on tortuous roads, and tasted all kinds of joys and sorrows of life, but I feel, as always, no regret at all!

Notes

For events, sequences, and dates, see Chronology of the Development of the Jiangxi Communist Labor University, and for other chronologies, see Qiu Chaodong, "Major Events in Jiangxi Communist Labor University," in Collection Committee of Materials about the Party's History — Jiangxi Provincial Party Committee and Jiangxi Agricultural University, *Founding and Evolution of Jiangxi Communist Labor University: Materials of the Party's History in Jiangxi (Item 38)* (Beijing: Central Documents Publishing House, 1966), and Wen Liming and Qiu Chaodong, "Major Events in the Communist Labor University," in *The Road of China's Rural Education Educational Research on Jiangxi Communist Labor University*, ed. Huang Dingyuan (Nanchang: Jiangxi Tertiary Education Press, 1997). Interviews were recorded by the author at Jiangxi Agricultural University in June 1991 and September/October 1992, and off campus in October 1998; correspondence was received 1993–99.

Introduction
Setting the Scene

1. Wang Dongxing, "Carrying Out the Party's Principle of Education: Run the Communist Labor University Well, 13 September 1959," in *The Communist Labor University* (Nanchang: Jiangxi Education Press, 1960).
2. W. Bauer, *China and the Search for Happiness*, trans. Michael Shaw, (New York: Seabury Press, 1976), 341.
3. *Mao Tse-tung Unrehearsed Talks and Letters: 1956–1971*, ed. Stuart Schram (Harmondsworth, England: Penguin, 1980), 18.

4. R. F. Jackson, "Education in China," in *The Year Book of Education, 1932*, ed. Eustace Percy (London: Evans, 1932), 957–962.
5. S. Y. Chiu, "Public Education," in *The Year Book of Education, 1949*, ed. George B. Jeffrey (London: Evans, 1949), 609.
6. "Chronology of the Two-Road Struggle on the Educational Front in the Past Seventeen Years," in Peter J. Seybolt, *Revolutionary Education in China Documents and Commentary* (White Plains, NY: International Arts and Sciences Press, 1973), 7.
7. Leo A. Orleans, *Professional Manpower and Education in Communist China* (Washington: National Science Foundation, 1961), 117.
8. Seybolt, *Revolutionary Education*, 25.
9. Seybolt, *Revolutionary Education*, 31.
10. Wang Dongxing, "Hold High the Red Banner of Mao Zedong: Educational Thought and Advance with Great Strides," in *Communist Labor University*.

One
Great Expectations

1. Wang Dongxing, "Education as the Foundation of National Development: Reminiscences of Jiangxi Communist Labor University," *Scientific Research on Jiangxi Education*, vol. 1, Jiangxi Institute of Education (1995).
2. Wang Jin Xiang, "How I Became a New Student at Gongda," ms., n.d.
3. The Number of Students Admitted and the Graduates of Jiangxi Agricultural University (1940–1991).
4. Wang J. X., "How I Became."
5. Jen-chi Chang, *Pre-Communist China's Rural School and Community* (Boston: Christopher Publishing, 1960), 77.
6. Xiao Fan, "Raise a Red Banner and Lead the Way: Reflections on How the Provincial Party Committee of Jiangxi Supported Gongda," in *The Red Sun Shines over the Journey: Essays on the Jiangxi Communist Labor University* (Shanghai: Shanghai Education Press, 1978).
7. "Note," *Peking Review* 3:36 (6 September 1960), 5.
8. Interview with the author.
9. Wang D., "Education as the Foundation."
10. Provincial Party Committee and People's Congress of Jiangxi Province, "Decision on Setting-Up the Jiangxi Labor University" (9 June 1958), in *Communist Labor University*.
11. Wang, D., "Education as the Foundation."
12. Interview with the author.
13. Chen Ping,"Recollections of My Stay in Jiangxi Communist Labor University," Chen Ping Memoir, 1949–1984.
14. Liu Junxiu, "On the Combination of Education and Labor: My Impressions

on the Opening of the Communist Labor University," in *Communist Labor University*.
15. Du Juan, "The Proletarian Mold Should Never be Broken: Comrade Liu Junxiu on Gongda," in *Red Sun Shines*.
16. Interview with the author.
17. See Liu Junxiu, "How We Established the Communist Labor University," in The Main Campus of the Communist Labor University and Jiangxi Education Press, *Training New Type Personnel through Half-Work and HalfStudy; A Collection on the Running of Jiangxi Communist Labor University* (Nanchang: Jiangxi Education Press, 1965); and interview with the author.
18. Wang, D., "Education as the Foundation."

Two
The Founding

1. Donggushan Branch, "Doing a Good Job in Production through Arduous Effort," in Main Campus, *Training New Type Personnel*.
2. From Liu Junxiu, "Hailing the Birth of a New Kind of Communist Labor University, 5 August 1959," in *Communist Labor University;* Du, "Proletarian Mold"; and Liu, "On the Combination."
3. Yu Yingen, The Development of Jiangxi Communist Labor University, Jiangxi Education Committee, typescript, n.d., 1.
4. Liu, "On the Combination."
5. See Li Chao, "Reminiscences of Working at the Jiangxi Communist Labor University," Collection Committee of Materials about the Party's History — Jiangxi Provincial Party Committee and Jiangxi Agricultural University, *Founding and Evolution of Jiangxi Communist Labor University: Materials of the Party's History in Jiangxi (Item 38)* (Beijing: Central Documents Publishing House, 1966).
6. Interview with the author.
7. Party Committee of Jiangxi Communist Labor University, "Give Prominence to Politics, Go in for Production, Reform Teaching, and Cultivate New People," in Main Campus, *Training New Type Personnel*.
8. "Decision on Setting-up the Jiangxi Labor University," in *Communist Labor University*.
9. "Instructions Concerning the Enrollment of the Communist Labor University, 5 August 1959," in *Communist Labor University*.
10. Tang Chenggong, "Several Experiences in Going in for Production in the Part-Work, Part-Study School," in Main Campus, *Training New Type Personnel*.
11. Hualin Branch, "Carrying Out the Class Line in Enrollment and Improving the Methods of Enrollment," in Main Campus, *Training New Type Personnel*.

12. Zhang Yuqing, "Applying the Half-Work, Half-Study Educational System to Train New Type Personnel for Socialist Construction," in Main Campus, *Training New Type Personnel*.
13. Li C., "Reminiscences," and interview with the author.
14. Figures Wang Dongxing, "Report to the Representatives' Assembly of the State-Run Multiple Production Reclamation Farms and Report to the Communist Labor University, 13 December 1959," in *Communist Labor University*; Liu Junxiu, "Strive to Run the Communist Labor Well, 20 December 1959," in *Communist Labor University*; and, "Run the Communist Labor University Well," *Jiangxi Daily*, 2 August 1959; and Wang D., "Hold High the Red Banner."
15. Interview with the author.
16. Chronology of the Development of the Communist Labor University, 1 November 1958.
17. Yu, Development, 1.

Three
Branches of Gongda

1. Yunshan Branch, "Taking the Road of Running the School through Self-Reliance and Thrift," in Main Campus, *Training New Type Personnel*.
2. Interview with the author.
3. Tang, "Several Experiences."
4. From Li Guangchun, Zhong Huannian, and Wan Shangwen, "The Proletariat Should Have This Kind of University: A Lecture Given by Shao Shiping at the Huanggangshan Branch," in *Red Sun Shines*.
5. See Yunshan Branch, "Taking the Road"; and, Yunshan Branch, "Some Experiences in Strengthening the Party's Educational Principles," and, "How We Consolidated the Combination of Teaching and Productive Labor," in Main Campus, *Training New Type Personnel*.
6. Xiao, "Raise a Red Banner."
7. Yunshan Branch, "Taking the Road."
8. Fu Shaogao and Du Weiguo, "From Beggar to University Student," in *Red Sun Shines*.
9. Agnes Smedley, *The Great Road: The Life and Times of Chu Teh* (London: John Calder, 1958).
10. Qiu Chaodong, "Major Events in Jiangxi Communist Labor University," in Collection Committee, *Founding and Evolution*, 2–12 August 1959.
11. Yun Xiao, "Spring Warmth in Yunshan," in *Red Sun Shines*.
12. An Article Written by Zhu De's Nephew, 1977, in Collection of Documents, Leaders' Articles, Articles from Various Institutions and Newspaper Correspondents and Students and Staff, Jiangxi Agricultural University.

13. Zhu De's Instructions Concerning the Running of Gongda, 7 February 1966, in Collection of Documents.
14. Yun, "Spring Warmth."
15. Wang, D., "Education as the Foundation."
16. Interview with the author.
17. Lei Fenling, "A Broad Road: The Manifold Schooling at the Gaoan Branch of Gongda," in *Red Sun Shines*.
18. Tai Guozhen, "The Party's Principle of Education Yields Positive Results at Guanghaizai," in *Communist Labor University*.
19. Correspondence with author.
20. Interview with author.
21. Lan Gongwen, "A Visit to Lin Gang," in *Red Sun Shines*.
22. Interview with author.
23. Wang, D., "Carrying Out the Party's Principle."
24. Qiu, "Major Events," 15 February 1959, 1963.
25. Li, Zhong, and Wan, "Proletariat Should Have."
26. See Xiao, "Raise a Red Banner."
27. Chen, "Recollections of my Stay."

Four
A Dark Side

1. Interview with the author.
2. John Farley, *Bilharzia: A History of Imperial Tropical Medicine* (Cambridge: Cambridge University Press, 1991), 201–215.
3. Tien-Hsi Cheng, "Schistosomiasis in Mainland China: A Review of Research and Control Programs since 1949," *The American Journal of Tropical Medicine and Hygiene* 20:1 (1971), 26.
4. Cheng, "Schistosomiasis," 27–28.
5. Farley, *Bilharzia*, 8–9.
6. Interview with the author.
7. Cheng, "Schistosomiasis," 39–41.
8. Farley, *Bilharzia*, 203.
9. David M. Lampton, *The Politics of Medicine in China: The Policy Process, 1949–1977* (Folkstone: Dawson, 1977), 116.
10. Cheng, "Schistosomiasis," 45.
11. Sheila M. Hillier and J. A. Jewell, *Health Care and Traditional Medicine in China, 1800–1982* (London: Routledge and Kegan Paul, 1983), 191.
12. Seybolt, *Revolutionary Education*, 9.
13. Wei Wenbo, "Farewell to the 'God of Plague,'" in *Mao Zedong Biography-Assessment-Reminiscences*, Zhong Wenxian, comp. (Beijing: Foreign Language Press, 1986), 218–221.

14. Quoted in Farley, *Bilharzia*, 208–209.
15. *The Poetry of Mao Tse-Tung*, trans. Hua-ling Nieh Engle and Paul Engle (London: Wildwood House, 1972), 72–77.
16. Joshua S. Horn, *"Away with All Pests...": An English Surgeon in People's China* (London: Paul Hamlyn, 1969), 179.
17. Cheng, "Schistosomiasis," 37.
18. Luo Songsheng and Wen Renzhi, "Fresh Flowers: The Achievements of Gongda Main Campus in Three-in-One Research," in *Red Sun Shines*.
19. Chronology of the Development, 14 October 1965.
20. Qiu, "Major Events," 28 February 1966.
21. Seybolt, *Revolutionary Education*, 16.
22. Wu Ningkun, *A Single Tear* (London: Hodder and Stoughton, 1993), 333.
23. Cheng, "Schistosomiasis," 45.
24. Interview with the author.
25. Wang, D., "Carrying Out the Party's Principle."
26. Liu, "How We Established."
27. Interview with the author.

Five
Classroom and Farm

1. Wang Jiming, "Cultivating Personnel for the Construction of Mountain Areas and Serving the Mechanization of Agriculture," in *Communist Labor University*.
2. Interview with the author.
3. Wuyishan Branch, "Doing Political and Ideological Work Well, and Revolutionizing Educated Youth and Integrating Them with Laboring People," in Main Campus, *Training New Type Personnel*.
4. Interview with the author.
5. Qiu, "Major Events," 5 July 1961.
6. Wang, D., "Carrying Out the Party's Principle."
7. Nancheng Branch, "Carry Out the Class Line and Cultivate New Type Labor for the People's Commune," in Main Campus, *Training New Type Personnel*.
8. Wang, D., "Carrying Out the Party's Principle."
9. Quoted in Barry Keenan, *The Dewey Experiment in China: Educational Reform and Political Power in the Early Republic* (Cambridge, Mass.: Council on East Asian Studies, Harvard University, 1977), 90.
10. Chang, *Pre-Communist*, 36.
11. Geoff Chapple, *Rewi Alley of China* (Auckland: Hodder and Stoughton, 1980), 153.
12. Rewi Alley, *An Autobiography* (Beijing: New World Press, 1997), 14.
13. Wang, D., "Education as the Foundation."

14. Wang, D., "Hold High the Red Banner."
15. Chronology of the Development, August 1961.
16. Party Committee of Jiangxi, "Give Prominence to Politics."
17. Rewi Alley, *Travels in China, 1966–1971* (Beijing: New World Press, 1973), 311.
18. Zhang, "Applying the System."
19. Nancheng Branch, "Carry Out the Class Line."
20. "Criticism of Revisionism and Rectification of the Style of Work Brings Jiangxi's Communist Labor University a New Style of Atmosphere," *People's Daily*, (3.8.73), cited in *Survey of People's Republic of China Mainland Press*, no. 5438, 178.
21. Interview with the author.
22. Party Committee of Jiangxi, "Give Prominence to Politics."
23. Yunshan Branch, "Some Experiences in Strengthening."
24. Party Committee of Jiangxi, "Give Prominence to Politics."

Six
"Staffers, Laborers, and Researchers."

1. Wang, D., "Education as the Foundation."
2. Interview with the author.
3. Party Committee of the District of Shangrao, "We Exercised Leadership of the Gongda Branch School," in Main Campus, *Training New Type Personnel*.
4. Wang, D., "Hold High the Red Banner."
5. Wang, D., "Carrying Out the Party's Principle."
6. Interview with the author.
7. Qiu, "Major Events," 5 April 1978.
8. A Minute Summary of Zhou Enlai's Meeting with Representatives of the Teaching Staff and Students of Jiangxi Communist Labor University, 18 September 1961.
9. Party Committee of Jiangxi, "Give Prominence to Politics."
10. Nancheng Branch, "Carry Out the Class Line"
11. Chronology of the Development, 1961.
12. Party Committee of Shangrao, "We Exercised Leadership."
13. "The Flower of Education, the Furnace of Revolution," in *Communist Labor University*.
14. Wang Jin Xiang, Some Initial Considerations of the Rise and Decline of Gongda, 1 August 1988.
15. Qiu, "Major Events," 3 August 1962.
16. Interview with the author.
17. Liu, "How We Established."
18. "Kiangxi Communist Labor University," Nancheng, 19 August 1976, cited in *Survey of People's Republic of China Press*, no. 6167, 202.

19. Jing Shan, "A Leader in Learning from Dazhai: The Exemplary Gongda Graduate Leng Baoyu," in *Red Sun Shines*.
20. Jing Dai, "Militant Review," in *Red Sun Shines*.
21. Qiu, "Major Events," 14 July 1977.
22. Xin Gan, "Combining Scientific Research with Agricultural Production and Teaching, and Going in for Breeding Fine Varieties," in Main Campus, *Training New Type Personnel*.
23. Lan, "Visit to Lin Gang."
24. Interview with the author.
25. Wan Guohua, "Planting China Firs in Red Soil," in *Red Sun Shines*.
26. Huang Gang, "Liberated from the Rice Red Lady Bug," in *Red Sun Shines*.
27. Luo and Wen, "Fresh Flowers."
28. Interview with the author.
29. Liu, "How We Established."
30. Zhang Yuqing, "Holding High the Red Banner of the General Line by Running the Communist Labor University Well," in *Communist Labor University*.

Seven
Guidance from the Chairman

1. Du, "Proletarian Mold."
2. Wang, D., "Education as the Foundation."
3. Quoted in Ross Terrill, *Mao: A Biography* (New York: Harper & Row, 1980), 45.
4. Mao Zedong, "Report on the Peasant Movement in Hunan, March 1927," *Selected Works of Mao Tse-Tung*, Vol. 1 (London: Pergamon Press, 1965), 54.
5. Li Rui, "Mao Zedong in His School Days," *Beijing Review*, part 2 27:19 7 May 1984, 29.
6. Jonathon Spence, *To Change China: Western Advisers in China, 1620–1960* (Harmondsworth, England: Penguin, 1980), 161–183.
7. Mao Zedong, "Letter to Luo Xuezan, 26 November 1920," in *Mao's Road to Power: Revolutionary Writings, 1912–1949*, ed. Stuart R. Schram, vol. 1, *The Pre-Marxist Period, 1912–1920* (Armonk, NY: M. E. Sharpe, 1992), 605.
8. Quoted in Dick Wilson, *Mao, The People's Emperor* (London: Hutchison, 1979), 68.
9. Wang, D., "Education as the Foundation."
10. Quoted in Jane Price, *Cadres, Commanders, and Commissars: The Training of the Chinese Communist Leadership, 1920–1945* (Folkstone: Dawson, 1976), 17.
11. "Appendix: Elementary School Educational Methods of the Hunan-Kiangsi Provincial Soviet Cultural Committee," *Chinese Education* 6:3 (Fall 1973), 40.

12. Yang Xianjiang, "Education and Labor," *Republic Daily*, 1 May 1921, cited in *The Educational Writings of Yang Xianjiang*, extracts (Beijing: Education Science Press, 1982), 37.
13. "K'ai Feng's Conclusion to His Report, 23 October 1933," *Chinese Education* 6:3 (Fall 1973), 30.
14. "Chairman Mao on Educational Revolution, 1929: Teaching Methods," *Chinese Education* 6:4 (Winter 1973), 9.
15. Party Committee of Jiangxi, "Give Prominence to Politics."
16. "School Song: The Situation at K'angta," *Chinese Education* 6:1 (Spring 1973), 5.
17. Hubert Freyn, *Chinese Education in the War* (Hong Kong: Kelly and Walsh, 1960), 131.
18. "A College of the Newest Type That Is Most Revolutionary and Progressive," *Peking Review* 9:32 (5 August 1966), 12–14.
19. Wang, D., "Education as the Foundation."
20. Wang, D. "Hold High the Red Banner."

Eight
A Role for Ideology

1. Minute Summary of Zhou Enlai's Meeting.
2. See Jinggangshan Branch, "Strengthening Education in the Revolutionary Tradition, and Carrying Forward the Revolutionary Spirit of Jinggangshan," in Main Campus, *Training New Type Personnel*, and Jinggangshan Branch, "A New Kind of University on the Heroic Mountain," in *Communist Labor University*.
3. Jinggangshan Branch, "New Kind of University."
4. Jinggangshan Branch, "Strengthening Education."
5. Vivian Chiu, "Comrades of the Old Red Soldiers Club," *South China Morning Post International Weekly*, 7 December 1996, 6.
6. Jinggangshan Branch, "Strengthening Education."
7. Wang, D., "Report to the Representatives."
8. Party Committee of Jiangxi, "Give Prominence to Politics."
9. "Chronology of the Development," 19 August 1961.
10. Qiu, "Major Events," 1960.
11. Jing S., "Leader in Learning."
12. Gao Zhihong and Xiao Shaozhang, "A Woman Veterinary Surgeon in a Mountainous Village," in *Red Sun Shines*.
13. Wuyishan Branch, "Doing Political and Ideological Work."
14. Liu, "How We Established."
15. "Chronology of the Development," 30 September 1962.
16. Wuyishan Branch, "Doing Political and Ideological Work."

17. Qu Shaojian, "The Communist Labor University Is Marching Forward with Giant Strides Repudiating the Slander of the Right Opportunists," in *Communist Labor University*.
18. Zhang, "Red Banner of the General Line."
19. Wang, D., "Carrying Out the Party's Principle."
20. Yunshan Branch, "Some Experiences in Strengthening."
21. Interview with the author.
22. Fu and Du, "Beggar to Student."

Nine
On Political Movements

1. Correspondence with the author.
2. William Hinton, "Dazhai Revisited," *Monthly Review*, March 1988, 34–50.
3. Interview with the author.
4. Department of Politics, Communist Labor University, "Strengthening the Basic Construction of Political Education and Organize Students in the Study of Chairman Mao's Work," in Main Campus, *Training New Type Personnel*.
5. See John F. Cleverley, *The Schooling of China, Tradition and Modernity in Chinese Education*, 2d ed. (Sydney: Allen and Unwin, 1991), 157–158.
6. Qiu, "Major Events," 26 May 1966.
7. "Minute Summary of Zhou Enlai's Meeting."
8. *Serve the People: Five Articles by Chairman Mao Zedong* (Beijing: Foreign Language Press 1976).
9. Spence, *To Change China*, 223.
10. Department of Politics, "Strengthening the Construction."
11. Yunshan Branch, "Some Experiences in Strengthening."
12. Department of Politics, "Strengthening the Construction."
13. Jing, S., "Leader in Learning"
14. Yunshan Branch, "Some Experiences in Strengthening."
15. Interviews with the author.
16. See Wuyishan Branch, "Doing Political and Ideological Work"; Yunshan Branch, "Some Experiences in Strengthening"; Party Committee of Jiangxi, "Give Prominence to Politics"; Hualin Branch, "Class Line"; and Nancheng Branch, "Carry Out the Class Line."
17. Department of Politics, "Strengthening the Construction."
18. Jing, S., "Leader in Learning."
19. Interview with the author.
20. Nancheng Branch, "Carry Out the Class Line."
21. Department of Politics, "Strengthening the Construction."

Ten
Famine and Fortitude

1. Party Committee of Shangrao, "We Exercised Leadership."
2. J. Becker, *Hungry Ghosts: China's Secret Famine* (London: John Murray, 1997).
3. Party Committee of Jiangxi, "Give Prominence to Politics."
4. Interview with the author.
5. Cheng Chung, "Agricultural Science in New China," *Peking Review* 3:47 (22 November 1960), 21–23.
6. Interviews with the author.
7. Li, C., "Reminiscences," and interview with the author.
8. Party Committee of Shangrao, "We Exercised Leadership."
9. Interview with the author.
10. Party Committee of Jiangxi, "Give Prominence to Politics."
11. Interview with the author.
12. Figures, Party Committee of Jiangxi, "Give Prominence to Politics," and Qui, "Major Events," 25 August 1960.
13. Interview with the author.
14. Party Committee of Jiangxi, "Give Prominence to Politics."
15. Interview with the author.
16. Zhou Yuliang, et al., *Education in Contemporary China* (Changsha: Hunan Education Publishing House, 1990), 209, 270, 561.
17. Seybolt, *Revolutionary Education,* 41.
18. "Chairman Mao's Brilliant Directive Illuminates the Road of Advance for the Communist Labor University," *People's Daily*, 30 July 1976, cited in *Survey of People's Republic of China Press*, no. 6167, 196.
19. Party Committee of Gaoan County, "Strengthening the Leadership over the Branch School Directly under the County to Run Gongda Better," in Main Campus, *Training New Type Personnel.*
20. Interview with the author.
21. Qiu, "Major Events," 4 April 1961.
22. Party Committee of Gaoan, "Strengthening the Leadership."
23. Ji Dian, "The Red Blossom of Meiling: Comrade Tian Jiecai and His Colleagues in Defense of Gongda Enterprise," in *Red Sun Rises,* and "Mao's Brilliant Directive," 196.
24. Qiu, "Major Events," 4 April 1961.
25. Ji, "Red Blossom."
26. "Chronology of the Development," University, 22 September 1961.
27. Qiu, "Major Events," 4 April 1961.
28. The Basic Situation of the Branch Schools of Jiangxi Communist Labor University (1958–1984).
29. The Number of the Students Admitted and the Graduates of Jiangxi Agricultural University (1940–1991).

Eleven
A Letter from Mao Zedong

1. Mao Zedong, "Letter to Comrades, Communist Labor University of Jiangxi Province, 30 July 1961,"*Peking Review* 33 (12 August 1977), 3–4.
2. See, Wang, D., "Education as the Foundation."
3. Wei Zhi, "The Magnificent Document, the Red Battle Flag," in *Red Sun Shines*.
4. Wang, D., "Education as the Foundation."
5. "Comrade Mao Tse-tung on Educational Work," excerpt, 1958, *Chinese Education* 2:3 (Fall 1969), 45–46.
6. Wang, D., "Carrying Out the Party's Principle."
7. Wang, D., "Education as the Foundation."
8. Interview with the author.
9. Minutes of a Meeting Presided over by Premier Zhou Enlai, 20 October 1963.
10. Interviews with the author.

Twelve
Good Friends Rally

1. Wang, D., "Education as the Foundation."
2. See Chae-Jin Lee, *Zhou Enlai: The Early Years* (Stanford, Calif.: Stanford University Press, 1994).
3. See Lu Songting, "Impressive Footprints: Notes on Premier Zhou's Inspection of the Lushan Branch of Gongda," in *Red Sun Shines*.
4. Minute Summary, of Zhou Enlai's Meeting.
5. Wang Jin Xiang, Yuan Zhaofen, "A Memorable Day," in *Red Sun Shines*.
6. See Minute Summary, of Zhou Enlai's Meeting.
7. "Mao's Brilliant Directive," 195.
8. Interview with the author.
9. See Li, C., "Reminiscences," and Li Chao, "A Meeting at Ziguange Pavilion," in *Red Sun Shines*.
10. See Minutes of a Meeting Presided over by Zhou.
11. Interviews with the author.

Thirteen
"The Golden Years"

1. Chen, "Recollections of My Stay."
2. Interview with the author.
3. Chen, "Recollections of My Stay."
4. Wang, J. X., "Initial Considerations."

5. Chronology of Development, 27 June 1963.
6. Wei Z., "Magnificent Document."
7. Party Committee of Shangrao, "We Exercised Leadership."
8. Chronology of Development, September 1965.
9. Qiu, "Major Events," 19 June 1965.
10. The Basic Situation of the Branch Schools of Jiangxi Communist Labor University (1958–1984); Liu, "How We Established"; Party Committee of Jiangxi, "Give Prominence to Politics."
11. Jerome Ch'en, *Mao Papers* (Oxford: Oxford University, 1970), 22.
12. Seybolt, *Revolutionary Education*, 26.
13. "Speech at Hangzhou, 21 December 1965," in *Mao Tse-Tung Unrehearsed*, 236.
14. "Talk on Questions of Philosophy, 18 August 1964," in *Mao Unrehearsed*, 212.
15. Ruth Gamberg, *Red and Expert: Education in the People's Republic of China* (New York: Schocken Books, 1977), forepage.
16. Yen Ke, "Grasp Well Popularization of Science," *Guangming Daily*, (20 July 1977), in *Survey of People's Republic of China Press*, no. 6394, 96.
17. Interview with the author.
18. "Mao's Brilliant Directive," 195.
19. Interview with the author.
20. "Theory and Practice in Higher Education," *China Higher Education*, no. 4, (1992), 34.
21. Wang, D., "Education as the Foundation."
22. Zhou et al., *Education in Contemporary China*, 587.
23. Chronology of the Development, 12 August 1964.
24. Chronology of the Development, 21 December 1964.
25. Chronology of the Development, University, 15–23 July 1965.
26. Chen, "Recollections of My Stay."
27. Interview with the author.

Fourteen
Cultural Revolution

1. Interview with the author.
2. Ch'en, *Mao Papers*, 117.
3. Ch'en, *Mao Papers*, 25.
4. Ch'en, *Mao Papers*, 129.
5. Ch'en, *Mao Papers*, 115.
6. See Cleverley, *Schooling of China*, 167–169.
7. Qiu, "Major Events," 21 September–4 October 1966.
8. Interviews with the author.

9. Alley, *Travels in China*, 279.
10. Revolutionary Rebel Liaison Station, Second General Head Quarters, "The East Is Red," no. 172, Beijing (11 February 1967), cited in *Survey of China Mainland Press*, 21.
11. Interviews with the author.
12. Chronology of the Development, 21 February 1972.
13. Interviews with the author.
14. Qiu, "Major Events," 11–23 October 1968.
15. Interviews with the author.
16. Chen, "Recollections of My Stay."
17. Chronology of the Development, 30 June 1968.
18. Donggushan Branch, "A Fierce Battle at the Foot of Bai Yun Mountain," in *Red Sun Shines*.
19. Correspondence with author.
20. Chen, "Recollections of My Stay."
21. Qiu, "Major Events," 17 October 1968.
22. *Take the Road of the Shanghai Machine Tools Plant* (Beijing: Foreign Language Press, 1968), i.
23. "Mao's Brilliant Directive," 198.
24. Interview with the author.
25. Ch'en, *Mao Papers*, 35.
26. "Indictment of the Special Procurate," *Beijing Review* 23:14 (1 December 1980), 22.
27. Interview with the author.

Fifteen
An Open Door

1. William Hinton, *Hundred Days War: The Cultural Revolution at Tsinghua University* (New York: Monthly Review Press, 1972), 14.
2. *Take the Road*, 2.
3. Interviews with the author.
4. The Basic Situation of the Branch Schools of Jiangxi Communist Labor University (1958–1984), and The Number of the Students Admitted and the Graduates of Jiangxi Agricultural University (1940–1991).
5. Alley, *Travels in China*, 563.
6. Chronology of the Development, 15–25 July 1970.
7. Chronology of the Development, 17 March 1972.
8. Party Committee of Jiangxi, "Give Prominence to Politics."
9. Huanggangshan Branch, "A Survey of Teaching and Learning at Huanggangshan Branch of the Communist Labor University," in Main Campus, *Training New Type Personnel*.

10. Xinhua News Digest, no. 071603, 16 July 1977, 2.
11. "Continue the Revolution," *Guangming Daily*, 7 May 1977, cited in *Survey of People's Republic of China Press*, no. 6355, 61.
12. Talks with Mao Yuan-hsin, 5 July 1964, in *Mao Tse-tung Unrehearsed*, 248.
13. Remarks at the Spring Festival, 13 February 1964, in *Mao Tse-tung Unrehearsed*, 204.
14. "Continue the Revolution," 615.
15. Xinhua News Digest, no. 032602, 26 March 1977, 5.
16. Xinhua, News Digest, no. 071603, 16 July 1977, 2.
17. Quoted in John F. Cleverley, "China's School Factories," *Insight for Decision Makers in Asia* (January 1975), 32.
18. Remarks at the Spring Festival, 13 February 1964, in *Mao Tse-tung Unrehearsed*, 205.
19. Alley, *Travels in China*, 568.
20. Interview with the author.
21. "New-type College Students Trained in Jiangxi Communist Labor University," Nanchang, 7 May 1976, cited in *Survey of People's Republic of China Press*, no. 6097, 95.
22. Compiling and Writing Group, "A Brand New Socialist University: A Brief History of Chaoyang Agricultural College," *Historical Research*, no. 2 (20 April 1976), *Selection of People's Republic of China Magazines*, no. 874, 1.
23. Interviews with the author.
24. The Basic Situation of the Branch Schools of Jiangxi Communist Labor University (1958–1984), and The Number of the Students Admitted and the Graduates of Jiangxi Agricultural University (1940–1991).

Sixteen
Trial by Media

1. Chu Lan, "A Battle Song of Proletarian Educational Revolution: Comments on the Movie *Break*," *People's Daily*, 7 January 1976.
2. Wang, J. X., Initial Considerations.
3. See *The Break*, and Chu Lan, "A Battle Song."
4. Liu Zhishen and Luo Qingzhen, "Holding High the Great Banner to Fight Devils," in *Red Sun Shines*.
5. Jiangxi Provincial Party Committee, "Advance in Triumph Holding High the Brilliant Banner of Chairman Mao's 'July 30th Directive,'" *People's Daily*, 30 July 1977, cited in *Survey of People's Republic of China Press*, no. 6399, 119.
6. Correspondence with author.
7. Liu, Z. and Luo, "Fight Devils."
8. Interview with the author.

9. See "Brand New Socialist University," 1–30.
10. "Talk with Mao Yuan-hsin," 5 July 1964, 248.
11. "The Party's Policy on Intellectuals Brooks No Abuse," *People's Daily*, 22 February 1977, cited in *Survey of the People's Republic Press*, no. 6293, 2.
12. Chronology of the Development, 20–29 May 1975.
13. "A Graduation Paper: The Deeds of a Peasant College Graduate," Shenyang, 17 July 1976, cited in *Survey of the People's Republic of China Press*, no. 6146, 214.
14. Interviews with the author.

Seventeen
Attacked by Left and Right

1. Interview with the author.
2. Liu, Z. and Luo, "Fight Devils."
3. Parris H. Chang, "The Cultural Revolution and Chinese Higher Education Change and Continuity," *Journal of General Education* 26:3 (Fall 1974),192.
4. Liu, Z. and Luo, "Fight Devils."
5. Interview with the author.
6. David I. Chambers, "The 1975–1976 Debate over Higher Education," *Comparative Education* 13:1 (March 1977), 7.
7. Jiangxi Provincial Party Committee, "Advance in Triumph," 120.
8. Jing, D., "Militant Review."
9. Interview with the author.
10. Wang Ting, *Chairman Hua Leader of the Chinese Communists* (London: C. Hurst, 1980), 150.
11. Xiang Wen, "A Shining Example," in *Red Sun Shines*.
12. See Cleverley, *Schooling of China*, 220.
13. Chen Xueyong, "The Torch Lights Up Mountain Villages: Notes on the July 30 Instruction Propaganda Team of the Yecheng Branch of Gongda," in *Red Sun Shines*.
14. The Basic Situation of the Branch Schools of Jiangxi Communist Labor University (1958–1984), and The Number of the Students admitted and the Graduates of Jiangxi Agricultural University (1940–1991).
15. Wang, J., "Initial Considerations."
16. Interview with the author.
17. "Encyclopedia of Education, 1980," *Chinese Education* 14:4 (Winter 1981–1982) 7.
18. Deng Xiaoping, "Speech at the Opening of the National Science Conference," *Beijing Review* 21:12 (24 March 1978), 18.
19. See Deng Mao Mao, *Deng Xiaoping, My Father*, (New York: Basic Books, 1995).
20. Interview with the author.

Eighteen
Decision Point

1. Qiu, "Major Events," 14 February 1979.
2. Correspondence with the author.
3. Chronology of the Development, 18 May 1980.
4. Interview with the author.
5. Correspondence with the author.
6. Interviews with the author.
7. Chen, "Recollections of My Stay."
8. Department of Agriculture, Vocational, and Technical Education, Jiangxi Agricultural University, The Experience of the Communist Labor University and the Running of the Department of Agricultural, Vocational, and Technical Education, Jiangxi Agricultural University, n.d.
9. Interview with author.
10. Chen, "Recollections of My Stay."
11. Wang, J., "Initial Considerations."

Chapter 19
Life After Death

1. Interview with the author.
2. Chen, "Recollections of My Stay."
3. Suzanne Pepper, *China's Universities, Post-Mao Enrollment Policies and Their Impact on the Structure of Secondary Education: A Research Report* (Ann Arbor: Center for Chinese Studies, University of Michigan, 1984).
4. Interview with the author.
5. Report on Reception, 5 December 1980, Jiangxi Communist Labor University.
6. Department of Agriculture, Experience.
7. Quoted in Chen, "Recollections of My Stay."
8. Department of Agriculture, Experience.
9. Interview with the author.
10. Zhang, "Applying the System."
11. Interview with the author.
12. Correspondence with the author.
13. Interview with the author.
14. Wang, D., "Education as the Foundation."
15. Kingsley Fairbridge, "A Lecture on Agricultural Education," no. V1, ms., 934A/9, Battye Library, South Australia.
16. "Chairman Mao's Instructions Light Up the Road of the Communist Labor University," *People's Daily*, 30 July 1976.

17. State Education Commission, *Educational Development in China* (Beijing: SEDC, 1997), 2.
18. Greg Kulander, "Agricultural Universities: Engines of Rural Development?" in *Higher Education in Post-Mao China*, eds. Michael Agelasto and Bob Adamson (Hong Kong: Hong Kong Press, 1998), 168.
19. Department of Agriculture, Experience; and Chronology of the Development, 17 May 1984.
20. Yu, Development, 5.
21. Interviews with the author.
22. Correspondence with the author.

Bibliography

This bibliography list Chinese sources which, unless otherwise cited, comprise non-print, typescript or duplicated materials. Such records are typically held in the general office or archives of the institution. Serial and other sources are listed in the Notes.

Account of Professor Cleverley's Visit to Zhanggongshan Gongda, Wuyuan County, October 1992, and collection of Associated Papers.
The Basic Situation of the Branch Schools of Jiangxi Communist Labor University (1958–1984).
A Brief Introduction to Jiangxi Communist Labor University, n.d.
Chen Ping Memoir, 1949–1984.
Chronicle of Educational Events in the People's Republic of China, *1949–1982*, ed. Central Institute of Educational Research (Beijing: Education Science Press, 1983).
Chronology of Foreign Affairs of Jiangxi Agricultural University, 1949–1990.
Chronology of the Development of the Communist Labor University.
Collection Committee of Materials about the Party's History — Jiangxi Provincial Party Committee and Jiangxi Agricultural University, *Founding and Evolution of Jiangxi Communist Labor University: Materials of the Party's History in Jiangxi (Item 38)* (Beijing: Central Documents Publishing House, 1996).
Collection of Documents, Leaders' Articles, Articles from Various Institutions and Newspaper Correspondents and Students and Staff, Jiangxi Agricultural University.

Communist Labor University, The (Nanchang: Jiangxi Education Press, 1960).
Department of Agricultural, Vocational and Technical Education, The Experience of the Communist Labor University and the Running of the Department of Agricultural, Vocational and Technical Education, Jiangxi Agricultural University, n.d.
Educational Annals of Jiangxi Province, Editing Committee, n.d.
Guide to the Archives of Jiangxi Agricultural University.
Jiangxi Communist Labor University, Nanchang, 19 August 1976.
Long Live Chairman Mao's Educational Thought, (Wuhan: CPC Committee of the Great Proletarian Cultural Revolution, 1967).
Major Events in the History of Jiangxi Communist Labor University, 31 May 1958–15 October 1985.
Mao Zedong, Letter to Comrades, Communist Labor University of Jiangxi Province, 30 July 1961, *Peking Review*, no. 33 (12 August 1977), 3–4.
Minutes of a Meeting Presided Over by Premier Zhou Enlai, 20 October 1963.
Number of the Students Admitted and the Graduates of Jiangxi Agricultural University, The (1940–1991).
Outline of Educational Research on Jiangxi Communist Labor University. n.d.
Red Sun Shines over the Journey: Essays on Jiangxi Communist Labor University, The (Shanghai: Shanghai Education Press), 1978.
Report on Reception, 5 December 1980, Jiangxi Communist Labor University.
The Road of China's Rural Education Educational Research on Jiangxi Communist Labor University, ed. Huang Dingyuan (Nanchang: Jiangxi Tertiary Education Press, 1997).
Table of Statistics Regarding the Archives of Jiangxi Agricultural University.
Table of the Evolution of the Departments of Jiangxi Agricultural University, 1981–1991.
Training New Type Personnel Through Half-Work and Half-Study: A Collection on the Running of Jiangxi Communist Labor University, Main Campus of the Jiangxi Communist Labor University and Jiangxi Education Press (Nanchang: Jiangxi Education Press, 1965).
Wang Dongxing, "Education as the Foundation of National Development: Reminiscences of Jiangxi Communist Labor University," in *Scientific*

Research on Jiangxi Education, vol. 1 (Jiangxi Institute of Education, 1995).

Wang Jin Xiang, How I Became a New Student at Gongda, ms., n.d., and, Some Initials Considerations of the Rise and Decline of Gongda, 1 August 1988.

Yu Yingen, The Development of Jiangxi Communist Labor University, Adult Education Office, Jiangxi Education Committee, n.d.

Index

ABC of Educational History, The, 81
Academic Committee, 191
Acupuncture, 45, 158
Adminisration Office, 101
Africa, 41, 90, 133, 164, 171
Afro-Asian Writers' Emergency Meeting, 141
Agricultural Group of the Command Post for Grasping Revolution and Promoting Production, 161
Albania, 90
All-China Women's Federation, 211
Alley, Rewi, 56, 141, 146, 148, 163
Analects of Confucius, The, 76
Anhui Province, 107, 108, 170
Anti-Japanese Political and Military University, xxi, 10, 32, 33, 83, 84, 120, 127, 174, 179
Anti-Lin Biao, Anti-Confucius Campaign, 187
Anti-Local-Nationalism movement, 20
Anti-Rightist movement, 64–65
Anyi County, 109
Arts Institute, 152

Asia, 41, 90, 210
Association of Science and Technology, 211
August 1 Branch, 34, 72
Australia, 208
Automobile Production Factory, 169

Bai Dongcai, 13
Bailie, Joseph, 56
Bailie Schools, 56
Ba Mao Ling, 4
Bao Gong, 69
Basedow, J. B., 208
Bayi Reclamation Farm University, 140
Bayi River Bridge, 4, 94
Beijing, xxiii, 7, 10, 18, 22, 23, 31, 33, 37, 75, 83, 112, 123, 125, 129, 136, 138, 140, 141, 147, 149,150, 162, 169, 170, 176, 177, 189, 191, 192, 204, 207
Beijing Agricultural College, 170
Beijing Agricultural University, 141, 152

Beijing Film Studios, 173
Beijing Gongda, 170
Bethune, Norman, 99
"born reds," 92
Boyang Lake (Dam),17, 31, 41, 111
Break, The, 173–181, 192, 197, 199
Britain, xxiii, 141

Cai Yuanpei, xxi
Cao Zhonghe, 174
Capital College, xix
Central Bureau of Guards (Guards Regiment), 7, 119, 120
Central Party School (Yan'an), 7, 12, 82
Central Revolutionary Base Area, 80
Chang Ge County, 121
Changsha, 76, 77, 78, 79, 80, 136
Changxindian Railway Works, 79
Chang Yi County, 111
Chaoyang Agricultural College, 178, 179, 180, 181, 184, 185
Chaoyang Communist Labor University, 178
Chaoyang County, 178
"Charting a New Path," 175
Chen Duxiu, xxi
Chengdu Higher Normal School, 32
Cheng Shiqing, 152, 153, 154, 164, 199
Chen Ping, 11, 39, 135, 136, 140, 200, 208
Chiang Kaishek, 55, 184
Children's Corps, 80
China Constitution (1954), xxii
Chinese Academy of Science, 22, 191
Chinese Board of Management, 77. *See also* Changsha
Chinese People's University, xxi, 18
Chinese Women's University, xxi, 37, 82
Chi Qun, 176, 183, 184, 185, 186, 187, 188, 199

Chongqing Preparatory School, 192
Chu Lan, 173
Ciping, 80, 89, 148
Cixi, 28
classics, xix, 55, 76, 77, 191
Confucius, xix, xx, 7, 13, 16, 26, 27, 98, 102, 125, 146, 209
Communist Manifesto, 80
Communist Party of China (CPC), xxi, xxiv, 7, 11, 77, 82, 85, 87, 89, 97, 108, 186, 213; Central Committee (Office), 119, 120, 121, 140, 185, 188, 205; Central Committee Party School, 7, 10, 12; Central Files, 119; Central Propaganda Department, 22; Cultural Office, 10; General Office, 10, 141; Propaganda Department, 11, 22, 121, 129
Communist Labor Team, 13
"Communist Labor University Marches Ahead, The," 185
Communist Youth League, 3, 19, 21, 46, 205
Cowherd, 44
"Creating a New Way," 175
Cultural Revolution, xxiii, 10, 21, 56, 71, 83, 96, 98, 102, 122, 123, 137, 161, 165, 170, 175, 179, 180, 184, 189, 190, 191, 192, 199, 209, 213; Cultural Revolution decade, 145–159
Cultural Revolution Office, 146
Culture Bookshop, 77

Dagangshan, 17, 23
Da Jing, 87
Damaoshan, 33, 37, 45, 54, 56, 72, 141, 196
Danish Folk High School, 209
Dai Shuirong, 33
Dazhai, 95, 96, 169, 170, 171, 179
"Declaration of War," 176

INDEX 239

Democracy Wall, 189
Deng Xiaoping, xx, xxiii, xxiv, 23, 115, 149, 177, 186, 188, 189, 190, 191, 192, 195, 199, 200, 203, 205
Deng Yingchao, 126, 200
Department of Agricultural Machinery, 71, 100, 169
Department of Agriculture, 35
Department of Animal Husbandry (and Vetinary Medicine), 45, 126, 177
Department of Forestry, 97
Department of Industry in Mountainous Areas, 5
Department of Public Health, 45
Department of Rural Medicine, 46
Department of Social Sciences, 5
Deshengguan, 22
Dewey, John, 56
Ding County, 55
Donggushan Branch, 15, 155
Dong Peilin, 23
Draft Higher Education Sixty Articles, 115

Eagle's Mouth Mountain, 179
Education Research Office, 136
Eighth Plenary Session (Eighth Pary Congress), 23, 75
Enrollment Committee, 19
Europe, 32, 77, 80, 141, 208, 210
Evergreen Commune, 31

Faculty of Professional Education, 206
Fairbridge Kingsley, 208, 209
Fang Zhichun, 13
"Farewell to the God of Plague," 44
Fellenberg, 208
Fengjing County, 110
Fengxin County, 17
Fifth Educational Work Conference, 191
First Machinery Ministry, 157

First National Health Conference, 43
First Plenary Session, Third National People's Congress, 141
First Provincial Normal School, 76, 80, 188
"Five Old Men Mountains," 126
Five Ridges, 44
Five Year Plan (1953–7), xxii
"Foolish Old Man Who Removed the Mountain, The," 99, 100
Foreign Affairs Offices, 214
Four Clean Ups, 96
Fourth Red Army, 33, 81, 89, 126
France, French, 125, 171, 192
Fruit Tree Research Institute, 31
Fudan University, xix, 4
Fuhkien Christian University, xx
Fujian Province, 9
Fuzhou Vocational and Technical College, 196

Gan dialect, 14
"Gang of Four," 151, 180, 181, 189, 190
Gan River, 6
Ganzhou, 56
Ganzhou Forestry Technical College, 4, 65
Gaoan County, 20, 55
Gao Xiaoren, 25
German (Shandong), 125
Gong Qing city, 205
Gorki Colony, 57
Graduates of the Gongda Revolution, The, 149
Great Education Debate, 187
Great Leap Forward movement, xix, xxiii, 20, 43, 107, 112, 113, 120, 122, 123, 173, 175, 198, 199
Guangdong Province, 70
Guangxi Province, 153
Guangzhou, xix, 79, 170

Guazhou (Farm), 111
Gui Xi Branch, 67
Gung Ho, 56
Guo Moruo, 191

Hainan Island, 70
Hangzhou, 43, 137
Harbin, 23
Harbin Polytechnic, 179
health and hygiene, 41–47, 68, 200
Hebei Province, 7, 55
Heilongjiang Province, 140, 170
Heiwulei, 155
Henan Province, 96, 107, 121, 148, 153, 170
Historical Research, 185
Hofwyl, 208
Hongda, see Red Army University
Hong Kong, 101
Horn, Joshua, 44
Hua Guofeng, 188, 189, 191, 192, 199
Hualin, 20, 35, 100, 114, 170
Hua To, 44
Hubei Province, 170
Hunan Province, 8, 9, 29, 77, 78, 79, 80, 123, 149, 153, 170, 185, 188, 204
Hunan Provincial Library, 76
Huanggangshan, 26, 29, 34, 36, 38, 152, 155, 196, 211
Hu Rigao, 31–32
Hu Shi, xxi
Hu Yaobang, 205

Indonesia, 43
"In Memory of Norman Bethune," 99, 100

Japan, xx, xxi, 56, 82, 125, 171
Ji'an (Communist Labor University), 55, 154
Jiang (teacher), 35

Jiangjunzhou, 112
Jiang Nanxiang, 190, 200
Jiang Qing, 164, 179, 187, 190, 192
Jiangsu, 97, 108, 125, 204
Jiangxi Agricultural College, 17, 65, 69, 70, 151, 152, 153, 159, 197, 198, 206, 207, 208
Jiangxi Agricultural University, 22, 177, 197, 198, 200, 203, 205, 206, 207, 208
Jiangxi Branch, China Academy of Sciences, 151
Jiangxi Daily, xxiii, 176, 186, 187
Jiangxi Hall, 23
Jiangxi Hotel, 4, 204
Jiangxi Industrial College, 114
"Jiangxi's New Seedlings," 175
Jiangxi Labor University, 13
Jiangxi Nongda Bao, 213
Jiangxi Provincial Games, 37
Jiangxi Provincial Government, 110. 195
Jiangxi Provincial Party Committee, 11, 13, 18, 21, 68, 111, 114, 126, 128, 129, 134, 141, 154, 170, 176, 185, 186, 187, 195, 196, 197
Jiangxi Provincial People's Congress, 13, 111, 126, 134, 154, 197
Jiangxi Provincial Revolutionary Committee, 152, 170
Jiangxi Technology University, 152
Jiang Yizhen, 133
Jiaotong, 4
Jingdezhen, 91
Jinggangshan Branch, 16, 33, 34, 80, 87, 88, 99, 123, 126, 147, 148, 152, 196, 205
Jinggangshan Forest Pioneer Farm, 87
Jin Xiang Branch (County Party Committee), 70, 71
Journal on Educational Revolution, 150

July 30 Medical Factory, 72
July 30 Institution, 186

Kangda. *See* Anti-Japanese Political and Military University
Kang Keqing, 33, 149, 200
Kang Youwei, 28
Kant, 76
Ke Qingshi, 67
Khrushchev, xxii, 109
Kuomintang (KMT), xix, 7, 26, 28, 55, 56, 87, 101, 162

Labor University, Soviet Union, 10
Landlord's Courtyard, 102
Lanzhou, 56
Language fusion, 20
"Learn from Comrade Lei Feng," 97
"Learn from Dazhai," 95
"Learn from Gongda," 188
"Learn from the PLA," 96, 97
Leng Baoyu, 91
Lei Feng, 97
Lenin (Leninism), xxi, 11, 15, 19, 118, 179, 188; elementry schools, 80; Normal School, 80
Li (teacher), 35
Liang Shuming, 55, 209
Liao, Minister, 141
Liaoning Province, 178, 179, 180, 184
liberated areas, xxi
Liberation Army Daily, 185
Li Chao, 11, 21,23, 29,109, 110,111, 112, 114, 126, 128, 129, 131, 132, 133, 135, 145, 150, 151, 159, 163, 183, 191, 204, 208
Lichuan County, 55
Li Dehou, 169
Li Na, 76
Lin Bao, 7, 96, 97, 98, 102, 152, 156, 159, 170

Li Min, 76
"Lingzhi grass," 72
Lin Zhong, 21, 67, 68, 192
"Little Red Book, The" (*Quotations from Mao Zedong*), 98, 99, 169
Liu (teacher), 71
Liu Junxiu, 11, 12, 15, 16, 19, 21, 34, 59, 68, 72, 75, 111, 116, 117, 141, 150, 208
Liu Shaoqi, xxii, 63, 102, 112, 113, 137, 139, 140, 145, 147, 148, 149, 150, 170, 184
Liu Xiyao, 170, 188
Long Guozheng, 173, 174, 175, 176
Long Live Chairman Mao's Educational Thought, 185
Long March, 7, 10, 12, 88
Long Quan Dam, 170
Lou Jinglin, 37
Luddites, 49
Lu Dingyi, 22, 112, 141
Luo Ruiqing, 126, 149
Luo Shangde, 89
Lushan, xix, 33, 60, 109, 114, 117, 119, 126, 127, 128
Lushan Branch, 126
Lushan Party Conference, 126

Ma Chaomang, 37, 204
Main Campus, 4, 5, 11, 13, 17, 18, 20, 21, 22, 26, 33, 34, 37, 42, 46, 53, 57, 59, 61, 65, 66, 67, 68, 69, 72, 89, 94, 96, 97, 108, 109, 110, 112, 114, 115, 116, 119, 120, 136, 137, 141, 146, 149, 150, 152, 153, 154, 156, 161, 162, 163, 164, 168, 172, 176, 177, 187, 189, 190, 196, 197, 198, 199, 204, 205, 207, 212
Mao Bingjie, 23, 213
Mao's Brilliant Directive," 145
Mao, *Selected Works*, 33, 98

Mao Yuanxin, 179, 180, 187
Mao Zedong, xx, xxi, xxii, xxiii, xxiv, (role in founding) 6–9, 10, 12, 13, 19, 27, 31, 32, 34, 35, 43, 46, 47, 45, 55, 56, 67 (on CLU 75–6), (educational experiences 76–9), (in Jiangxi 80–2), (in Yan'an 82–5), 87, 88, 90, 96, 97, 98, 99, 100, 102, 103, 107, 109, 111, 112, 116, (letter 117–123, 133, 159, 170, 175, 176, 183, 185, 188, 205), 125, 126, 127, 128, 129, 130, 133, 136, 137, 138, 139, 140, 145, 146, 147, 148, 149, 150, 152, 155, 156, 157, 158, 159, 161, 162, 167, 169, 170, 174, 176, 177, 178, 179, 180, 184, 186, 187, 188, 189, 190, 192, 198, 199, 203, 205, 210, 212, 213, 214,
Mao Zedong Thought Propaganda Team, 162, 165, 166, 178, 190
Mararenko Anton S., 57
Marx (Marxism, Marxist), xxi, 7, 11, 15, 19, 34, 57, 77, 81, 85, 90, 91, 102, 111, 119, 126, 127, 139, 156, 166, 179, 188
Marxism Leninism University, xxi
Mass Criticism Group of Beijing and Tsinghua, 183
"mass-line," 60, 196, 207
Ma Xulun, 41
May 4 movement, 10, 125
May 7 Agricultural College, 170
May 7 Agricultural, Science and Technology University, 178
May 7 Cadre Schools, 156, 157
McClure, William, 208
Meiling Mountain, (site), 4, 13, 115, 156, 162, 175, 196
Mencius, 16
Methodists, 55
middle schools, (No 2, No 22,) 17, 153–4, 162, 164, 207

Military Commission, 188
Ming tombs, xxiii
Ministry of Agriculture, 18, 137, 140, 147, 207
Ministry of Cultivation and Reclamation, 129
Ministry of Education, xxii, 113, 121, 132, 138, 139, 140, 146, 170, 186, 190, 191, 200, 206, 209; Vocational Education Division, 200
Ministry of Finance, 18, 129
Ministry of Fisheries, 129
Ministry of Forestry, 129, 137
Ministry of Higher Education, 18, 146, 170
Ministry of Labor and Personnel, 129, 140
Ministry of Light Industry, 18
Minister of Public Security, 189
More, Thomas, 208
Morrell Act, 208
Moscow, xxi, 192
Moscow Labor University, 13
Mount Yueli, 78

Nanchang, 4, 23, 31, 33, 55, 87, 94, 98, 110, 128, 147, 149, 152, 154, 164, 187, 189, 198
Nanchang Branch, 59
Nanchang Forestry, 4, 13, 15, 65
Nanchang Hospital, 23
Nanchang Hotel, 126, 187
Nanchang Machine Tools Plant, 162
Nanchang middle schools. *See* middle schools
Nanchang Municipality, 109
Nanchang Power Plant, 162
Nanchang Railway Bureau, 162
Nanchang University, 152
Nancheng Branch (County Communist Labor University), 37, 55, 59, 68, 70, 162, 196, 204, 211

INDEX 243

Nanhu Farm (Lake), 17, 99, 205
Nanjing, 43, 55, 209
Nanjing Forestry Institute, 90, 141
Nankai Middle School, 125
National Association for the Promotion of Mass Education, 209
National Conference on Educational Work, 183
National Conference on Part Work Colleges, 147
Nationalists, 55, 57, 79, 82, 83, 87, 88
Nationalities Pictorial, 185
National People's Congress, 32
National Representative Conference of Advanced Workers in Socialist Culture and Education, 192
National Resistance University, 83
National Science Conference, 191
National Tertiary Entrance Examination, 190
National Zhongzheng University, 152
Neef, Joseph, 208
Nepal, 137
Never Forget Class Struggle campaign, 100, 101
New Education Movement, 80
New Life Movement, 55
Nine-Man Subcommittee, 43, 46
No. 1 Army School, Jiangxi, 7
No. 1 Lu Lin, 118
North Shanxi Public School, 82

Office of Inspection, 156
Officer Instruction Regiment, 33
Offices of Hydropower, Agriculture, Water, Forestry, 129
On Capital, 8
"On Practice," 99
On the Spot Meeting . . . (Chaoyang), 180
Ou Yangliang, 207

Party Committee of Main Campus, 21, 92, 145, 151, 197, 199, 206, 209
Party University of Chaoyang Agricultural College, 179
Paris, 33, 125, 192
Paulsen, 76
Peasant Movement Training Institute, 79
Peiping Normal College, 10
Peking University, xix, xxi
Peng Dehua, 80
People's Daily, The, 43, 139, 176, 184, 186
People's Liberation Army (PLA), 15, 27, 34, 96, 97, 140, 151, 158. 161, 163, 170, 173; PLA Pictorial, 185; PLA Unit 6012, 150
Pepper Suzanne, 204
Pestalozzi, 208
Pingxiang County, 212
Politburo, 10, 183, 180, 189
Political Bureau of the CPC, 119
Political Department (University), 97
PLA. *See* People's Liberation Army
President's Office, 22
Program for Agricultural Development, 120
Protestant educators, 91
Provincial Agricultural Bureau, 196
Provincial Cultural and Educational Bureau, 188
Provincial Educational Bureau, (Commission), 21, 114, 170, 196, 205
Provincial Farms and Reclamation Division, 170
Provincial Finance Department, 21
Provincial Forestry Division, 170
Provincial Forestry Research Unit, 69
Provincial Grain Authority, 170
Provincial Propaganda Department, 18, 22, 90, 196
Putonghua, 20

Pu Yi, 141

Qing Dynasty, xix, 28, 76
Qinghai warlord, 12
Qiu Chaodong, 204
Quotations from Mao Zedong. See "The Little Red Book"
Qu Shaojian, 22

Reception Office, 152
Red Army, 26, 80, 81, 87
Red Army Hospital, 88, 89
Red Army University, xxi, 82, 120, 127
Red Family, The, 149
Red Flag, 185
Red Flag General Headquarters, 149
Red Flag Headquarters, 149
Red Guards, 12, 98, 146, 147, 149, 150, 155, 158, 159, 162
Red Lantern Brigade, 178
Red Sun Shines Over the Journey, The, 190
Republic of China, xx, xxi, 77
Revolutionary Committee, University, 37, 151, 163
Revolutionary Committees, 154, 161, 162, 164, 165, 166, 190
Rightists. See Anti Rightist movement
Road of China's Rural Education, The, 214
Robinson Crusoe, 208
Rousseau, 208
Ruijin, 11, 80
Rural Industry Conference, 31
Russia (experts), xxii, xxiii, 10, 16

Sandan Bailie School, 56, 146
Sanmen Gorge, 169
Schistosomiasis, see Health, Hygiene
Science and Education Group, State Council, 180, 183
second session of the National Soviet Conference, Jiangxi, 8

Self-Study University, 79
"Serve the People," 99
Shanggao, 69
Shanghai, xix, 3, 4, 5, 17, 23, 53, 59, 67, 94, 95, 129, 136, 157, 213
Shanghai Education Press, 190
Shanghai Machine Tools Plant, 157
Shanghainese, 67–68, 92, 93
Shangrao, 55, 114
Shangyanpun, 41
Shaoshan, 188
Shang Jing Forestry Brigade, 89
Shangrao, 55, 114
Shangyou, 115
Shanxi (North), 7, 82, 83, 95
Shanxi-Gansu-Ningxia Border Region, 82
Shao Shiping, 9, 10, 12. 13, 16, 17, 19, 21, 22, 23, 27, 28, 29, 30, 34, 38, 60, 68, 82, 83, 84, 87, 90, 91, 94, 109, 110, 111, 114, 117, 119, 139, 150
Shaoxing, 126
Shao Yi Lan, 37
Shandong Province, 125, 170
Shandong Rural Reconstruction Institute, 209
Shen Vice Minister, 132
Shenyang Agricultural College, 178, 180
Sheperd, George, 55
Shun, 44
Shun Yuan Academy, 78
Siberia, 174
Sichuan Province, 23, 191
Silkworm Branch/Factory, 34, 59, 152, 208
Sino-French work-study project, 125
Sixth Army Group, 12
"Smash Old Gongda and Construct a New One," 150
Snow, Edgar, xx

INDEX

Socialist Education Movement, 96, 102
Socialist Spiritual Civilization, 102
Song Dynasty, 54, 82
South America, 41
Soviet Union, xxii, xxiii, 34, 57, 85, 91, 112, 149
Spanish Civil War, 99
"Spring at Daomaoshan," 175
"Spring Comes to the Withered Tree," 43
State Council, 121, 133, 158, 180, 189
State Plan, 45
Stalin, xxii, 57, 131
St. John's University, xix
Strong, Anna Louise, 141
Students' Union executive, 37
Sungshan Branch, 174, 175, 176
Sun Yat-sen, 28
Sun Yat-sen University of the Toilers of China, xxi, 192
Sun Ziqing, 174
Switzerland, 208

Taihe Branch, 55
Taiwan, 55, 90, 101
Tan Zhenlin, 129, 131, 141
Tao Mao, 22
Tao Xingzhi, 55, 209
Taxation Bureau, 21
Teachers College Columbia, 55, 170
Teili, 170
Tenth Worker and Peasant Red Army, 7
Thailand, 43
Third Plenum, Eighth Party Congress, 96, 191
Three Character Classic, The, 54
Three Kingdoms, 44
Tiananmen, 214
Tian Jiecai, 115

Tianjin, 121, 136
Tianjin University, 120
Tibet, 165
Tolstoy, 78
Topographical Survey Class, 88
Training New Type Personnel Through Half-Work and Half-Study, 141
Triple River, 44
Tsinghua University, 146
Tsinghua University Middle School, 162, 170, 186

United States, xxiii, 56, 77, 78, 125, 140, 206, 208, 210
Utopia, 208

Versailles Treaty, 125
Veterinary Science. *See* Department of Animal Husbandry

Wang Dongxing, xix, xxiii, 3, 12, 14, 15, 16, 17, 18, 21, 22, 34, 35, 37, 38, 54, 55, 56, 57, 64, 65, 72, 75, 78, 79, 111, 117, 118, 119, 120, 121, 122, 127, 129, 130, 140, 141, 163, 169, 184, 186, 187, 188, 192, 199, 204, 208, 214; role in founding 6–10
Wang Hairong, 137
Wang Jie, 97
Wang Jiming, 51
Wang Jin Xiang, 3–5, 17, 22, 33, 37, 41, 43, 47, 63, 67, 68, 94, 101, 108, 110, 122, 126, 127, 135, 145, 149, 150, 151, 152, 154, 170, 171, 173, 180, 183, 189, 200, 203, 204, 206, 210, 213, 214
Wang Zhen, 140
Wan Jianhai, 163
Warship 571, 7
Washington, George, 78

Water Conservation Department, 69, 178
Wayaobao, 82
Wei Wenbo, 43
West China Union University, xx
Whampoa Military Academy, 126
"White Haired Girl, The," 178
WHO Division for the Control of Tropical Diseases, 43
Worker and Peasant Red Army, Jiangxi, 81
Worker-peasant-soldier students, 164
World War I, xxi, 32, 99, 125
World War II, xxi
Wuhan, 136
Wuyishan, 25
Wuyuan, 211
Wu Zhengcai, 69

Xiangtan District, 188
Xiao Gao, 126
Xiao Jing, 88
Xiao Li, 126
Xiaoli, 188
Xiaozhuang Experimental Normal School, 209
Xie Caiyan, 91
Xie Min, 180
Xinanjiang, 37
Xin Gan, 70
Xinhua Printing Plant, 162
Xinjiang, 6, 56, 67
Xin Ming, 3
Xiyang County, 95
Xu Jiawu, 188

Yale Foreign Missionary Society, 77
Yale-in-China, 77
Yan'an, 7, 8, 10, 33, 34, 37, 82, 83, 84, 85, 99, 120, 127, 152, 170
Yandi Branch, 114

Yang Cai, 126
Yang Shangkui, 13, 189
Yangtse River, 4, 31, 41
Yang Weiyi, 151
Yang Xiangjiang, 81
Yang Xui County, 109
Yan Xishan, 83
Yan Yangchu, 55, 209
Yan Zhu Hu, 88
Yao, 44
Yao Wenyuan, 185
Yecheng, 189
Ye Jianying, 187
Yellow River, 55, 169
Yenching University, xx
Yi (Comrade), 70
Yifeng County (Communist Labor University), 26, 196
Yingchen, 170
Yishen, 170
Yiyang County, 7, 10
Yongxin County, 11
"*Young Generation, The*," 133
Youth League. *See* Communist Youth League
Youth Vanguard, 80
Youxian, 188
Yuetan, 170
Yugoslav film, 185
Yujiang (Yukiang) County, 43, 44
Yunnan Military Academy, 32
Yunshan, 21, 25, 29, 30, 31, 32, 33, 34, 141, 152, 200
Yushan Branch (County), 41

Zeng Shenguan, 18
Zhang Chunqiao, 166, 176, 186
Zhanggongshan Communist Labor University, 211
Zhang Shimei, 69, 191, 204
Zhang Tiesheng, 184, 187

Zhang Xianpeng, 118, 119
Zhang Yuqing, 22, 101, 129, 131, 150, 151, 207, 208
Zhang Zhongyu, 129, 132
Zhao Daoqiu, 23
Zhao Guohua, 97
Zhejiang, 37
Zhongnanhai, 7, 8, 34, 119, 120, 129, 133, 179
Zhongshan University, xix, 21
Zhou Enlai, xx, 7, 23, 24, 32, 33, 46, 56, 67, 84, 87, 94, 98, 107, 121, 122, 135, 136, 137, 139, 140, 149, 150, 164, 183, 184, 186, 187, 198, 199, 200; intervention 125–134
Zhou Rongxin, 186, 187, 188
Zhu De, xx, 32, 33, 56, 80, 84, 88, 125, 139, 146, 149, 184, 187, 199, 200
Zhu Hu Brigade, 32
Zhu Min, 187
Ziguange Pavilion, 129
Zouping, 209

About the Author

John Cleverley has had a long engagement with the study of education, and has written extensively on China's activities based on firsthand experience and personal contacts. His book, *The Schooling of China: Tradition and Modernity in Chinese Education,* presents a comprehensive account of its educational development. His other studies explore agricultural and rural schooling and business and education. He has also published on education in Australia and Papua New Guinea and on the history of ideas in childhood.

Currently John is an honorary professor in the School of Social, Policy, and Curriculum Studies at the University of Sydney. He is principally engaged in studying international and comparative education. He also does educational consulting for both governmental and nongovernmental agencies on educational cooperation and aid assistance and training. He is an honorary professor of South China Normal University and of Jiangxi Agricultural University and is a member of the Advisory Committee for Chinese Education and Society.

www.ingramcontent.com/pod-product-compliance
Lightning Source LLC
Chambersburg PA
CBHW031546300426
44111CB00006BA/199